Inside Story
Official Real Estate Manual

FOR NEW AGENTS WHO DON'T KNOW HOW,
AND OLD AGENTS WHO KNOW HOW,
BUT DON'T

Barbara Nash-Price

Prentice Hall
Upper Saddle River, New Jersey 07458

Library of Congress Cataloging-in-Publication Data
Nash-Price, Barbara
    Inside story : official real estate manual : for new agents who
don't know how, and old agents who know how, but don't / Barbara
Nash-Price.
       p.   cm.
    Includes index.
    ISBN 0-13-281164-2
    1. Real estate business. 2. Real estate agents. I. Title.
HD1375.N265 1997
333.33—dc21   97-1583
                                                          CIP

Acquisitions Editor: Elizabeth Sugg
Production Liaison: Eileen O'Sullivan
Editorial Production Services: WordCrafters Editorial
    Services, Inc.
Managing Editor: Mary Carnis
Director of Production and Manufacturing: Bruce Johnson
Prepress Manufacturing Buyer: Mark Bove
Marketing Manager: Danny Hoyt
Editorial Assistant: Emily Jones
Cover Designer: Susan Newman
Printer/Binder: Banta—Harrisonburg

Published by Prentice-Hall, Inc.
Simon & Schuster/a Viacom Company
Upper Saddle River, NJ 07458

Printed in the United States of America

10 9 8 7 6 5 4 3 2 1

ISBN 0-13-281164-2

Prentice-Hall International (UK) Limited, *London*
Prentice-Hall of Australia Pty. Limited, *Sydney*
Prentice-Hall Canada Inc., *Toronto*
Prentice-Hall Hispanoamericana, *Mexico*
Prentice-Hall of India Private Limited, *New Delhi*
Prentice-Hall of Japan, *Tokyo*
Simon & Schuster Asia Pte. Ltd., *Singapore*
Editora Prentice-Hall do Brasil, Ltda., *Rio de Janeiro*

Contents

Foreword

It took me years to REALLY KNOW the ins and outs of real estate. In fact, I'm still finding things out. However, from the time I started twenty years ago, through today, I've yet to find a good manual—a self-help book that can walk you through the entire gamut of real estate, a book that can take you to a listing and show you just what to do, a book that can tell you how to get that appointment and how to get clients and keep them, a book that can give you examples from the "best in the business" of:

How to run your daily schedule!

How to keep your books!

How to work each and every day!

How to keep track of everything in one single book!

How to be able to simplify it all and yet "be so successful!"

How to write a certain ad and attract the right clients!

How to know what is expected of you!

How to know if you are going to stay in the business!

This book is especially for those already **in the business** and looking for a fresh start by simplifying it all!

There had to be an easier way, and with hard work, I found it each and every day!

I just hope you can have the stick-to-it-iveness to enjoy great success!

Preface

This book is written for all fellow real estate salespeople like myself in hopes of shortening your trial-and-error experiences and making the most out of your appointments with future business contacts.

This business is RISKY.

This business is ONLY AS STABLE as you are each and every day.

This business is waiting for you to take charge in a simplified fashion.

Be sure to remember three things, if you forget everything else I have written in this book:

1. Keep your sense of humor!
2. Be disciplined and follow through with a CMA (competitive market analysis) regardless of how futile it may seem at the time.
3. Try to stay enthusiastic (at least for part of the day). The dictionary defines enthusiastic as en-thuous: inspired by God.

By being disciplined and simplifying your schedule of work habits, hopefully you will be able to save countless hours of wasted time and energy pursuing avenues that are fruitless.

I prefer to look at this book as a "tour guide." It is filled with many positive examples of success and helpful hints acquired after twenty years of successfully selling real estate.

I hope by sharing this knowledge with you and others that you will grow to enjoy the "art of selling real estate" by utilizing a simplified formula within the *Inside Story*.

Happy reading.

CHAPTER 1

At the Start

big deal
by "Lorayne n' Neil"

At the Start . . .

Getting started and staying "active" in the real estate business require one crucial element: **ORGANIZATION** followed by determination and enthusiasm!

A real estate professional could not begin to think that he or she can keep every number and detail in his or her head. However, most agents will get a call at home, messages at the office, and calls referred at odd times from friends. And then there are those calls when least expected in the car, at odd hours of the evening, and so on.

Where are all of these messages stored? What about daily schedules? What about personal secretaries that are lacking if your business can't or won't warrant them at present?

There absolutely must be *organization* right from the beginning and every day in order to maintain discipline, balance, and order.

Real estate has lots of little odds and ends numbers, little pieces of paper where this number and that number have been quickly jotted down. They must be kept in a **daily planner.** This is covered later in this chapter.

When I first started in the business about twenty years ago, I realized after much trial and error that a lot of business was quickly lost from disorganization!

It took me years of trying various methods before I came to grips with which tools were definitely needed and which could be abandoned.

Getting started can create a completely new perspective on how to work effectively and how to make the most of your time each and every hour of your day.

Some agents feel that getting started means finishing a "quick start" program at their company, and then they feel ready to dive right in! Just go out and list and sell a house. . . . Little do most agents realize (until it is too late) that agents must be prepared to sell themselves first. They must be able to show (sometimes on first impressions) that they are extremely professional, confident, successful, trustworthy, and pleasant to be with. **Seldom do they get a second chance.**

A real estate agent who does not have the tools of the trade down pat is similar to the person who has studied for the driving test without getting behind the wheel. It can't be done.

Real estate is pretty much a sink or swim business. There are very few agents out in the field who go out of their way each day to indoctrinate a new agent. That is normally what the sales manager is for, and other agents usually have their hands full. It is up to an agent to completely know his or her business when he or she is ready to get started. Unfortunately, there are two little things called experience and wisdom. No one can just give it to you, but like a very good outline of anything, certain ideas and ways can be explained so that a person can at least know the ground rules.

If I were starting in the business all over again, I would do two things:

1. select one of the most productive agents at the office and ask if I could tag along to a few open houses to watch him or her in action, and

2. find someone who would have my least favorite area of real estate down pat and see if that agent would want to team up for some future business.

I have teamed up with many agents in the past to call on "For Sale by Owners," and we usually decide to: *Split all commissions down the middle regarding the subject property.*

I like associating with a large, reputable real estate firm which gives a person added credibility that he or she would not normally have on his or her own, starting out with a tiny firm.

ALWAYS . . . LOOK YOUR BEST! YOU REPRESENT HOW SUCCESSFUL YOU ARE. Don't be concerned whether or not your friends think you are making too much money. You want to look, act, and be successful. Always talk optimistically about real estate in general. For example, say, "This is my twentieth year in real estate and it still provides loads of excitement for me."

Remember that enthusiasm is contagious. Become enthusiastic, and you will stay that way longer and longer.

The more you worry, the more you lose your self-confidence.

In real estate you must also remember:

> *NEVER LEAVE ANYTHING TO CHANCE.*
> *MAKE THE MOST OF THE MOMENT.*

When you show a home or are ready to list a home, don't think that it can wait. By waiting, even until morning, buyers and sellers cool off.

Getting started in the real estate business will take a tremendous amount of perseverance and persistence. Another good word for it would be "stick-to-it-iveness." Don't let up on a plan for calling:

a buyer to buy a home
a seller to sell a home
a client to see a home
a seller to list a home

My normal plan of action for all of the above is to:

allow six weeks to find a home, and
allow six weeks to sell a home.

Then regroup.

If a listing doesn't sell, reevaluate the entire program that you have instituted with the seller. Begin by trying for a price reduction after 30 days.

If a buyer hasn't bought a home, reevaluate your program for showing and see if:

OTHER AREAS SHOULD BE INVESTIGATED

THE PRICE RANGE SHOULD BE INCREASED

THE PRICE RANGE SHOULD BE DECREASED

THE BUYER LACKS MOTIVATION

THE BUYER CANNOT DETERMINE WHAT HE OR SHE WANTS

If a seller hasn't sold his or her home, reevaluate your program for selling and see if:

THE HOME IS OVERPRICED

THE HOME NEEDS SERIOUS ATTENTION

THE HOME IS MARKETED POORLY

THE HOME IS DIFFICULT TO SHOW

In order for you to be successful in today's real estate market, you are going to have to use a lot of imagination and be able to bounce back.

Getting started in the real estate business means you must be informed. Nowadays, in most states it is essential to have at least a certain number of accredited courses to your favor before the end of each year. Each local real estate board sponsors seminars, conferences, and classes to take for continuing education. Keep abreast of what is happening in the real estate market across the country. Subscribe to real estate journals and periodicals. Become a CRS (Certified Real Estate Specialist). Obtain your real estate agent designation and attend graduate Real Estate Institute classes for your GRI designation.

Keep your eyes open to all that is around you and watch yourself in interactions with clients. Constantly improve your style. Watch for signs of your own weaknesses and work in these areas with self-help tapes and seminars. Discover special strengths that can distinguish you and sell your uniqueness.

Getting started with good habits is extremely important. With the Clean Air Act in force and more and more people aware of air pollution, try not to smoke or offend a client with foul odors of any type. Always keep a breath spray or peppermint in your pocket for those close encounters.

Get started with a good attitude (which is covered in Chapter 2) and a good sense of humor. Many, many transactions have been:

SAVED AND CLOSED

with a good sense of humor and a light touch at the right moment. Learn to become discerning. Learn to listen better and take constructive criticism when it is fair and truthful!

When getting started in the business, there is another reality that I have to touch on: there will be salespeople in the business who are doing better than you, about the same as you, and much worse than you! Don't waste time wondering **why**. Don't wallow in self-pity if this day Jane J. Jones got one more sale than you did. **Don't be envious.**

It's amazing how jealousy can be felt. Be genuine! Compliment a fellow agent on a sale. Don't wonder who is getting fed listings and buyers. It doesn't matter in the long run. What does matter is that you are doing all you can do to stay in the real estate business.

You will be so busy that when you take a breather it will be to go to sleep.

There is one important note to mention here in regard to sales commissions. Don't count on them until they are in the bank. In other words, too often an agent becomes overly confident that there will be a closing and that he or she is getting a check.

> *Real estate is definitely a hands-on business.*
> *Real estate is definitely a hand-holding business.*

Getting started in the real estate business is somewhat like getting started in the counseling business. You have to learn to understand people's needs and try to imagine yourself in their place.

Real estate people are looked upon to fix things, such as:

FIX MY HOUSING NEEDS WHEN I GET DIVORCED.
LET ME YELL AT YOU BECAUSE I'M FRUSTRATED.
FIX THE BIND I'M IN FINANCIALLY—GET ME MORE.
FIX THE PRESSURE BECAUSE WE BOUGHT BEFORE WE SOLD.
FIX IT!
FIX IT!
FIX IT!

Getting started in real estate means:

LETTING GO OF EGO
NOT GETTING YOUR NEEDS MET
LONG, TIRESOME HOURS; THANKLESS EXTRA EFFORT

Getting started in real estate also means making large sums of money when you *least* expect it, having your own hours and literally being your own boss, making wonderful, new friends, sometimes for life, and becoming very well known and popular.

It would not be a bad idea to do some role playing with your spouse or significant other regarding:

1. an open house

2. asking a buyer to sign a purchase agreement

3. asking a seller to sign a listing agreement

4. answering an ad-call off an ad in the newspaper

5. looking at houses

6. overcoming an obstacle regarding listing or buying

7. dealing with a client that just walked in

8. talking to a friend, relative, or neighbor about real estate

9. referring yourself to your local "frequently frequented" establishments

10. going over papers at a final closing (settlement and/or close of escrow)

Finally, real estate generally goes in cycles. Sometimes it is very hot and then there is a cooling off period. Know when it is important to stay "hot" and work those buyers and sellers rather than taking long periods of time off. In the beginning it is much more difficult to take off a lot of the time. As the years go by, a person should develop a lot of networking among contacts and lots of referral business!

However, it is vital to take time off to avoid burnout. Learn to pace yourself and know yourself.

Perhaps your idea of setting yourself up involves designating duties to another individual. If this is the case, you will want to have a personal assistant. This person can do all of the detail work and usually can get paid by the hour. A personal assistant can leave the networking to you and let you just sell, sell, sell! (See Personal Assistant Sheet at end of this chapter.)

. . . and so goes it in the real world of real estate. Overall, it's fun. It's challenging. It's rewarding. And it's never, ever boring!

What Do You Need to Buy?

The following information is created for a real estate agent. This information should help you to work effectively from one day to the next.

1. good, preferably leather, daily planner, size 5″ × 8″ or 8½″ × 11″
2. good calculator, prefer flat to fit into the planner
3. good pen and pencil set
4. plain pad of white paper to fit into back of planner
5. 8½″ × 11″ or legal size daily ruled notebook (perfect for notes at seller's house, daily notes from buyers, addresses of homes to see with combinations for showings)
6. large and small paper clips
7. highlighter pens
8. current mapbook of your city
9. stationery with your name, picture, and real estate company on it
10. stickers for envelopes with your name, picture, and real estate company on them (order 1,000 minimum)
11. promotional brochure with your name, picture, and real estate company on it (order 1,000)
12. business cards and business reply cards with your name, picture, and real estate company on them (order 1,000 minimum)
13. colored index tabs and 3″ × 5″ colored cards in an index card holder
14. large construction-type tape measure
15. polaroid instant camera and/or other very good camera
16. car phone and/or portable phone
17. laptop computer/modem/software packages
18. fax machine
19. tape recorder (for good PMI tapes)
20. Through the company or independently, acquire
    a. lockboxes (12)
    b. signs and name riders (12)
    c. home highlight stands (12)
    d. open house signs (6)
21. large wall calendar and large desk calendar
22. box of legal-size folders
23. file folder labels
24. "sold" and "initial" stamps
25. typewriter
26. standard-size leather or good vinyl book with plastic inserts for personal promotion book. This will be your promotional book in which all promotional material regarding yourself and your company and your sample best material can be put. Ask fellow agents if they mind if you use some of their best highlight sheets from their current listings, and you will help promote their property for them.
27. Real Estate "Blue Book" from Professional Publishing Corp., 1212 Paul Drive, San Raphael, CA 94903
28. personal assistant

How to Work Effectively

1. Use your index tabs in the following manner: index tabs are for separating the areas of work in your planning book.

   a. **Red tabs: current listings (See sample on page 18.)**
   b. **Blue tabs: potential sellers/buyers**
   c. **Yellow tabs: FSBO (for sale by owner) expireds canceled**
   d. **White tabs: current buyers—only top priority buyers (See sample on page 17.)**
   e. **Green tabs: transactions**

2. (e.) Transaction sheet (just behind green index tab) (See sample on page 19). Take a sheet of paper that is graphically lined and separate *vertically* as follows:

3. (d.) Current Buyer Sheet (just behind white index tab) (See sample on page 17.) This sheet should also be graphically lined and able to hold up to twenty large rectangle shapes.

Keep a file system for buyers and sellers and use your colored index cards. Use your white index cards and keep them handy. Pull out a white index card to keep under a paper clip on the front of your daily minder as you are working with specific buyers or want to remember to check something for them. Otherwise check your list of buyers daily under each "Current Buyer Sheet." Constantly look at the date you met that buyer. Log the date next to the name as you call him or her twice weekly.

4. (c.) For Sale by Owners, canceled and expireds *(just behind yellow index tab)*. This sheet should also have quadrants also ruled off to be able to house twenty rectangle shapes. If you have a larger daily minder (such as $8\frac{1}{2}'' \times 11''$) then it is also easy to keep sheets that have punch holes in them that the sellers have given you or information from the previous listing if it is canceled or expired. At any rate, this section should contain that information that you acquire as you contact sellers and convert them. Keep a cover sheet at the front so you can quickly glance over quite a few at a time to help reference in calling sellers weekly. Also note on the quadrant sheet to date each time to telephone a For Sale by Owner, a Canceled or an Expired.

I seldom, if ever, allow myself more than *six weeks* with either a FSBO or an expired or a canceled unless it is very, very unusual circumstances. It is imperative that you can get on with other business.

(Always let the sellers know and get the message across that it is imperative that you stay active with all your current business and that you have an MLS book filled with homes that have contracts signed to give a commission to "if sold," and *that is the book that you generally work out of* rather than with a Canceled, Expired, or FSBO who may not be in a position to sign a contract for any service rendered.)

5. (b.) Potential Sellers/Buyers (just behind *blue index tab*). This section should also hold quartered sheets. The first sheet should be able to hold approximately twenty names, addresses, and phone numbers and the date you met each of them. Keep track of the dates you call them. Make sure that you are in touch at least *twice a month*. Are you sending them computer information? Are you asking them to go out and look with you because you just happen to have Tuesday or Thursday available and *which one would work better for them*? Are you listening to what they have to say and making notes?

6. (a.) Current listings *(just behind the red index tab)*. This section should contain a sheet with each listing that you have with a computer sheet on it and/or the MLS picture with the date that you listed the home on the side of the sheet and record each time you call them. You should call weekly to update the seller on how the home is selling. You should be recording each time you run an ad and keep that ad (cutout) in your daily minder, under the day that you ran the ad.

After thirty days from the time the house has been listed, are you reviewing price with the sellers?

In your file system the pink 3 × 5 index cards are for CURRENT LISTINGS. Should you have something to do on a particular listing on a particular day such as: Remove lockbox, change highlight sheet, drop off papers, etc. Just keep the *pink index card* on the outside of your daily minder.

7. Keep *alphabetical index* for calling past clients and all important numbers. Get list of important numbers for city inspectors, taxes, building inspection, etc. Also have your own current list of who is good for plumbing, painting, etc.

Home Office

Find a place at home to call your office.

Keep your home office stocked with the same contracts and information that you use at your office "away from home."

Be able to do business from your home if necessary.

Keep your home office stocked with the following if possible:

> **ALL SETS OF CONTRACTS**
> **GOOD CALCULATOR**
> **LARGE LEGAL-SIZE NOTEBOOKS**
> **AMORTIZATION CHART**
> **LARGE WALL CALENDAR**
> **TYPEWRITER**
> **REAL ESTATE CONTRACT BOOK**
> **MAP BOOK OF YOUR CITY**
> **GOOD SHARP PENCILS AND PENS**
> **LEGAL NOTE PADS OF PAPER AND PENCILS/PENS BY EVERY PHONE—KEEP ON HAND POST-IT NOTEPADS**
> **COMPUTER (LAPTOP)**
> **FAX MACHINE**

Office Away from Home

Set your desk up in order to be able to create new business each and every day.

Have your Multiple Listing Books in order.

Keep records and charts (either at home or at the office or both) of all:

> **current listings**
> **current buyers/potential buyers**
> **potential sellers**

Update your computer constantly. This is essential.

Keep charts on the wall next to your desk of all current clients and all current listings. (You may prefer to keep this list at home.)

Make a chart of *buyers* to call for the following *month*.

Make a chart of *sellers* that you have currently and when to call them *weekly*.

BUYER'S CHART should read as follows:

Buyer's Name	Address and Phone	(Price)	Date Called

SELLER'S CHART should read as follows:

Seller's Name	Address and Phone	(Price)	Date Called

Your Car

Keep your car sparkling clean!

Keep *at least* three sets of blank client listing contracts and three sets of purchase agreements with you at all times in the car.

Also keep six net sheets and six buyer information sheets. Keep these in a file folder. You may choose to carry a briefcase. Perhaps they could stay in there. If not, just keep them tucked safely away. You never know when you may need them.

Keep your personal brochures and extra business cards in the glove compartment.

Affix a stick-on notepad and pen to the dashboard. Keep messages up front.

Keep your tape measure in the glove compartment.

Keep your personal brochure with you at all times.

Keep your *daily minder* with you at all times.

Keep your open house signs in the trunk.

Keep a recent listing book either in the car or in the trunk.

Have on hand children's books for ages four to ten (just some inexpensive books that you keep in the trunk in a small bag in case you are showing a property to a mom with small children that must tag along). Oftentimes this is a godsend.

Keep a flashlight with you in your car.

Keep a calculator, tape measure and camera in your trunk!

If possible, make the best investment of all . . . have a car phone or a portable phone. It saves hours and hours of hassle if showing and you happen past a home that is newly listed and need the price right now or especially if you have arrived at a home with the wrong lockbox combination and you do not see a store or a place from where you can phone anywhere in sight.

How to Work Effectively

When putting your *daily planner* together, try to do the following:

Label your insert tabs as follows:

Red tabs:	**Listings**
White tabs:	**Buyer**
Green tabs:	**Transactions**
Yellow tabs:	**FSBO/Exp./Canceled**
Blue tabs:	**Potential sellers and Buyers**

(Under the blue tab section, make sure that your sellers and your buyers are on different colored paper. When going to that section, even if not in order, you can immediately decipher when it is a buyer or a seller).

Make sure your daily minder starts out first with:

1. Your yearly agenda planning calendar.
2. Behind this start your index tabs.
3. Behind your tabbed off sections get a clear plastic insert that holds business cards. I have two of these. Behind this, place your telephone index.
4. The back of your book should hold a ruled notebook pad.
5. On the *inside cover* keep:
   a. some of your business cards,
   b. a flat amortization schedule,
   c. the daily mortgage rate sheet,
   d. some of your brochures if possible, and
   e. a flat calculator.
6. Inside the back cover underneath the notepad keep:
   a. one blank listing,
   b. one blank purchase agreement, and
   c. three pieces of blank stationery and envelopes.
7. Keep large paper clips on your daily planner sectioning off the week and any important notes in front to remember.
8. Keep one or preferably two pens and pencils on your daily minder.
9. Record everything you do each day that involves money, your time, and people that you meet and see each day.
10. Also keep track of your daily mileage in your **daily planner**.
11. Keep three large legal pads for:
    a. "FSBOs"/"canceleds"/"expireds" (notes on home),
    b. daily to do lists (See page 12.), and
    c. daily telephone messages.

Daily To Do

Showings	Previews	FSBOs	Signs	Other

Getting Started

1. Call an architect. Ask him or her to send you some information in case you have a buyer who wants to design his or her own home. (This could be an instant referral.)

2. Find a good real estate attorney and have lunch with him or her. You may need to refer him or her time and time again. He or she may wish to refer clients to you!

3. Find good heating and plumbing contractors in your town. Have lunch with them and tell them that you would love to give them referrals and vice-versa.

4. Talk to two or three good builders in areas that you feel comfortable working. Look at their projects. Keep information on hand. See if they need real estate representation for their project.

5. Go to your local courthouse. Become familiar with the Records of Deeds office.

6. If possible, call the telephone company and have a second line just for business installed in your home.

7. Find two or three good title companies (or just one if you wish). Tour the company. Meet the closers. Become comfortable with someone who you feel is an expert at his or her job.

8. Call two or three moving companies. Have them send you information on their rates and charges. Give them your name and ask for referrals.

9. Call your Chamber of Commerce. See if there are openings for community involvement. This is an *excellent resource for clients.*

10. Call the Welcome Wagon representatives in your area. Give your name. Offer any assistance to incoming buyers that they may know of.

11. Call five new companies in town. Ask for the relocation department. Offer to work with relocation clients. Bring your personal résumé, brochure, and personal promotion book.

12. Run a personal advertisement in the weekend edition of your local newspaper. Make sure that it is catchy.

13. Watch the financial and business sections of your local newspaper. See if there are any newsworthy articles that may make a good point of reference in a monthly newsletter that you would consider sending out to a farm area.

14. Get a very good picture taken of yourself. *Put your picture on everything* that you send out or advertise in.

    a. postcards
    b. stationery
    c. post-it notes
    d. desk reminder notes
    e. monthly mailers
    f. large pencils
    g. calendars
    h. bus stop bench placards

    i. brochures

    j. personal promotional book

15. Set up your real estate office, your home office, and your car. Keep enough duplicate sets of everything that you might need at your fingertips.

16. Make some sample schedules for yourself.

17. Set some goals for a week, a month, a year, five years.

18. Join a good health club. If it has a newsletter, put in a promotional piece about yourself.

19. Become part of an organization in your area. If it has a directory, ask to put in a word about yourself. You may want to become involved with a church.

What to Wear

REMEMBER ONE THING IF YOU FORGET EVERYTHING ELSE IN THIS BOOK:

A real estate agent is expected to look successful, even if he or she is not!!

If you have been in the business for one day or one year, look as though you have been selling real estate all of your life!

How can you do this?

START BY ACQUIRING SOME "MUST-HAVES"

1. A basic tailored dark (100% cotton or silk) suit of very good quality (woman—$100+; man—$250+).

2. White or cream colored blouses/shirts (100% cotton or silk), again of quality material.

3. Well-kept, good-quality dark shoes and dark stockings. Shoes should cost 35–40% of what you pay for your clothing.

4. If you must wear jewelry, make it as real as you are and simple. Wear a watch and always be on time. So often you won't get that second chance.

5. I prefer a shoulder strap, dark leather purse that zips or stays closed.

6. If you carry a briefcase (I don't—I only carry my daily planner), be sure that it is leather. (briefcase stays in car until listing)

7. Your nails should be well-groomed at all times. Short or long, they should be well-manicured at all times.

   Because your hands are used for writing details and miscellaneous information about houses the majority of the time, your nails are always in the spotlight. How you take care of your nails and your shoes are a direct reflection of your success. Always show that you care about outside appearance.

   A good rule of thumb: a home's outside appearance reflects the inside character. It has always rung true to form. If I call on a seller that has a chipped outer door and messy landing, I can usually plan on an inside setting that needs immediate attention. The same rings true for an individual.

8. Make sure that each day your clothing is pressed and fresh-looking. If you have to avoid dry cleaners to save money, use an iron and a wet towel to press over a suit or a pair of pants. Blouses and shirts should be fresh-looking and free from wrinkles at all times.

9. Before leaving the house each day, make sure that all spots and any dirt marks are removed from clothing. Invest in an inexpensive lint remover brush. Keep it by the door and use it each day before you leave for work.

10. Refrain from garish colors. Real estate professionals should be easy on the eyesight. I know of a fellow real estate agent that literally lost a sale with a buyer because of clothing color. The agent was wearing a bright orange suit and it obviously made the buyer ill at ease. And not knowing her at all, the agent was unable to close with her.

11. In the summer, an overcoat is usually unnecessary. However, in the winter make sure the overcoat is a neutral color. A trench coat is always a safe investment.

12. Part of your dress is your car. Keep it spotless.

I am not advocating that people must go out and fill their closets with dark suits and cream and white colored shirts and blouses. However, I do feel that a basic part of a well-groomed real estate agent's wardrobe will always be the clothes I have spoken about.

Personal Assistant

There are many duties that a personal assistant can perform for a real estate agent throughout the day. Following is a list that was composed of many of the designated jobs I have given to my personal assistant.

1. Prepare a FSBO packet.
2. Prepare a listing packet.
3. Prepare a buyer's packet.
4. Prepare seller's weekly report.
5. Call with feedback to all agents.
6. Answer telephone calls and messages.
7. Track all pending files before closing.
8. Input listing, price changes, etc. in computer.
9. Contact title companies.
10. Take picture of property.
11. Help to measure home.
12. Get printout of current new listings, solds, and expireds.
13. Clip and save all FSBOs in newspaper.
14. Update computer daily.
15. Send out fax to other company and/or client.
16. Write ad for paper.
17. Write ad for a real estate magazine and/or TV.

18. Update client list and mailer after closing.

19. Make all appointments for buyers.

20. Send highlight sheet on listing to other agents.

21. Do a CMA on the computer.

22. Do an area market survey on computer.

23. Purchase cards and gifts for closing.

24. Give all information to appraisers on property.

25. Order any and all self-marketing tools for agent.

26. Send listing renewal to clients ahead of schedule.

27. Note all showings on listing files.

28. Constantly update wall and desk calendars.

29. Keep files on important real estate articles for newsletters.

30. Use the computer for mailings of postcards and mass mailings.

31. Take care of any and all travel arrangements.

32. Set up open houses.

33. Set up tour for other agents.

34. Install highlight homes boxes at listing.

35. Call lender for update on buyer's mortgage.

36. Send thank you notes to clients and/or agents.

37. Go to post office; receive and distribute mail.

38. Send out highlight sheet on listing to top agents.

39. Send out sheet of all listings to top agents.

40. Type all correspondence and proofread it.

41. Keep office neat and orderly.

42. Pick up and deliver lunch on busy days in the office.

43. Pull comparable listings for all FSBOs.

44. Xerox any and *all* information needed daily.

45. Deliver papers to buyers and sellers at their homes.

46. Take various materials to printer.

47. Deliver and pick up pictures at local photo developer.

48. Keep inventory and stock of all office supplies needed.

49. Take notes at office meetings if agent is unable to attend.

50. Telephone FSBOs ahead of time to say you're in the area.

51. Mail just sold listed card.

52. Call lenders on update of interest rates and financing.

53. Handle rental properties.

54. Retype purchase agreements.

55. Oversee vacant properties.

Current Buyers

Name	Address	Phone	Date Met	Needs

Current Listings

Address	Name	Phone	Date Listed	Price	Combo Lockbox	Date Sold

Transaction Sheet

Address	Seller/Buyer	Commission Paid	Closing Date	Agents Name/ Coop. Company Loan Officer/ Phone No.

Conference Planner	Date_____

CHAPTER 1

CHAPTER 2

Attitude

big deal
by "Lorayne n' Neil"

Attitude

The following is a quote from Charles Swindoll:

> *The longer I live, the more I realize the impact of attitude on life. Attitude, to me, is more important than facts. It is more important than appearance, gift or skill. It will make or break a company . . . a church . . . a home.*

> *The remarkable thing is we have a choice every day regarding the 'Attitude' we will embrace for that day. We cannot change our past. We cannot change the fact that people will act in a certain way.* **WE CANNOT CHANGE THE INEVITABLE**. *The only thing we can do is play on the one string we have, and that is our "attitude." I am convinced that life is 10% what happens to me and 90% how I react to it . . . and so it is with you . . . we are in charge of our attitudes.*

My definition:

> *Attitude is the reaction you take and maintain to any given situation, either spontaneous or thought out. An attitude is directly attributable to the value you place on happiness and peace of mind. An attitude, more than any other one thing, will make or break you in the real estate business.*

Guess what?

Attitude is 93% of everything that you do.

Guess what else?

Almost 83% of all communication is what you see.

The amount of money you make in real estate depends on how you feel about yourself.

What About Your Attitude?

Your attitude might as well sum up your whole career in a nutshell.

Here's the best example of attitude that I can think of to give to you:

> *Don't listen to "no."*
>
> *Carefully . . .*
>
> *Constantly . . .*
>
> *Consistently . . . maintain a positive approach.*
>
> *Don't listen to "no."*

If a client mentions that he really doesn't want to list his home right now, and he's had the *best* of all real estate agents over to his house and he's sick and tired of the whole thing, tell him that you understand completely and you really are going to be in his area next Monday, and you really do have either 4:00 or 7:00 P.M. open right now, and you really could stop by on Monday. Which time would be best for him? And if not then, when? And if not, why not?

And be kind.

And listen.

And if all else fails and he still says "*no*,"

Then *that's okay*! Because *you won't get all of them.*

Go on to the next one, and the next one.

And suddenly someone will really want you to come over and *list his or her home.*

And the wait wasn't so bad after all!

It works. I know it does because that's how I get all of my business. *I just don't give up.*

Good luck eventually finds me.

I could write chapter after chapter on *attitude*, *how to stay enthusiastic*, how to constantly keep the smile on your face when all else is horrible around you. But actually maintaining a good attitude is a bit simpler than that.

Try to remember to keep disciplined! Have a schedule each and every day from which you *cannot* and *will not* and *do not* deviate. Take certain days that you call on the FSBOs, certain days that you work with your buyers, certain days that you call on "expireds," and certain days that are just for you! In all my years in the business, I still reserve Sundays for "opens." I have two open houses on Sundays: 12:00 to 2:00 P.M. and 2:30 to 4:30 P.M. I still call For Sale By Owners on Sunday nights. I still go over all my notes from my opens on Mondays and call buyers to set up showings for the week. I send out mailings and call more For Sale By Owners on Mondays to set up appointments for all week!!

You are only as busy, successful and motivated as your *daily calendar* shows that you are!

Your attitude is your lifeline in the real estate business!

Be your own manager! Set up your own schedule for the *entire week* at the *beginning of the week*. Start with Sunday after your two open houses!

You need to fill in the blanks for the week *by Monday*. Call and work with two buyers a week. Call and work on at least two listings a week. Call and work on at least five future listings (FSBOs) each week. Call and work on at least five expired listings each week. Your attitude should tell you to *just do it*! Don't think about how you feel. Don't think about needing money, not having money, not feeling like it, not wanting to do it, or possible rejection. Don't think beyond the disciplined schedule that you have created for yourself.

Just pick up the telephone. Call each number. Try to follow a belief system in which you do not listen to "no." There is always a way around a situation. If someone has a way of reaching you with the fact that they want to buy or sell a home, the simple fact remains that they reached you. Now reach them!

Be *consistent*. Be careful to remember to ask for the appointment. Don't let a potential buyer leave you at an open house without an appointment (even an appointment for you to call on a given date). Don't hang up without making an appointment with a buyer to schedule a time to look at some houses. *Always get an appointment.* If you are at a For Sale By Owner for the first time, *don't leave without the next appointment.*

I like to think that:

Real Estate Agent + Appointment + Appointment + Appointment = Transaction

I must add an important point regarding timing here.

I spend no more than *six weeks* with For Sale By Owners, Expireds and Buyers (usually trying to list FSBOs by the second or at most third appointment).

See Chapter 10 for details on price reductions as well as Chapter 4 for additional information on making a sale.

Ways That You Can Improve Sales

1. Replace a negative thought with a positive one.
2. Read a *positive* motivational book.
3. Buy a *"real" piece of jewelry*.
4. Discover what makes you *look your best*.
5. *Change your diet* by eliminating sugars, meats, alcohol, tobacco, caffeine and salt and go for "low fat."
6. *Eat more fiber foods*, like fruits and vegetables.
7. *Exercise* fifteen to twenty minutes every other day.
8. *Say something positive to yourself* every day, such as, "I am important."
9. *Update your finances* and budget twice a month.
10. *Try to laugh* more than frown each day.
11. Tell yourself *something good* about yourself.
12. When showering each morning, try to *say positive affirmations to yourself.*
13. Do *something nice* for somebody each and every day.
14. *Listen to good motivating tapes* (keep them in your car), and limit TV viewing time.
15. When frustrated, take deep breaths and relax by replacing negative thoughts with positive ones.
16. Find a *hobby* other than your job. Work on it weekly. (Consider volunteer work, something you've always wanted to do or some kind of lessons.)
17. Become aware that you can control your own destiny.
18. Every *third* weekend *plan a special event* or trip.
19. *Try smiling* more each day.
20. When you schedule your work schedule, *schedule your fun schedule.*
21. Keep lists of your goals.
22. *Keep lists of things* that you want to do daily, weekly, and monthly.
23. Before you leave the office, make sure that you *feel good about yourself.*
24. Take time for your family with a *planned event.*
25. *Surprise someone* with a gift.
26. Make or attend a good sit down dinner with friends or family at least *twice a week.*
27. *Let go of grudges.*
28. *Learn something* new each day.
29. *Replace a bad habit* with something you have always wanted *to do for yourself.*
30. Introduce yourself to your neighbors.
31. *Join an organization* that creates some sort of positive inner effect on you.
32. Give someone a compliment *each day.*
33. Talk to people who are *positive.*
34. Avoid gossip.
35. Subscribe to a magazine that reflects inner growth.
36. Keep a journal to record your thoughts and to see how you change.
37. Keep your daily planner current.
38. Maintain *good posture.*
39. Buy yourself something to improve your looks once every month. (If money is tight, sometimes getting a haircut, a new tie, a new hair clip, or even a new color of lipstick or nail polish will suffice.)
40. *Read this book again!*

DEFINITION OF ATTITUDE IN THE REAL ESTATE BUSINESS

"Be honest from the beginning."

The way you look is the way the client looks at you!

Be prepared to close from the day you meet your first client, including the day you hold your first open house.

Any *client may want to buy right away!*

I'll never forget the time I held one of my first open houses almost twenty years ago. I watched as a fellow colleague asked permission to bring his people through my open house. Of course, I agreed because my objective is to represent the seller and sell the house! The agent came—very professional and well-dressed. He brought his clients, including a husband, a wife and a three year old daughter. After spending a good forty minutes in the home, the people decided to buy it!

I remember thinking, "Thank goodness I don't have to help them! What would I do . . .?" I didn't even bring purchase agreements with me! They were back at the office. Also I didn't think I could fill one out very well. Being in class and taking the real estate test was one thing, but this was the real thing! That day I went home and practiced for two hours writing and rewriting purchase agreements.

I was determined that when the opportunity presented itself again, I would be ready.

Upon further reflection I was also a bit self-conscious about the shoes I had worn and the jacket I had grabbed. My outfit was acceptable, but the shoes and the jacket were an afterthought. I could have done better.

Remember: "Dress to close" from the beginning.

It's a feeling of knowing, you are, you can, and you will be the best when you decide to be the best dressed and best prepared agent from the start.

Make More Money in Less Time

Two ways of making big money are:

1. to know that "time is a gift," and
2. to realize that we never know how much time we have!

Learn from your past experiences.

You will never really change the amount of time you put into the business, so how can you get better using the same amount of time? Don't just work nights. Work by appointment. Reorganize the time you are using.

COMMITMENT:

The real estate business is you! To be in the business unconditionally in rain, sleet, snow, hard times, good times, high interest rates, low interest rates, happy customers, etc., you must have an UNCONDITIONAL desire to succeed.

Some time-saving devices include:

1. car phone
2. computer (laptop)
3. fax machine
4. phone mail
5. personal assistant

Increase productivity without increasing your activity.

Life is a gift and a game you've already won. *To maintain a leading edge, be true to yourself!*

Is there a best attitude to approaching real estate?

Is there such a thing as being able to turn a positive attitude on and off?

Can a person actually achieve success in the real estate business, even when his or her life is in a quandary and depression is weighing heavily on one's mind?

Let's just say the answer for myself, to all of the above is "yes"!

I have developed a formula for success for myself over the years by applying a technique that works well using a "time management" solution for buyers, home, office, open houses and sellers.

Attitude with Buyers

When I meet with a buyer either from a phone call, through an open house, or from a referral, I try to use the following formula for working with them to keep them as clients:

I sit down with my clients and have at least one meeting during which I can listen to their needs. I listen to what is important to them *and put a* time limit *on how long they want to look for a house. I always frame-in a time from the very beginning.*

I let buyers know that my attitude toward selling them a house is based on when *they* want to be in a property. I do not allow myself to listen if they tell me that "if and when" they find the *right* house they will buy. This is not appropriate dialogue for myself and my clients. I find it extremely imperative that I get across to them how important it is to be working within a *time frame* for all parties considered.

I stress the fact that once a home is found, usually a mortgage commitment is affixed at or around 60 days, and also the interest rate is usually set for that period of time.

I also stress the fact that the good properties that are found are usually uncovered immediately and sell fairly quickly. Buyers need to know, especially for themselves, some sort of time frame to be working within.

I explain to my clients that I assign them to one of *three categories: A, B, or C.* The A buyers are the buyers who get the *majority* of my attention and rightly so. Once you establish boundaries on your own *way of working*, the respect that comes from your buyers is *automatic.* Buyers instinctively don't want to miss out on a good deal. If they feel that they can get the best from you just by rerouting their own thought patterns on how and when to buy, it will be in everyone's best interest to use a time frame to work within. (The B and C buyers are not in a hurry.)

IMPORTANT RULE OF THUMB: FIND OUT YOUR POTENTIAL BUYER'S SCHEDULE. Make sure that you allow yourself time in the beginning to discover client flexibility and to set up future appointment times. Also cover the ground rules from the start. Have an attitude that is *enthusiastic, fun and exciting* to entice the potential buyer to want to be with you more than any other real estate agent. How can you achieve this?

TELL THEM THAT YOU ARE THE BEST AGENT FOR THEM. *Keep your personal life separate.* Don't allow the buyer to peek into your private life! Talk about *them.* Ask lots of questions. Be cheerful and talkative and upbeat about real estate.

Attitude at Home

Is your business life tied with your family life? How important is it to mix? Should, and can you take real estate calls at home, at any time and allow them to overlap with family time? The answer to all of the above questions is "yes."

You just need to know how to do this. Your attitude regarding real estate must be very, very broad-minded. You must be able to cope and bend and be flexible in ways that you did not need to be before. This is all okay if you can allow yourself the opportunity to say "no" at the appropriate times and work within a fixed schedule for yourself and your family.

Your family should know that the home phone is essential to success in real estate. The phone at home must, should, and can be answered in a professional manner at all times. Let your family know how important it is for everyone who calls to hear an appropriate response at your end. Let them know that good manners come across with a good attitude on the telephone. Many missed calls, wrong numbers and loss of time can be eliminated by just stating the following when answering the telephone:

"Hello, this is the Johnson residence, Jim speaking" or "Anderson residence, may I help you?"

Keep a pencil and pad of paper by each and every phone in the house. Instruct all people living at home *how* important a telephone message is and that not only the name and phone number, but the time that they called is very important also! Tell your family how important they are to you and that you *do not* intend to let business interfere with family time for such and such hour(s). Try to work around this time frame. If the dinner hour is from 6:00 to 7:00 every night, make this the time that the answering service automatically receives the calls at home. With an appropriate message on your recorder, you should have no trouble retaining any and all calls that come into the home. If you work in the evening, make sure that when you come home after your appointments, you put the rest of your business calls on the answering service. There is such a thing as burnout in the industry, and it usually occurs in agents who do not know when to stop! A family cannot be expected to tolerate without resentment one member working around the clock. There must be balance in order to have harmony at home while working real estate.

Even if there are no other family members, a successful agent must set aside appropriate time for relaxation and enjoyment. Life is very much like a teeter-totter; it goes up and down, but must have equal weight on both sides to achieve balance.

Attitude at the Office

Is it right to be at the office *more* than not? Should you be going to lunch and making friends with other salespeople at the office? Or should you just skip office meetings and do your own thing?

THE ANSWER TO ALL OF THE ABOVE IS "NO."

It is very important to maintain the correct attitude toward your office. *How* important is it to be at the office all the time? There again, your attitude should encompass the fact that you are definitely "minding the store for yourself" so to speak. No one can ever tell you how to work effectively, except for yourself. It is not prudent, nor in your best interest to be in the office all the time. There, again, your attitude will determine your success. Your attitude is imperative in addressing time tables which include when you are expected to go to a sales meeting for your own knowledge of what new listings are perhaps available among the sales people in your office, and what new office requirements or sales data have gone into effect. "No man is an island," and although you are your own boss, so to speak, in order to work successfully and completely effectively, you need to include yourself in meetings, seminars, and talk sessions that improve you as a whole in the industry.

We all benefit from sharing information, and this is also vital in real estate. I make sure that every single week in preparing my daily schedule, I block out a certain amount of time for sales meetings, touring new properties, and some or all office get-togethers. In the real estate business you not only list and sell homes, but also network with your fellow associates to keep abreast of the latest techniques. Success and failure stories help you and others as well.

Attitude at Open Houses

Should you be enthusiastic *all the time* at an open house, even if you are depressed that day? Should you have an open house if you have an opportunity to do something that is more fun? Should you put out extra *Open House* signs even if the property doesn't really warrant them?

THE ANSWER TO ALL OF THE ABOVE IS "YES."

It is imperative that your attitude reflect your optimism in real estate because often you will not get another chance! I cannot emphasize enough the importance of a good attitude, a cheerful disposition and how contagious *enthusiasm* really is.

When you are at an open house, and people come through, they immediately *size you up*. I know this isn't fair, but *life isn't fair*. That's the way it is.

Buyers will come through an open house, and they will decide, sometimes on the spot, whether or not they want to work with you.

YOUR ATTITUDE CANNOT BE COMPROMISED

You must decide when going to an open house that your attitude will be upbeat, cheerful, and enthusiastic!

When meeting buyers at an open house, remember to act and talk the way you would want to be treated if you were them. Try going to open houses to gauge how you are impressed by attitudes of other agents. What turns you on or off?

Never take anything for granted.

You most likely will not have another opportunity to impress them!

Attitude with Sellers

Should you treat all sellers the same? Should you answer a seller's question just to satisfy him or her, even before you have checked into it? Should you assume that you probably will not get the listing from a seller because he or she mentioned another company?

THE ANSWER TO ALL OF THE ABOVE IS "NO."

The correct attitude to have regarding sellers is to treat every potential sale as a unique situation in and of its own merits. Rely on your good judgment to tell you when to back off and when you should ask more questions. But have the attitude that you can help them regardless of their difficulty with selling their home. Do your homework first. Your attitude should consist of genuine concern and undivided attention to their entire situation. You should have an understanding nature about what has brought them to this point and let them know that you are the professional and that you will make every conceivable effort to help them in the best way that you know how. Be sure to relate an attitude of trust and assuredness. Your demeanor should be impeccable, and your appearance should be professional at all times. You should reflect an attitude of irreproachable honesty and unique style. Sellers should be left feeling that *you* are the best professional that they could hope to find, a confident person whom they can trust.

Your attitude toward sellers will be a deciding factor in your success in the real estate business.

Never, under any circumstances, take anything for granted.

Your attire should be the best groomed, your attitude should be the best in the room.

Attitude

Attitude reduces to one definition:

> Basic hard work = terrific results

A common denominator of life is that most successful people have the habit of doing things that other people don't like to do.

Be all that you can be. Give yourself continual reassurance.

You need to work the business from all of these angles:

1. out-of-town buyers
2. local buyers and sellers
3. corporate relocation clients
4. expired listings
5. past customers
6. retired people

TAKE ON THE GOAL TO MAKE A SALE, SOME WAY, EVERY DAY! (SOMETIMES THIS MEANS THAT YOU SOLD A CLIENT ON AN APPOINTMENT.)

You will get ahead because most people are unwilling to make even a good effort! To achieve this goal, you must

1. have a plan, and
2. prospect all the time.

In real estate, if you come to and leave work without appointments, you are out of business!

ALL WE HAVE TO OFFER PEOPLE IS OUR *PRODUCT KNOWLEDGE.*

To determine your sales appeal, ask yourself if you **would hire yourself to sell your own home.**

People hire real estate agents for three things:

1. to manage their properties,
2. to help with the decorating,
3. to get a property bought or sold.

REMEMBER:

> People will always want to work with enthusiastic individuals.
> People get hung up on ego.
> Take control of your own destiny!

Seven Important Statements for Real Estate Salespersons

1. Stop focusing on what is not, and start creating what can be.

2. Take an honest look at all the negative practices in your life and business, and eliminate them.

3. Revoke your membership in the "Knock Yourself Down" Club.

4. Start all over again with the basics.

5. Look ahead instead of backward. Only spend time in your past if you really must.

6. Change your mental diet by watching what you feed yourself (TV, radio, paper, magazines, etc.).

7. Do something that you normally wouldn't do or couldn't afford to do. In other words, *take a risk!*

THE KEY TO GROWING IS EXPANDING YOUR KNOWLEDGE.

If you *want* success in real estate, you can have it!

ABCs of a Successful Attitude

A Arguing with a seller or buyer is unacceptable.

B Begins a sales effort with full knowledge of the customers' needs.

C Careful in the way the agent dresses *at all times*.

D Delivers answers to buyers and sellers without dodging them.

E Emphasizes the right statement at the right time.

F Follows through after a sale to keep in touch with the buyer and seller.

G Guarantees top performance at all times.

H Has heart in the business at all times.

I Interested in the customer and asks lots of questions.

J Joins the buyer and seller together successfully. Jots down notes from meetings with clients.

K Knows what to do *every* day.

L Looks at all possible alternatives in a transaction.

M Manages his or her business in a professional manner.

N Numbers "to do" items daily.

O Organizes time daily in making appointments and sales.

P Praises oneself for good effort.

Q Quits only when the job is done.

R Realizes that success in real estate depends on personal hard work.

S Services clients with 100% dedication to the business.

T Time management in all things.

U Understands the situation of the buyers and the sellers.

V Vacations at least one full weekend a month with family and/or friends to avoid burnout.

W Walks, jogs, or exercises during the week to eliminate stress.

X Xeroxes all necessary information as clients' needs arise.

Y Yearly reviews all goals and ambitions and reorganizes files.

Z Zestful whole-hearted interest, gusto, and spirited enjoyment of life.

AFFIRMATIONS:
Alternative Ideas for Negative Attitude

I am doing the best job I can to succeed in real estate.

Every day I will somehow try, some way to better myself.

Nothing can disturb my thinking or upset me if I do not allow it to.

"In all ways, at all times, for all purposes, I will guard against negative thoughts and negative behavior."

I will survive through all kinds of adversity and discouragement.

Today and every day, I commit to loving myself and forgiving my mistakes.

Decisions I make are based entirely upon the truth that is.

All people and all things depend upon good. I will seek to do good.

I am completely filled with good feelings, good thoughts, and good intentions, at all times.

These positive affirmations can be used on a daily basis. Try one at a time for a week at a time.

ANYTHING GOOD IS WORTH TRYING ONCE.

How to Work Best with Your Body's Timeclock

Each and every day it is important to know how to make use of the best hours of that day. Did you know that your body has a natural timeclock and that you subconsciously follow what your body says, regardless of what you want to do?

This is a general guide for taking full advantage of your body's daily rhythm.

7:00–9:00 A.M.	Short-term memory is at its peak. Problem solving skills are at their peak. Overall alertness is generally very high.
8:00–10:00 A.M.	Pain tolerance is highest.
9:00 A.M.–12:00 P.M.	Analytical and reasoning skills are high. Good time to solve problems. Good time to map strategy. Good time to balance books. *Good time for thinking things through.*
10:00 A.M.–12:00 P.M.	You are wide awake. You are the most alert and most aware. Your speaking skills are at peak. Excellent time for business meetings. Excellent time for presentations. Good time for closing arguments and important lunches and brunches.
1:00–3:00 P.M.	You naturally feel dull and sleepy at this time. Exercise at this time revitalizes you. Good time for walking, jogging, or swimming.
3:00–4:00 P.M.	Alertness rises again. Long-term memorization skills peak. Time to deliver a speech or sell-job. Recall is 8% higher on material studied. Hand to eye coordination is at peak. This is a good time for a game of tennis.
3:00–5:00 P.M.	You might expect to experience a mood swing. Disposition improves throughout the day. Cheerful afternoon high.
4:00–5:00 P.M.	Your ability to handle confrontation is at its highest.
4:00–6:00 P.M.	Your manual dexterity is the sharpest. This is a good time to type contracts.
6:00–9:00 P.M.	Your thinking skills and reflexes are winding down. Not a good time to exercise. You need to regroup. Good time for mental affirmations. Low key.
7:00–9:00 P.M.	Your five senses are most acute now. Great time to appreciate music. Excellent time for rescheduling activities for the next day. Excellent time to meet with people because you are so responsive to their needs and wants.
11:00 P.M.–1:00 A.M.	Late night genius creativity burst is possible. Good time to write snappy, catchy ads. Compose copy for self-promotion.

Scientists have found that the afternoon dip persists regardless of whether people skip lunch, eat at odd times, or eat at identical times every day. We are at our sleepiest every twelve hours, typically in midafternoon and a few hours before dawn. In your afternoon make sure to include some sort of distraction, such as a walk, a very short time out, whatever can work for you.

Real estate agents must work long, hard hours into the evening, or shorter time managed hours even when making the most out of their entire day. So find a way to relax your mind and your body.

Guaranteed Stress Reducers

1. Sit quietly, close your eyes, and take ten very long, deep breaths. Nothing is ever as important as it seems!

2. Take a scenic drive to where there is water, country, quiet and peace.

3. Play a relaxing tape, such as George Winston's "Autumn," for twenty minutes.

4. Read an uplifting book, such as *The Great Thoughts* by Geo Seldes.

5. Play golf.

6. Make a reservation at a nice hotel, even if it's close by.

7. Walk very hard and fast outside in fresh air.

8. Do some kind of exercise for no less than twenty minutes.

9. Go for a swim for no less than fifteen minutes at a local health club.

10. Go for a bicycle ride.

11. Take time to just be alone.

12. Go window shopping and people watching at a mall.

13. Get a massage, pedicure, facial, and haircut.

14. Play cards.

15. Stop working, and do something with your family.

16. Go to a north woods cabin.

17. Go out country western dancing.

18. Go to a comedy movie, even alone, and eat popcorn.

19. Go somewhere quiet and private to pray and/or meditate.

20. Curl up with a cozy blanket by a crackling fire and watch an old movie.

21. Learn to play the piano.

22. Take drawing lessons, or paint with no lessons.

23. Go to a craft store and decide to do a project.

24. Go to a health foods store, and purchase good vitamins.

25. Reorganize your closets, your bedroom, and your drawers.

26. Paint a room in your house a positive, cheerful color.

27. Learn to play tennis.

28. Learn to speak a foreign language.

29. Volunteer to work at an organization that needs help. The quickest way to forget your problems is to *help someone else*!

30. Think way back about what you used to like to do for relaxation or fun. **Could you do it now?**

Stress

The dictionary defines stress as "mentally or emotionally disruptive, disquieting . . . distress." Stress is a funny thing. It has a way of creeping up and building up on you until all of a sudden you just want to explode! Your body often takes such a pounding that your head doesn't stop pounding even when the stress's source is removed. Unless you're selling homes to ostriches (and you're one too) you will undoubtedly encounter some stress in the real estate business!

NO ONE WILL EVER TAKE CARE OF YOU THE WAY YOU DO.

No one can ever know how a deal affects you. No other person can actually feel the pleasure you get from a sale or the discouragement you get from rejection . . .

> *a lost buyer*
> *a house that didn't sell*

You absolutely must learn to balance your professional and private lives and to watch for certain warning signs.

1. extreme fatigue

2. becoming overtired

3. doing too many things at once

4. making mistakes because of overload

5. doing everything you can and still not getting business.

It's sometimes important to:

1. delegate jobs (maybe you really *do* need a personal assistant),

2. find a partner (maybe another agent could work better with you),

3. regroup (if time management is the biggest problem, you may need to give yourself more space), and

4. change jobs (maybe you're working with the wrong people or doing the right things with the wrong kinds of buyers).

No single real estate agent has been able to go through a year with every transaction falling into place perfectly.

REAL ESTATE TAKES A LOT OF WORK AND
TAKES ITS TOLL,
SO LEARN TO PREPARE AND HELP YOURSELF!

WHAT'S YOUR ATTITUDE REGARDING MONEY?

Would you rather have $1,000,000

or . . .

a penny each day of the month that doubles itself in value?

Day

Day	Amount	Day	Amount	Day	Amount
1	$ .01	11	$ 10.24	21	$ 10,485.76
2	$ .02	12	$ 20.48	22	$ 20,971.52
3	$ .04	13	$ 40.96	23	$ 41,943.04
4	$ .08	14	$ 81.92	24	$ 83,886.08
5	$ .16	15	$ 163.84	25	$ 167,772.16
6	$ .32	16	$ 327.68	26	$ 335,544.32
7	$ .64	17	$ 655.36	27	$ 671,088.64
8	$1.28	18	$1,310.72	28	$1,342,177.28
9	$2.56	19	$2,621.44	29	$2,684,354.56
10	$5.12	20	$5,242.88	30	$5,368,709.12

31 (Last day) . . . $10,737,418.24

How Do You Spend Each Day?

Twenty-One-Point Plan

1. What is your logo?

2. When will your personal brochure be ready for distribution?

3. How can you set yourself apart from other agents?

4. What is your personal motto?

5. What real estate area will you specialize in?

6. Where will you farm?

7. What is your self-marketing plan?

8. What will you offer sellers?

9. What will you offer buyers?

10. How will you promote yourself and your company through community involvement?

11. What is your personalized marketing plan?

12. What is your sellers' marketing plan?

13. Have you purchased your lockboxes? Do you take your lockbox with you on every second appointment with potential sellers?

14. How many listings will you get this week?

15. How many buyers will you sell this week?

16. How many listings will you sell this month?

17. How many buyers sold this month?

18. How many listings will you get this year?

19. To how many buyers will you sell this year?

20. Do you want to work with a partner? FSBOs?

21. Do you have a four-week schedule in your daily planner?

Have you practiced closing on a buyer this week?

Have you practiced closing on a seller this week?

How many appointments do you have for this week?

Where have you promoted yourself this week?

A "Best Attitude" Regarding Life . . .

Risk . . .

To laugh is to risk appearing the fool
To weep is to risk appearing sentimental
To reach out for another is to risk involvement
To expose feelings is to risk exposing your true self
To play your ideas and dreams before the crowd is to risk their loss
To love is to risk not being loved in return
To live is to risk dying
To hope is to risk despair
To try is to risk failure . . .
. . . but risk must be taken,
Because the greatest hazard in life is to risk nothing
The person who risks nothing does nothing, has nothing, and is nothing
One may avoid some suffering and sorrow
But one simply cannot learn, feel, change, grow, live, and love
Chained by one's certitudes,
One is a slave, one has forfeited freedom
Only one who risks . . .
. . . is truly free

—author unknown

Weekly Objectives

1. PUT TOGETHER YOUR REAL ESTATE PLAN.

2. DEVELOP AN INDIVIDUAL MARKETING SYSTEM THAT YOU PROMOTE THROUGH YOUR MOTTO OR LOGO.

3. CLOSE DAILY ON A NEW BUYER OR SELLER.

4. GET A MINIMUM OF TWO NEW BUYERS THIS WEEK.

5. GET A MINIMUM OF TWO LISTINGS THIS WEEK.

6. CALL SIX FSBOS THIS WEEK, WORKING A 6-2-6 PROGRAM.

7. START YOUR OWN REFERRAL SHEET WITH YOUR CLIENTS.

8. PRIORITIZE AND CAREFULLY SCHEDULE YOUR TIME.

9. WEEKLY, WRITE DOWN TEN WAYS TO IMPROVE YOUR TIME MANAGEMENT.

10. KEEP A DAILY, COMPREHENSIVE "TO DO" LIST.

CHAPTER 3

Advertising
Ads to Write,
Sample Ads

big deal
by "Lorayne n' Neil"

Advertising

Did you know that 5% of all homes are sold from an ad?

When writing an ad for the seller of a particular piece of property, I try to include the following important items:

1. number of bedrooms and baths
2. style of the home (especially if it has a walkout lower level)
3. main floor family room and/or den and fireplaces
4. major new improvements
5. interior square footage
6. special amenities of the lot or interior
7. price or price range
8. location

These items reflect the overall type of home that you are selling.

An ad that reflects the above items will target potential buyers for this particular home. Because you include the price range and talk about the particular style and area you narrow the market for a more specific buyer who can qualify for the home. Therefore, you will be more likely to keep a potential buyer who calls on the telephone.

Placing Ads in Newspapers

When designing a newspaper ad, I try to structure it according to the following formula:

I try to design a two-cap headline with no more than seventeen letters, such as:

Just Listed
Great Listing
Gorgeous Home
None Like It
It's the Best

The second line should also be two caps with no more than seventeen letters. This line might reflect the times the home is open, such as Sunday from 2:00 to 4:00 P.M. or if the home is not being held open. It might also describe the style and area of the home, such as:

Colonial in Woods
Lakeside Retreat
Country Rambler
Sensational Split
Beautiful Bungalow

Hillside Haven
Two-story Sun-filled
Breathtaking View
Unique Area
Close to School

The rest of the ad describes the kind of home, numbers of bedrooms and baths, interior square footage, and something about a special feature that you like about the home.

When Writing the Ad

1. Give the facts.

2. Don't exaggerate.

3. Be descriptive.

4. Avoid hard to understand abbreviations.

5. Include the price.

6. Be available.

Ad Writing

1. *Remember* your two-line headline.

2. *Get across* to the reader that this home is a real bargain.

   Examples: "no home with this square footage for the money . . ."

   "least priced home in the neighborhood . . ."

3. *Stress* a main benefit.

   Examples: "park across the street . . ."

   "located in desirable area of . . ."

   "lowest maintenance around . . ."

4. Be *specific* on the address and provide clear directions.

   Example: 425 Maplewood Drive (2 blocks so. of North St. and 1 block w. of Alameda, left to 4th house)

5. Be *specific* in the body of the ad.

   Example: "3 br, 2 bath, family room off kitchen, formal dr, huge finished lower . . ."

6. Make the ad *interesting* as well as specific.

   Example: "3 huge brs! fantastic family room off country kitchen . . ."

7. Find something *unique* to the home.

   Examples: "no other lot like this one"

   "very unusual floor plan"

   "a gourmet cook's dream kitchen"

8. *Ask yourself* if you would call on your own ad.

9. *Remember* to include your name and phone number and the price of the home.

10. Short and sophisticated ads = satisfied clients who call!

Thesaurus for Real Estate

ACREAGE:

private land
rolling greens
luscious estate

AIR CONDITIONING:

zoned heating and cooling
climate controlled

ALCOVE:

secluded area
music alcove

AMENITIES:

assets of the home
pleasantries the home includes

APPLIANCES:

like new
built-ins
subzero refrigerator

APARTMENT:

mother-in-law apartment
lower level apartment
teenage apartment

AVAILABLE:

take advantage now
accessible immediately

AVENUE:

wide thoroughfare
ivy-covered lane

tree-lined path
approach to home lined with trees

BASEMENT:

lower level
downstairs den
crawl space under house

lower family room
lower level walkout

BATHROOM:

master bath	his and her vanity
jacuzzi in master bath	sumptuous Roman bath
therapeutic, whirlpool spa	health club with spa in your own home
private spa	

BEDROOM:

master bedroom suite	teenage hideaway
skylit master suite	beautiful, big bedrooms
panelled bedroom or den	dormitory-size bedroom
extra bedroom ideal for rental	second master suite
private, palatial suite	bunk beds go great in this room
master suite with fireplace	secluded master

COLONIAL:

two-story center hall	Currier and Ives colonial
charming southern colonial	picture-book colonial
4 bedroom dutch colonial	Williamsburg white colonial

CONDOMINIUM:

corner unit	private end unit
upgraded designer unit	strategically located end unit

CONTEMPORARY:

classic contemporary	art deco contemporary
provocative contemporary	exciting and open contemporary

COUNTRY:

over the meadow	short drive to country seclusion
country estate	rustic and rural countryside locale
country cottage	

CLEAN:

model condition throughout	impeccable interior
superbly maintained	flawless condition
refreshingly mint condition	white-glove condition
sparkling, move-in condition	

CARPETING:

all-wool carpet throughout

plush, luxurious carpeting

white wool carpeting

genuine berber carpet

neutral carpet throughout entire home

CEILINGS:

vaulted and soaring

softly lighted ceilings

soaring ceiling

spectacular ceiling

skylights

beautiful and beamed

cathedral and open-beamed ceilings

crown molding

soaring and spacious

CIRCLE:

cul-de-sac location

CITY:

in the heart of town

community involvement

the center of it all

central location

COLORS:

neutral colors throughout

wonderful white tones

bathed in soft pastels

softly decorated throughout

decorator decor

earth tones prevail

warm, soft colors prevail

muted tones

fresh, cool colors

DECK:

private, sunny deck

sunrise deck

B.B.Q. on your dynamite deck

fully landscaped deck

multiple-leveled deck

spacious terrace

oversize cedar planked

relax and watch sunsets from your . . .

wonderful, wraparound deck

extensive deck

private courtyard

DEN:

home office

music room

separate entry for home office

sneak-away spot

separate study

cozy library

convenient office, bedroom, den

convertible office/bedroom

DINING ROOM:

elegant formal dining

New England formal dining

entertainer dining

French doors off formal dining

light, airy, formal dining

unique, formal dining room

informal dining room

combination living and dining room

gourmet dining room

oversized, grand dining room

cozy, formal dining

intimate formal dining

massive, open, formal dining

full-windowed dining room

sensational formal dining

ENTRY:

palatial entrance

stone archway

impressive entry

graceful foyer

gleaming marble entry

dramatic entry

massive double-doored entrance

EXPOSURE:

southern exposure

sun-drenched

sun-filled

sun-splashed

EXTERIOR:

maintenance-free

wonderful wood

stunning stone

vinyl siding

genuine cedar slabs

brick beauty

sensational cedar

stone and stucco

low-maintenance masonite siding

FAMILY ROOM:

informal family room

leisure room

private studio

enchanting family room

shuttered family room windows

drawing room

handsome hearth accents family room

classic kitchen off family room with fireplace

combination kitchen and family room

two-story family room/great room

FENCING:

split rail fencing

protective privacy fence

chain-linked fencing

fabulous fenced grounds

white picket fencing

cross-fencing surrounds property

ranch rail fencing

FINANCING:

below market owner financing

owner financing

no qualifying mortgage to assume

assumable loan below market

assume huge mortgage

FIREPLACES

beautiful brick hearth

fieldstone fireplace

corn-poppin' fireplace

cozy hearth

woodburning fireplace

old-fashioned featherstone fireplace

toe-warming fireplace

master suite with fireplace

franklin stove

firelit breakfast

FIXER-UPPERS:

make this livable

realize huge profit

only cosmetic surgery

bushels of nails

how would you paint it?

needs lots of love

paint a little, make a lot

prepare to paint

repair and plaster

loads of potential

barrels of paint

fabulous fix-up

FLOORS:

handsome hardwood floors

wonderful wood floors

authentic oak-pegged floors

Italian tile floors

Mexican quarry tile floors

marvelous maple floors

original oak floors

prestigious parquet floors

country-planked flooring

sensational ceramic tile floors

tremendous terrazzo tile floors

FURNISHED HOMES:

turnkey lifestyle

total furnishings stay

interior furnishings stay

decorator furnished to stay

furnished by designer to stay

just your suitcase needed

decor all-inclusive

gorgeous inclusions to stay

lavish appointments included

exciting accessories included

GARAGES:

oversize double garage

holds three cars

adequate single garage

terrific triple garage

attached, heated garage

fully finished tuck-under garage

GARAGES (continued)

complimentary carport

surprise tandem garage

garage with workshop

garage with separate storage room

gigantic garage

heated workshop garage

GARDEN:

perfect perennial gardens

gorgeous landscaped gardens

inviting English ivy garden

healthful organic gardens

perennial flowerbeds

farm-size, gigantic garden

areas for annual garden

masses of tulips

lavish, lush gardens

GOLF:

across from golf course

golf balls in your yard

one shot from the fairway

golf in your backyard

golf-oriented area

world class golf course

just bring your golf clubs

HEATING/AIR CONDITIONING:

high-efficiency furnace

zone heating and cooling

two-zone heat

state of the art heat pump

economical hot water heat

environmental climate control

super solar heat

wood furnace—heat home free

economical natural gas

HOME:

luxury lake address

most envied address

world class residence

no better lifestyle

magnificent estate setting

understated and elegant

unparalleled beauty

gracious and grand

one of the rarest pearls

embassy-size residence

classic country security

romantic and charming

from a bygone era

brings back memories

reflects colonial times

timeless and elegant

right out of history

beautiful bed and breakfast

ready to retire

comfortable and cozy

intimate hideaway

sophisticated and small

a simpler lifestyle

perfect getaway home

INTERIOR:

meticulously maintained
old world charm
exciting accessories
lavishly appointed
aura of elegance
ingeniously arranged
prestigious interior
cosmopolitan allure
enduring loveliness
exquisitely renovated
richly detailed

classical loveliness
sublime tranquility
extravagant appointments
dazzling innovation
impressive details
dramatically designed
decorator delight
magnificent interior
light-away
elaborate interior

KITCHEN:

firelit breakfast
genuine gourmet kitchen
sun-drenched kitchen
solid oak cabinet kitchen
English country kitchen
kitchen with a French flair
exquisite decorator kitchen
beyond belief kitchen
elegantly upgraded kitchen
sensational center island kitchen
breakfast bay-windowed kitchen
charming, cozy kitchen
handsome rich-tone kitchen
unbelievable condo kitchen
your best foods kitchen
southern charm kitchen
sensational ceramic kitchen

Julia Child's kitchen
European kitchen
cherry cabinet kitchen
skylit-windowed kitchen
old world, charming kitchen
kitchen accents breakfast room
style prevails in perfect kitchen
five-star rating kitchen
conversation area kitchen
wall of windows kitchen
massive country kitchen
contemporary open kitchen
best-applianced kitchen
perfect pullman kitchen
traditionally timeless kitchen
meticulously white kitchen
dramatic deck off kitchen

LAKES:

sunset over the water
luxurious lakeshore
landscaped lake views
luscious lake dwelling
beachfront property
wonderful water front
magnificent lakeshore
docking and beach
deeded lakeshore
beautiful boat slip

waterfront residence
looks out on lake
scenic pond views
fish from your yard
sunrise and sandy shores
float from your dock
sun-kissed shoreline
lake access
deeded docking

LAWNS:

artfully landscaped

sensational setting

magnificently manicured lawn

priceless, manicured grounds

terraced, landscaped beauty

formal gardens

grandiose gardens

premier landscaped lot

wonderful wooded grounds

lush landscaping

LOCATION:

distinguished address

nestled on the fifth fairway

set back in the woods

this location is a must

expansive views

captures the essence

marvelous, majestic locale

executive retreat

remarkable residence

backdrop of woods

expansive views

in the heart of town

view majestic mountains

gracefully situated

very important address

unsurpassed locale

secluded approach

revered address

breathtaking views

velvet lawn embraces home

waterfront residence

high on a hill

best country club locale

unparalleled views

storybook setting

distinctive address

exclusive area

private seclusion

sequestered behind trees

golf course community

award winning locale

superb views abound

fabulous foothills

oak-covered hill

priceless views

perfectly poised

year-round view

picture-book setting

elegant edge of acre

LOFT:

sun-filled studio loft

a real art studio

likable library loft

designer art studio

superb Swiss loft

hidden, high loft

balcony design studio

sleeping/studio loft

MASTER BEDROOM:

sensational master suite

fireplace accents master

master bedroom overlooks

master bedroom hideaway

exciting master spa

master bedroom with jacuzzi

beamed ceilings in master

master bedroom with walk-in

superb master suite

master suite glows

MASTER BEDROOM (continued)

firelit master suite	spacious master suite
magical master boudoir	embodied in sunshine
master suite indulges	master suite displays genius
banks of windows bask in sunshine throughout master	sumptuous master

NEIGHBORHOOD:

tree-lined street	prestigious locale
rewarding and rural	intimate cul-de-sac
winding boulevard	coveted community
exclusive enclave	successful address
private preserve	estate setting
country charmer	hidden pocket

OFFICE:

at-home office	oak-floored office
open, airy office	bay-windowed office
optimum office	office opportunity
old English office	old-fashioned office
old-time office	octagon office
obscure office	number one office

PORCH:

prestigious porch	a perfect porch
private and peaceful	sun-filled solarium
great garden room	superb Arizona room
classic conservatory	patio off porch
terrazzo tile porch	New England porch
summer days porch	

PRICE:

unbelievable value	unduplicated in price
rare offering	obvious value
priced to sell	don't hesitate
incredibly priced	solid value-priced
uncommon find	investment priced
carefully priced at	properly priced at

PRIVACY:

hidden corner

forest haven

God's little acre

sounds of silence

whispering woods

rare private setting

hidden hill

pampered in privacy

golden pocket

secret sector

wooded dream

acre of privacy

ultimate seclusion

private end unit

end of the road

REMODELED:

old with new

yesterday and now

handsome renovation

restored to capture

artistically restored

partially restored

modern and antique

dramatic updates

imaginative updates

yesterday's charm, today's decor

up-to-date elegance

restored to original elegance

ROOFS:

cedar tile shakes

Spanish tile roof

authentic slate roof

hand-split cedar roof

split shake roof

French mansard roof

mission tile roof

SCHOOL:

by schools

don't ride the bus

super school district

perfect playground

don't play chauffeur

elementary school areas

walk to school

walking distance

SECURITY:

Westinghouse security

hidden security system

feel safe and warm

central security

24-hour security

controlled access

peace of mind

secret security system

protection guaranteed

ultrasonic security

video security

monitored security

gate guarded

worry-free living

SHUTTERS:

plantation shutters

Bermuda shutters

colonial shutters

decorator shutters

oriental shutters

full-windowed shutters

privacy shutters

SPAS:

inviting jacuzzi

heated hydrotherapy

sensuous hot spa

health club bath

elite super spa

wonderful whirlpool

tantalizing hottub

a private spa

Hollywood hottub

STAIRS:

carved banisters

dramatic staircase

spiral staircase

grand staircase

center stairway

circular stairway

cherry balustrades

sweeping stairway

floating staircase

eighteenth-century stairs

STYLE:

English tudor elegance

European style

elegant Georgian colonial

traditional two-story

rewarding rambler

simplified split entry

exaggerated split level

beautiful brick bungalow

restored renaissance

from bygone era

Dutch colonial

monumental colonial

Williamsburg colonial

Nantucket colonial

English country estate

English country tudor

dramatic architect

country cottage

ivy-clad classic

storybook victorian

lavish lifestyle

French influence

Knob Hill distinction

exquisite contemporary

Cape Cod charmer

sensational salt box

wonderful walkout

distinctive style

storybook one-story

expansive two-story

sophisticated traditional

Currier and Ives

gone with the wind

federal colonial

timeless colonial

provocative contemporary

flawless tudor

Mediterranean villa

sumptuous French

Spanish adobe

crannies and collectibles

award-winning architect

landmark residence

intimate retreat

SWIMMING POOL:

inviting pool	luxurious pool
backyard vacation	private pool
year-round workout	vacation at home
steps to swim	sunshine and swim
want the water?	miss the lake?
like to swim?	free-form pool
diving pool/spa	

TENNIS:

steps to the court	home to tennis
your tennis court	definitely tennis
treat yourself to tennis	

TREES:

your own orchard	ask for apples
firewood forever	private woods
you'll love fall	trees and trees
hidden forest	enchanted forest
exclusive retreat	private and romantic

UNFINISHED ROOM:

space to create	full storage attic
hobby room area	easily converted
walk-up attic	

VACATION HOME:

holiday living	enjoy fishing?
family reunion?	summer relaxing
weekend getaway	a simpler life
summer hideaway	enjoy the water
happy retreat	

VIEW:

see forever	sunset views
white water view	million dollar view
tantalizing treetops	overlooks the city
sensational night lights	capture the landscape
get your binoculars	commanding views
treetop treasure	hilltop haven
majestic mountains	panoramic view

WALL COVERINGS:

imported paper

textured treatments

richly covered

picture frame paneling

designer walls

wonderful walls

lavish wall coverings

WINDOWS:

beautiful bay windows

wall of glass

bring in the outdoors

leaded glass windows

solar-bronze windows

French Provincial

stained-glass windows

skylighted ceilings

soaring windows

intricate etched glass

palladian windows

greenhouse windows

country style windows

clerestory windows

WORKSHOP:

wonderful workshop

handyman workshop

hammer and nails

perfect for projects

carpenter work area

crafts and arts

time for tool box

While it would be ideal if all your business could be generated just from an ad, you still would like to retain the call in as a client.

When Answering an Ad Call

1. GIVE THE FACTS.

2. SAY SOMETHING UNIQUE ABOUT THE HOME.

3. DESCRIBE THE HOME IN A POSITIVE TONE.

4. ARTICULATE CAREFULLY.

5. STATE THE PRICE.

6. BE AVAILABLE TO SHOW THE HOME AS SOON AS POSSIBLE.

Dialogue for Answering the Phone

Hi! This is Barbara Nash-Price from _____ Realty. This particular home that you are calling on is one of my favorite properties because . . .

> Examples: "of its big country kitchen."
> "it has a gorgeous family room off the foyer."
> "the lot is simply gorgeous and loaded with trees."
> "it reminds me of going to my grandma's house."
> "it has more character than any home I've seen in a long time."

Pick something *special* just for that home, and be sure to accentuate it. If the property is extremely plain and you are having difficulty finding an outstanding quality, imagine what you would *do* to the home if it were given to you. Spend a few minutes dwelling on its potential and hidden amenities.

ENTHUSIASM IS CONTAGIOUS!

If *you* are excited about the property, then you can excite a buyer.

Whenever you answer an ad call, try the following techniques.

Ask the buyer

1. Have you been prequalified for this price range of property? or Is this a price range that you feel comfortable with?
2. Have you been looking for a home for a while?
3. Do you have a home to sell first?
4. Is this the area that you are looking in?
5. Do you have a time frame for when you want to move?
6. Have you seen any homes that have come *close* to what you want?
7. Have you made any offers on homes as yet?
8. Can you meet me at the property later in the day or would after 2:00 P.M. tomorrow be better suited to your schedule?

If the buyer has been "prequalified," set up an appointment to meet the buyer at the property, keeping the schedule suited to your own needs.

An ad call can be converted easily with just three questions:

1. Have you been looking for homes for a long time?
2. When do you want to move?
3. Do you enjoy looking for homes?

An ad call can be converted easily with just three statements:

1. I have some excellent properties in this area that I have taken from the computer and will bring for you.

2. I specialize in your area and can take a look at your property sometime tomorrow between the hours of _____ and _____.

3. I enjoy uncovering new properties for clients that I meet and helping them find the best home possible.

If your answering machine is on at home, make sure that you include in your message that *you will be checking in frequently for calls*. Example: "Hi, this is Barbara Nash-Price from XYZ Realty, and I check in frequently for my calls. If you will leave your name and phone number, I will call you back shortly with the information that you need."

Additional Advertising Pointers

Also remember that you are always advertising. You are in the public eye and can meet a new buyer simply by wearing a lapel pin that says:

XYZ REALTY
BARBARA NASH-PRICE

Remember to accentuate your own name; put it in large print!

I cut out my Sunday ads from the newspaper and paste them in my daily planner on the date that they ran.

I also keep track of when I ran the ad for each seller's listing in a column on the outside of a legal-size folder.

I call the sellers weekly to tell them what kind of activity I had on the ad and if and when there were any calls. This is also an opportune time for a *price adjustment*.

I keep track of how many people were generated from any particular ad that I ran.

2-18-90
JUST LISTED!
1st Open 2:30-4:30
BELOW INDIAN HILLS

Nestled back on Samuel Rd sets this beautiful 3BR-2BA home!! Lovely gourmet eat-in kitchen ACCENTS HUGE FIRST FLOOR family room! Completely FINISHED lower level family room w/daylite windows & brick hearth. Att dbl gar-dynamic deck!

3-4-90
ITS LISTED!
OPEN 2-4
"EDINA CLASSIC"

The foothills of Indian Hills boasts a beautiful custom home featuring 3 br-3 bathrooms-double attached garage plus GORGEOUS first floor family room ALL IN WINDOWS walks out to private rear yard!! Formal dinning-2 brick fireplaces-all levels professionally finished-hurry!

3-11-90
OPEN
IT'S BIGGER

than it looks! 3 BR split at foot of Indian Hills. 1st floor fam room, nice lot, 2 fplc and more!

3-25-90
ITS LISTED!
OPEN 2:30-4:30
"CHARM GALORE"

NESTLED below Indian Hills sets this lovely 3 br-2 bath BEAUTIFUL home!! Accent on gorgeous 1st FLOOR family room! Totally finished lower-level w/daylite windows - 2 fplcs - formal dining - att. dbl gar!

4-8-90
ITS LISTED!
OPEN 2:30-4:30

"Wonderful Family..." Room LOADED with windows & charms just off beautiful kitchen!! This 3Br-2 1/2 BA home nestled at foot of Indian Hills features 2 fplcs - formal dining-att. dbl gar-LOVELY private lot-hurry!!

4-29-90
JUST LISTED!
OPEN 3:15-5:15
BELOW INDIAN HILLS

Nestled back on SAMUEL RD sets this beautiful 3BR-2BA home! Lovely gourmet eat-in kitchen-ACCENTS HUGE FIRST FLOOR FAM ROOM. Completely finished lower level, w/daylite windows 2 fplcs, dynamite deck!!

5-6-90
"FABULOUS AREA"!
OPEN 12-2
NESTLED BELOW

INDIAN HILLS sets the 3BR, 2 Bath Beautiful home! Accents on GORGEOUS 1st floor fam rm, 2 fplcs, formal DR.

5-13-90
IT'S LISTED!
OPEN BY APPT
"AND IT'S EVERYTHING"

Below Indian Hills set back on Samuel Rd is this 3 br - 2 bath split ranch style FANTASTIC family room (loaded w/windows & sliding door to private deck) off kitchen! 2 fplc - TOTALLY FINISH.

6-3-90
OPEN 3-5
BEAUTIFUL LOCATION
SPLIT FOYER

4 BR., 2 BA. Split. Great floor plan—1st flr. fam. rm. Neut. decor. Trees.

6-10-90
IT'S LISTED
OPEN 2-4
FANTASTIC FAMILY...

...ROOM off kitchen highlites this 3BR, 2BA home at the foothills of Indian Hills! BEAUTIFUL floor plan with 2 handsome fireplaces, delightful kitchen w/planning desk—gorgeous deck!!!

6-19-90
JUST LISTED!
OPEN 1-4
"DYNAMITE HOME"

4 BR, 2 ba split foyer. Great 1st flr fam rm off kitchen. Neut-decor. Trees.

7-1-90
JUST LISTED!
OPEN 2:30-4:30
CHARM GALORE!

Nestled below Indian Hills slts this lovely 3BR, 2BA beautiful home! Accent on gorgeous 1st floor family room! Totally finshed lower level w/daylight windows. 2 fplcs-formal dining -attached dbl garage.

7-15-90
OPEN 12:30-2:30
AFFORDABLE EDINA

Custom blt 3BR, 2BA split at the foothills of Indian Hills. Neutral decor thruout w/a fabulous flow. 1st flr fam rm, 2 fplc & more!

4-22-90

JUST LISTED!
"COUNTRY CLUB"

FABULOUS floor plan boasts formal LR-DR, library/study 1st fam room, SCREEN PORCH, 2 HUGE BR's up, amuse room w/extra BR down, dbl gar.

4-29-90

JUST LISTED!!
"COUNTRY CLUB"

2 STORY incredible home! Loaded with class...formal large LR w/2 French doors to perfect porch! Study or den off LR, formal DR, breakfast rm, 1st flr fam rm plus 2 pretty enormouns BRs on second floor, main flr laundry.

5-6-90

JUST LISTED
"DYNAMITE RANCH"

...style features 3+ BR, 2 baths, hardwood floors, 2 fplcs, "SENSATIONAL KITCHEN" workshop, office, amuse room, HUGE PRIVATE, LOVELY lot! Dble att. gar., CORNELIA SCHOOL DISTRICT.

5-6-90

IT'S OPEN!! 2:30-4:30
"CAPE COD CHARM"

UNBELIEVABLE classic 1940 2 story home...LOADED with: formal DR, french doors, sensational porch, private study, handsome 1st floor family room!!! NEW ENGLAND breakfast room w/ blt in Breakfast & floor to ceiling window,2nd floor: Two enormous bedrooms, 2 delightful decks, 2 fplcs, dble gar, 1st FLOOR FAM RM.

5-13-90

IT'S LISTED
OPEN 2:30-4:30
COUNTRY CLUB AREA

PRESTIGIOUS New England Colonial perfect for prof. nedding lots of 1st floor living! Library - french doors to PRIVATE PORCH - FORMAL Dining - 1st FLOOR Fam Rm! 2 Fplcs - Connecticut Kitchen w/floor to ceiling window & blt in Buffet!! Second floor features 2 ENORMOUS Bedrooms with their own sep. deck!!

5-20-90

IT'S LISTED
OPEN 2:30-4:30
COUNTRY CLUB AREA

PRESTIGIOUS New England Colonial perfect for prof. nedding lots of 1st floor living!! Library - french doors to PRIVATE PORCH - FORMAL Dining - 1st FLOOR Fam Rm! 2 Fplcs - Connecticut Kitchen w/floor to ceiling window & blt in Buffet!! Second floor features 2 ENORMOUS Bedrooms with their own sep. deck!!

6-3-90

IT'S LISTED!!
"CONNECTICUT CHARM"

Gorgeous 2 story COLONIAL nestled back - 1st floor fam room, fabulous screened porch, MAIN FLOOR laundry, DREAM kitchen won't last.

11-19-89

DELUXE CONDO
CLASSIC CREATION

JUST LISTED. Fabulous 2+ bedrooms w/library, guest quarters, 3 bathrooms, CUSTOM DOUBLE 2300 square foot unit o'looks breathtaking views of city.

2-11-90

CLASSIC CONDO
"FABULOUS INTERIOR"

Boasts the best! This 2+BR, 2BA, custom 2200 sq. ft. condo is one-of-a-kind! UNCOMPARABLE VIEWS of Mississippi - Fabulous hardwood floors - library - formal DR.

2-18-90

CLASSIC CONDO
"FABULOUS INTERIOR"

Boasts the best! This 2+BR, 2BA, custom 2200 sq. ft. condo is one-of-a-kind! UNCOMPARABLE VIEWS of Mississippi - Fabulous hardwood floors - library - formal DR.

6-12-88

JUST LISTED!!
"Classic Colonial"

Steps away from lake NESTLED back on CUL DE SAC sets this 4BR, 21/2 bath CUSTOM built 3 yr old ROBT MASON built beauty! FABULOUS fam room w/brick hearth - private porch - formal DR - Princeton trim - 6 panel doors - BRAND NEW Listing. Hurry!!

CHAPTER 4

Buyers

big deal
by "Lorayne n' Neil"

How To Get a Buyer Today!

WHERE *DO* YOU GET BUYERS TODAY?

Whether or not you are new to the business or have been in the business for a long time, you will be out of business if you do not have buyers and listings. How do you *get* buyers? The first step is to *have at least two open houses this next weekend*. If you do not have any listings, ask two fellow agents in the office if you might hold their listings open. Once at the open house, absolutely resolve to find one or two couples from each open house who sincerely want to buy a house in the near future. How do you identify these? *Ask a lot of questions*. Write down everything they tell you. Don't let these people leave your open house *without* making an appointment sometime in the coming week to see them.

If they have a house to sell . . .

> you are available either Monday or Tuesday night. Which would be better for them?

> you can come over and look at their house, walk through, take notes, and come back with a market appraisal for them.

> you also will bring your listing book, and they can look through it with you to help decide what price range and area would be most appealing to them.

If they don't have a house to sell . . .

> You have either Monday or Tuesday evening open, and you would be happy to meet with them at your office to help prequalify them for the price range that would be best suited to them and the area that they would want to consider.

BUYERS ARE NOT ALWAYS KNOWLEDGEABLE ABOUT WHAT THEY WANT

Buyers are *often confused* about areas and price ranges best suited for them.

Buyers are generally more interested in *aesthetic* appeal than potential.

Buyers are incredibly *unpredictable*.

Buyers are apt to go through open houses *without* you.

Buyers are often *difficult to read* at the first meeting.

Buyers more often than not, have a house to *sell first*.

Buyers don't always feel *loyalty* toward their agent.

Yet, most buyers stand firm on one point: they want to move *eventually*.

Because buyers are often *contradictory*, they often need help in deciphering the type of home best suited for them, through:

1. process of elimination (viewing at least six homes).

2. painting a scenario beforehand of a hypothetical transaction using a certain figure breakdown (such as, $100,000 mortgage with $2,000 annual taxes and $600 annual insurance would result in a specific PITI (principle-interest-tax and insurance). This breakdown allows buyers the opportunity to see exactly what specific payment would be based on a certain price of a home.

THERE IS A SUCCESS PATTERN TO APPLY WHEN WORKING WITH BUYERS.

1. It is *imperative* to prequalify buyers.

2. *Set limitations* and boundaries for areas.

3. Identify a *schedule* and time frame to work within.

4. Secure the buyer's *trust* and *loyalty*.

5. *Outline* the fact that because your salary is commission-based, you depend upon the resources from the time spent on each and every client. Some agents have buyers sign *buyer agreements*. (Do this after a minimum of one time out in the field showing preferably five or six properties *before discussion of loyalty*.)

6. Set up a *minimum* of one *in office* appointment to go over the above.

7. Provide potential buyers with a buyer's book which includes:

    a. map of your city
    b. highlights of yourself
    c. personal brochure and card
    d. highlights of your company
    e. sample properties that are for sale and/or sold
    f. some information about your city and/or suburbs
    g. sample purchase agreement contract
    h. sample financing addendum (way in which they will buy)
    i. buyer timeline for purchasing a home from start to finish
    j. buyer inspection cards

8. Use *inspection cards* with a rating system of one to ten as a systematic process of elimination for homes. Keep track of good and bad points on inspection cards.

9. At the end of each appointment day, ask the buyers, "If you had to move into or make an offer on one of the homes we saw today, which one would it be? Why?

IMPORTANT QUESTIONS FOR BUYERS:

How important is the **number of bathrooms?**
How important is the **number of bedrooms?**
How important is the **closing date?**
How important is the **condition?**
How important is the **lot? (flat, hilly, fenced, corner, cul-de-sac, etc.)**
How important is the **style?**

How important is an **eat-in kitchen?**

How important is a **finished lower level?**

How important is **closet space?**

How important are **older bathrooms?**

How important is a **formal dining room?**

How important is a **fireplace?**

How important is a **two-story (vs. one-story)?**

How important is a **busy street?**

How important is a **backyard?**

How important are **garages (attached/detached)?**

How important is an **office?**

How important is a **first floor laundry?**

How important is a **bath off the master bedroom?**

How important are **new mechanics (new roof, furnace, electrical, etc.)?**

How important is **structural condition?**

How important are **hardwood floors?**

How important is a **main floor half bath?**

How important is the **neighborhood?**

How important are **taxes?**

How important is **assumable financing?**

How important is **interior decorating?**

How important are **room sizes?**

KEEP TRACK OF YOUR NOTES.

Keep two sets of copies of the homes you look at:

1. one set for the buyer and
2. one set for you.

As the buyers look at each home, write down the negatives and positives. On each copy rate each home from one to ten after it is viewed.

Ask your buyers if they have seen a #10 home at all.

Learn to Read Your Buyers

Buyers usually buy a property in twos.

They are either a couple, a husband and wife, or in a partnership of some sort. When working with two buyers, try to listen between the lines. It is imperative to find out who is controlling the situation. One or the other will take over. If a man tells you he prefers a ranch style and his wife says she prefers a colonial, listen to the conversation. *Don't volunteer any comments.* Show them both styles of homes. They may surprise you and settle on an English tudor instead!

WATCH AND LISTEN CAREFULLY.

If one of the parties asks a question of the other, don't volunteer information for either of them. Listen to them to figure out what they both really want. Soon, you will see that even though they may not know *exactly* what style they are set on, they are participating as a couple in the process of elimination:

Try not to volunteer your own opinion on a home. Once I showed a property to some people to whom I had already shown ten to twelve homes. Before we opened the front door, I could tell the home had red carpeting. I was about to say how dreadful the color was, when I heard my buyer say, "Don, honey, look! The red carpet will go perfectly with our Mediterranean furniture." **They bought it on the spot!**

NEVER try to sell a buyer on a style of a home. The home should, and will, *SELL ITSELF.*

You are there to sell the *mechanics* of the entire situation. Learn to *listen* to the buyers' needs.

Learn to stay *concentrated* on what they need. Learn to have them *need your expertise.*

Types of Buyers

QUICK TO MOVE *Know just what they want.* Be ready with a purchase agreement so they won't surprise you. They are the best in knowing what they want.

SLOW AND EASY Want to look at lots of properties. They are very detailed and concise, so bear with them. They will buy, but be prepared to show them fifteen to twenty properties.

KNOW EVERYTHING Have seen *lots* of properties, have bought *lots* of properties. There isn't much they *haven't* done. They'll run out of hot air eventually. Bear with them. They just want to prove their knowledge to you and themselves. They may need to search for a *full eight weeks* and to see lots of homes.

PIG-HEADED Very set and determined. Try not to force them into a corner. They will be convinced eventually, but stand firm on your beliefs. A sale becomes a matter of earning respect.

QUEEN OF SHEBA The wife (or one of the parties) runs the show. Make sure that you find the opportunity to ask the other party's opinion.

LOVE THEM ALL These clients like all the homes you show them. It's hard to get *any opinion* from them at all! Try to pin them down and eliminate by asking them to close their eyes and imagine that if they had to move into one of the homes they saw today, could they make an offer and be happy with it?

HARD TO TELL These clients are devoid of expression. Regardless of what you show them, they are hard to get a reaction from. They do not know how to give you a direct answer. They cannot be specific. It is best to try to get to know them on a *different* level. Learn about them and what interests them in their lives. Talk a lot and ask them a *lot* of questions.

When Working with Buyers Out in the Field

1. Meet them at the office *first*.

2. Give them the *buyers book* for their own records.

3. Give them xeroxed copies of the homes that you will see the first day.

4. Never set up more than *six houses* to see at one time unless necessary. Out-of-town buyers may have little time; then you have no choice.

5. If showing a home that is open by another agent, make sure you have that agent's permission and have *called him or her first*.

6. Start working with your buyer by setting limits and time frames.

   Examples: "Should we find the home that you like today, would you feel prepared to *make an offer on it*?"

   "Have you *reviewed the sample purchase agreement* that I included in your buyers folder, and do you carry your checkbook with you?" (This is important in eliminating reasons for not making an offer.)

7. *Never leave a buyer at the end of your first appointment without* setting up the next appointment.

   Example: "Should we not be successful after we look at these homes today, would Thursday or Friday be better to *get together again*?"

8. *Never leave the buyer after the first appointment without* finding out where he or she stands *with the properties that you have seen and which one he or she preferred.*

9. Remember to *watch for emotional reactions* to homes they see.

   Example: "Oh, honey, our furniture would fit perfectly in the master bedroom!

10. *Remember that* timing is crucial *if they like it! "Once they sleep on it, they won't sleep in it."*

What Is the *Best Buyer to Work With?*

When I started out in the business almost twenty years ago and even today, *buyers are the same*. They fall into *three* categories:

1. *Buyers who want a home now!* These are A buyers. They either don't have a home to sell or, if they do, they want a new home now.

2. *Buyers who want a home soon!* They have a definite time frame in mind and will tell you so. These are usually A/B buyers.

3. *Buyers who want a home maybe!* These are usually C buyers. These buyers will buy if

   they can get top dollar for their present home,

   they retire,

   a certain home in a certain area with a certain floor plan comes along, they get a larger sum of money suddenly, and

they both decide to agree on what they both want.

Remember that good buyers, if married or in partnership, are only good buyers if they both want to buy a new home at the same time.

A Plan for Working with a Buyer

BUYERS YOU MEET AT AN OPEN HOUSE

1. Introduce yourself with your card and ask for his or her:

   a. name

   b. address

   c. phone number

2. Tell the buyer that you will immediately put him or her on your computer to receive a mailout list of all active properties that are available in the areas in which the buyer tells you he or she is looking.

3. Tell the buyer that you will mail this out immediately.

4. Tell the buyer that you will *call when you mail it out* and check to see when he or she wishes to set up an appointment during the next day or week to see homes.

IF THE BUYER SAYS, "WE ARE JUST STARTING TO LOOK . . ."

tell him or her:

> *I will send you information on homes that you are interested in from my home computer printout list. I will wait for you to call me on the homes that you are interested in. If you do not call me, I will wait to send you additional information until we touch bases.*

This is so important because it will *help you immediately decide* on whether your buyers are even *legitimate*.

BUYER . . . WHO CALLS ON AN AD

After you tell the buyer about the home, you ask the important questions:

1. "Does this home sound interesting to you?" (If the buyer says "no," you ask the next important question.)

2. "Would you like me to send you some of my favorite properties that are currently listed in the areas that you might have in mind? I could have them in tonight's mail." (Most people, if they are serious, will say "yes.")

It is critical to *categorize* buyers. It is crucial to *eliminate* time wasted.

I do not spend more than *two months* with A buyers if I do not feel that I have their *undivided loyalty*.

To get undivided loyalty, *ask for it*, but not until you have earned it and proved by at *least two meetings* that you deserve total loyalty.

How to Get Buyers Now

1. Hold at *least* two open houses a weekend in an area that is in a price range that you are comfortable with, and *preview* the homes first if they are not your listing. *Drive the area.*

2. Consider wearing a name tag with your name and company on it since it is an automatic conversation opener.

3. Call a FSBO (for sale by owner), an expired, or a cancelled. Make sure that you get an appointment now and visualize the listing as yours. *Three appointments maximum* should get you the listing, hopefully before the end of the week!

4. Make a list of all the people that are in your *warm farm* (a list of people that you know or have known). Call as many as you can, starting the conversation off with,

   "Hi, Bob. I haven't talked with you for a while and thought I would let you know that I have some extra time for a new client. If you would know of anyone thinking of buying or selling a house, I would be happy to work with him or her now."

5. Do a mailout in an area that you have chosen to farm. This means mailing real estate data to a select number of homes throughout the year, sometimes 400 to 600 or more. If you decide to mail out 1,000 or more, your chance of hearing back from one to five people in the next couple of weeks is *excellent!*

6. Drive a *different* way to work and look for FSBOs.

7. When you get gas or groceries or are involved in any purchase situation throughout the day, bring up *real estate*.

8. Make a deliberate attempt to *go to the source!* It will bring you more than just one client. Contact presidents of companies, lawyers, doctors, community leaders, teachers, coaches, ministers, hairdressers, barbers, PTAs, employment agencies, builders, and apartment landlords.

9. Read the *business section* of the newspaper, and collect names of people who have been promoted. Chances are excellent that they are considering moving.

10. Call your *past customers.* They already have a repertoire with you. Ask them who they know that you may be able to help move.

11. Contact sellers who are FSBOs and offer *relocation* services.

12. Ask *fellow salespeople* if there is a buyer whom they are not able to work with and whom you would be able to help. Work out an agreeable arrangement with the salesperson regarding commission before you work with the buyer.

13. *Meet your neighbors.* A great way is to do volunteer work. All of your neighbors should know you are in real estate and should be on one of your farm lists to receive a mailout.

14. Ask relatives if they know anyone through their work, etc.

Pledge of Performance to Buyers

Whether this is your first or fifth home-buying experience, *any* home purchase is, for most people, *their largest single expenditure.*

Following are some things that I pledge to give you, should you choose to utilize my services as your sole buying agent:

1. I'll help you identify the amount of *affordability* you would have on a new home.

2. I'll give you the most *vital information* on available homes.

3. I'll *recommend the price range* most suited to your finances.

4. I'll *keep you aware* of any changes in the real estate market.

5. I'll *arrange a tour* of areas, schools and key points of interest.

6. I'll *help you preselect* homes that are most suitable to your price range.

7. I'll give you *all the information* available on any home for sale.

8. I'll help you *arrange an inspection* of that "right" property and assist you in getting financing and homeowner's insurance.

9. I'll see that you get a *complete estimate of all costs* to you relating to purchasing a home.

10. I'll help you *write a purchase agreement*, present it to the sellers and coordinate all negotiation and communication between you and the sellers.

11. I'll *stay in touch* from the day you search for your new home until the day you move in.

12. I am reimbursed with a commission *only* if you choose to purchase a home through me.

Date:_____

Real estate agent: _____

      (PHONE)   (HOME)_____

                        (CAR) _____

                        (OFFICE) _____

Sample Master Buyer's List to Keep in Daily Planner

Name:	Ann Smith	Name:	
Address:	4200 10th St.	Address:	
Phone:	721-2444	Phone:	
Area:	West Suburbs Only	Area:	
Price:	150 + Tops	Price:	
Contacted:	4/10–5/6–6/3	Contacted:	
Originated:	Open House 4/6	Originated:	
Name:	Jim Jones	Name:	
Address:	1200 W. 3rd St	Address:	
Phone:	227-1044	Phone:	
Area:	Inner City Only (T-House)	Area:	
Price:	100 +	Price:	
Contacted:	4/6–5/3	Contacted:	
Originated:	Call on ad 4/4	Originated:	
Name:	Jeff James	Name:	
Address:	314 N.E. Maple	Address:	
Phone:	342-7717	Phone:	
Area:	Suburbs (East)	Area:	
Price:	125 Tops	Price:	
Contacted:	5/10–5/15	Contacted:	
Originated:	Sign Call (Girard Prop.)	Originated:	

Keep entries on this list active for *six weeks* to *two months,* then move them to an alternative file—depending on when they will buy.

Within the next *three to six months* (depending on how you want to keep this list), *replace* names.

Use sticky 2"× 3" post-it notes to add or replace a new quick addition to temporarily transfer it onto your master sheet.

KEEP *ACTIVE* "A" BUYERS ON LIST IN FRONT OF DAILY PLANNER
TO CHECK *DAILY*.

Buyer (Use Legal File Folder)

Property Address: _____

Sale Price: _____ Selling Date: _____

Closing Date:

Buyer: _____

Address: _____

Phone: (H) _____ (W) _____

Information: _____

Seller: _____

Address: _____

Phone: (H) _____ (W) _____

Information: _____

Agent's Name: _____ Company: _____

Address: _____

Phone: _____ Fax: _____

Additional Information: _____

MAKE COPIES OF ALL PURCHASE AGREEMENTS AND ADDENDUMS FOR:

1. buyer
2. selling agent and seller
3. mortgage company
4. your files.

Cold Calling for Buyers

"Mr. or Mrs. _____, please.

Hello, my name is _____ and I'm from _____ company. I am doing a special survey in our city, and I would like to ask you a few questions."

1. "Are you *thinking of moving* sometime with the next few years?"
2. "May I ask you about *when*?"
3. "Will you be *staying here* in the city or moving out of town?" "Thank you so much for *your time*, and have a nice day."

ADDITIONAL COLD CALL QUESTIONS:

1. "Would you like me to put you in touch with an excellent relocation firm from a different state?"
2. "I (or our company) just listed a home in your area. Do you know of any friends, business associates, or relatives who might be interested in my (our) services?"
3. "I'm having an open house in your neighborhood this Sunday. Would you be interested in dropping by?"
4. "Would you be interested in a free written analysis of your home, if I dropped by for about fifteen minutes sometime this week?"
5. "I (or our company) have a great newsletter, brochure, schoolhouse magazine, map, etc. of your area. Would you like me to drop one off?"

Calling Apartments for Buyers

1. Call until you find a buyer.
2. Get an appointment made. Ask for a referral.
3. Make your conversation light and professional, but to the point.

   "Hi, my name is _____, and I'm with _____ real estate company. This call will be very short but very helpful to me. We are looking for people who might be interested in buying or selling a home. Interest rates are extremely low right now, and there are some good properties available. Could this interest you?"

If yes . . .

Get their name. Set up an *appointment* with them. Talk a little about their *needs*. Talk a little about their *finances*. Buyers need at least $30,000 a year gross net to buy a reasonably priced home, and their house payment should be a little better than one-quarter of their gross monthly income.

   Example: If the payment is $500, they should gross $2,000/month. (4:1 ratio).

If no . . .

"Thanks so much for your time. If you should be interested in the near future, I am located at a convenient office near you."

How to Get Referral Business

1. Many good leads come from estate and garage sales. Don't hesitate to stop and visit.

2. Ask your relatives and your friends. Are people marrying, retiring, divorcing?

3. Refer to your mailing list daily, not just at the holiday season.

4. Neighborhood people are sometimes the best referral sources.

5. Perhaps a favorite sales clerk at a favorite store that you frequent knows someone who is moving.

6. Your best friend, spouse, or significant other always has a separate source of referrals that could help.

7. A hair stylist sometimes gives great referral business.

8. Pyramid businesses near you (Fuller Brush, Amway, Mary Kay, etc.) always have lists of different people.

9. Calling some large employers near where you live might provide you with future clients.

10. Wearing a name tag with your company logo on it to your gas station or your grocery store can be great for business!

Referral business in real estate is tricky. It can pass you by without your noticing. Yet every day there are more leads from referrals than you can imagine. So you must *always look the part of a good professional* and always ask for business.

Think of real estate in every facet of your day. **Aim to get at least two new good leads a week.**

Involve yourself in your neighborhood, even if you live in an apartment. You can become involved with a monthly newsletter and provide tasty real estate treats—a monthly recipe favorite or latest real estate trends—the latest scoop in what's happening in housing.

Where Do Buyers Come From?

40%	come from meeting a salesperson on site.
20%	come from a for sale sign.
18%	come from responding to an ad.
8%	come from meeting at an open house.
7%	come from relocation services.
3%	buy an advertised property.
1%	buy the open house they see.
3%	buy for a combination of reasons.

What to Give to a Potential New Buyer Looking for a Property

1. city map
2. city and state information
3. information about specific areas of interest
4. school information
5. religious directory
6. credit information sheet
7. information about you, the agent, or your brochure
8. information about your company
9. brief qualification guide to help them to determine what they qualify for
10. listings of some sample properties that are available for sale in areas that may be of interest to them
11. names and numbers of some good mortgage loan officers and lenders

Prepare this material in a *glossy folder* with the potential buyer's name typed on a sticker on the outside. Staple your card to the outside also.

Most buyers really want to know two things right from the start:

1. *How much* and what can I buy?
2. What can you *show me* in the price range I qualify for?

Most buyers really do want to see a mapbook of where the specific properties are for sale and what the neighborhood is like. So keep *copies* of a mapbook with inserts of subject properties.

Purchasing a Home from Start to Finish

1. Purchase agreement is accepted and copies are delivered to buyer and seller.

2. Meet with a loan officer at a good mortgage loan company to apply for a mortgage loan.

3. Give check to loan officer for an appraisal and credit report. (Appraisal is ordered, credit report is ordered on buyer, title work is ordered, and employment verifications are made.)

4. Credit report is received.

5. Review employment verifications.

6. Appraisal is reviewed by underwriter, and the value is issued on the property. Any work orders are issued.

7. Title work is reviewed for potential problems.

8. When all verifications are received, the value is confirmed by the appraiser, and title work has been completed and is acceptable, then the file is sent for loan approval.

9. Borrower *must sign* final application.

10. Loan file is submitted for underwriting review and returned as:

    a. *approved*

    b. *rejected,* or

    c. *additional information required.*

11. If loan is approved, sales associates, sellers, and buyers should be notified.

12. Listing agent schedules closing with the title company.

13. Attend the closing, sign all documents, and receive the keys.

14. Buyers move into new home (later that day if on contract).

Normal time to complete all of the above: 30 to 45 days

Interest rate lock-in: normally 60 to 90 days

It is essential for the agent to *stay abreast with the lender weekly* as to the progress of the loan.

Information on Buyer

Property Address _____

1st Buyer's Name _____

2nd Buyer's Name _____

Number of Children _____ Ages _____

Current Home Address _____

How long lived at the above address _____ Home phone _____

Previous address/how long _____

Employer _____ Phone _____

Position/Job _____ Years employed _____ Pay/month _____

Child support/Maintenance _____

Additional Income _____

Have you ever filed bankruptcy? _____ Date _____

Has the bankruptcy been discharged? _____Date _____

Do you have any judgments or liens pending? _____

If yes, please explain _____

Current Assets

Checking Account Balance	$_____	Bank	_____
Savings Account Balance	$_____	Bank	_____
Value of Stocks and Bonds	$_____		
Value of Real Estate Owned	$_____		
Personal Property	$_____		
Automobile(s) value	$_____		
Other _____	$_____	Total	_____

Current Liabilities

Real Estate Mortgages	$_____	Balance	_____
Home Improvement Loan	$_____	Balance	_____
Charge Accounts	$_____	Balance	_____
Automobile Loans	$_____	Balance	_____
Child Support/Maintenance	$_____		
Child Care	$_____	Total	_____
Total	$_____		

The undersigned hereby consents to the disclosure of the data on this form by the real estate agent to the property owner(s).

Signed _____ Date _____

Signed _____ Date _____

Sample Closing Remarks to a Buyer

Did you like that home well enough to cook dinner in the kitchen?

Do you think your furniture could fit well in the living room?

Can't you just see trimming a Christmas tree in the family room with a fire going?

Why don't we go back to the office and see if the numbers can work for both of you?

Why don't we sit down and see how the monthly payment can work on this particular property?

Let's go back to my office, and I can show you some information that could work for you to get into this property very easily.

Let's call a favorite loan officer of mine, and we could see how she thinks you would qualify for this new listing.

Why don't we go back to your house, and I could give you a quick idea of what your home might bring in order to get into this property?

Why don't we drive over to my office, and we could go through the added information I have on this home to see how the numbers add up for you?

Why don't we go back to your apartment, and you could see when your lease expires in order to get a good closing date and a low interest rate on this home?

Should we follow each other back to the office and put the numbers together to see if we can get this for you tonight?

Why don't we sit down, and I can show you how easy it would be to move into this home within the next couple of months?

Why don't you take a minute, and I will go over a purchase agreement with you to see when would be a good possession date for the two of you?

Let's take a few minutes to see whether or not your offer might work. You just might be able to get into this home!

Buyer Information Needed for a Mortgage Application

1. Seven-year address history that includes names, addresses, and phone numbers of any landlords.
2. Two-year employment history that includes names and addresses of all employers, a copy of the most recent pay stub, and W-2 forms for the past two years. If com-

mission employed, federal returns from last two years, and if self-employed federal tax returns profit and loss statements for last two years.

3. Banks names and addresses, account numbers, current balances, and last two or three month account statement for checking, savings and investment accounts.

4. Monthly payments and balances for debts and liabilities, mortgages, personal and auto loans, credit cards, and student loans. Creditors' names, addresses, phone numbers, and account numbers.

5. Child care information, including names, addresses, monthly amount owed, verification of amount, and terms of child support and/or alimony payments and/or income.

At application appointment buyer should be prepared to provide a personal check for

1. *property appraisal* and

2. *credit report on buyer.*

Buyer Closing Cost Guide

1. Origination fee—1% of the loan amount

2. Credit report—approximately $100

3. Appraisal fee—$250 to $350 (FHA/VA should be less than conventional)

4. Title insurance—approximately $500 (mortgagee should talk to loan officer since owner policy is optional)

5. Plat drawing—approximately $55 to $65

6. Recording fees—under $100

7. Name and judgment search—approximately $25 to $35

8. ARM title insurance endorsement fee—approximately $50 (applies only to conventional arm mortgages)

9. Mortgage registration tax—(Mn) $2.30 per $1,000

10. Settlement closing fee—The VA will not allow the buyer to pay the closing fee for a VA mortgage. It must be charged to the seller.

11. Discount points—each discount point equals 1% of the loan amount (example: 1 pt on a $40,000 loan = $400)

12. Commitment tax service fee—approximately $200 (not charged on VA mortgages)

13. VA funding fee—1.25% of the loan amount with less than 5% down, .75% with at least 5% down but less than 10% down, and .50% with a down payment of 10% or more

ADDITIONAL FEES:

1. The *daily interest* on new mortgages from the day of closing through the end of the month will be collected at closing.

2. *One full year of homeowner insurance* must be paid prior to closing and a paid receipt brought to the closing.

3. *Private mortgage insurance* is usually required on all conventional loans if the buyer makes less than 20% down payment.

4. *Two months* of homeowner insurance is collected at closing to start an escrow account. This account is maintained in addition to a one-year policy which is paid in advance.

5. If private mortgage insurance is used with a conventional loan, then two months of the renewal premium is escrowed to open the escrow account.

6. Flood insurance is required if the property is located in a specific flood zone. *A full year* premium is required, usually with two additional months for the escrow account.

Kinds of Mortgages for a Buyer

1. **CONVENTIONAL MORTGAGE**
   - *usually amortized over fifteen to thirty years*
   - *loan usually available for home purchase or refinance*
   - *fixed rate, adjustable rate or balloon loan*
   - *minimum down payment as low as 5% but usually 10%; less than 20% down payment requires PMI mortgage insurance*

2. **FHA MORTGAGE**
   - *loans insured against default by the United States government*
   - *down payment usually less than 10%*
   - *FHA adjustable rate mortgage has 1% rate increase with 5% lifetime rate increase*
   - *all FHA mortgages require mortgage insurance*

3. **VA MORTGAGE**
   - *buyer can finance up to 100% of sale price*
   - *buyer must have VA eligibility certificate*
   - *veteran can use VA program more than once*
   - *funding fee to guarantee the loan can be financed into the loan, or paid in cash by buyer or seller*

4. **CONTRACT FOR DEED**
   - *seller may hold the mortgage for the buyer*
   - *usually a balloon payment to the seller in five to seven years*
   - *seller determines down payment amount*

```
+--------------------------------------------------------------+
|                  Buyer Evaluation Form                       |
|                                                              |
|  _____        _____     |
|  Address                        Price                        |
|  _____        _____     |
|                                                              |
|  _____        _____     |
|                                                              |
|  _____        _____     |
|  Comments/condition:            Offer price                  |
|                                                              |
|  RATING SYSTEM:                                              |
|                                                              |
|  5 = superior                                                |
|  4 = above average                                           |
|  3 = average                                                 |
|  2 = below average              _____      |
|  1 = poor                       Rating                       |
+--------------------------------------------------------------+
```

These forms can be incredibly helpful in many ways:

1. When showing homes to a new buyer, give the buyer as many forms as the number of homes you are showing. At each house, ask the buyer to briefly complete each card. When you are finished showing properties, ask the buyers to give you the cards as they will help you evaluate which homes the buyers are leaning toward and which ones are absolutely not of interest.

2. The *evaluation card* is also helpful at your open houses.

   If you feel that there is a bit of a problem in the asking price, ask the buyers that come through to please leave their opinions on the card. They needn't give their name, so they will not feel pressured. This can also tell an owner exactly how a buyer feels about a home without compromising your own relationship with the seller.

Barbara Nash-Price

"SERVICE YOU CAN'T LIVE WITHOUT"

PROPERTY INFORMATION FOR:

7326 WEST 114TH STREET CIRCLE

- The builder of this home was Lecy Construction. A top builder in the metropolitan area.

- Upgrades include beautiful Princeton trim on the door and moldings.

- The formal living room and dining room have sensational skylights.

- Some of the neighborhood children are as follows:

Boys	*Girls*
1 baby	2 six-year-olds
2 three-year-olds	2 seven-year-olds
1 four-year-old	1 eight-year-old
1 five-year-old	3 nine-year-olds
2 six-year-olds	4 eleven-year-olds
3 seven-year-olds	2 thirteen-year-olds
1 eight-year-old	2 fourteen-year-olds
1 ten-year-old	1 sixteen-year-old
1 eleven-year-old	3 seventeen-year-olds
2 fourteen-year-olds	1 nineteen-year-old
Several also in college and senior high	

- Seldom has a home been offered with so many *upgrades*, additional *built-ins* and the best in quality workmanship available.

CHAPTER 5

CMAs
Competitive Market Analyses

big deal
by "Lorayne n' Neil"

What's the Best CMA?

I get just about every listing call that I go on!

I attribute 80% of my business to *the way* I do business!

I start with a professional-looking *market analysis* brochure.

I pull three properties that I feel are most similar in the following areas:

1. *location*
2. *floor plan type* or style
3. *square footage*
4. *age*
5. *number of bedrooms* and baths
6. *unusual amenities* (such as pool, security system, etc.)
7. *garage size*
8. property improvements (such as *additions, larger garage, new roof, furnace, electric, central air, appliances, and cosmetics*)
9. unusual financing opportunities
10. potential negatives (such as busy street or high hill)

When filling out the subject property part of the CMA, make sure that you fill in the high-light section (the part that talks about what the home is like) in descriptive, enthusiastic terms. Then immediately write an ad on the home!

When you do a CMA, write the information about the subject property in a *different color ink*. Often much of the information is provided to you by the seller. They have already made up a fact sheet on the home and have it at their property.

Doing a CMA is relatively simple. As you look at the following CMA you will notice some very specific information. I make it a point to bring the *most important information* about a home out and write it *in the margin*.

Example:

L.P.	list price
S.P.	sale price
Days	days on the market
BR	bedrooms
Bath	number of baths
Yr. blt.	year the home was built
Lot	lot size
Taxes	amount of yearly taxes

Fplc	how many fireplaces
Garage	number of garages
Exterior	exterior of the home
W.O.	walkout basement
**	space for extras, such as pool
Sq. ft.	main floor square footage
Ttl. sq. ft.	total square footage

Comparable price: original listing price

Difference: sale price

Indicated value of subject: I put the difference between *the home's asking price* and *sale price* in this box.

The difference can be used as a good marketing tool because the sellers can see that the comparable listings sold only after they adjusted the price or took a lower offer on the property.

Write notes about your properties all over the CMA!

The more notes you
take the better!

For example:

new roof
totally remodeled interior
attached triple garage
inground heated pool

If one particular home is the best comparable, note it by writing the words "best comparable" above it.

Write notes and highlight information in red pen.

When you have finished filling in the information on all three comparables, go to the bottom of the page where all the comparables are listed on the subject property.

Use a different color pen to fill in the information about the subject property. Under miscellaneous write the year the home was built, its style, its best feature, additional amenities, and any outstanding points of interest.

Do the same for the following comparables with the same color pen.

SUBJECT PROPERTY

Prepared for:

Price		Terms **SUBMIT**	# Bedrooms **3**
			# Baths **3**

				HS Tax $ **5445**	Map **33 4c**
1 Add					
2 Mun **EDINA**	Zip	Cty **HENN**		Tax W/Spec $ **SAME**	Lake **—**
3 Dist **585**	Lt Sz **63 x 137**			HS Filed **Y** 19 **92**	
4 Brk	#			Unpaid Spec $ **—**	Poss **ARRANGE**
5 Of Ph **920-1960**	Apt Ph			Pend Spec $ **—**	Yr Blt **38**
6 Agt **NASH-PRICE**	Hm Ph			Key **CLB**	C **3.15**	T **1**	#

7 SIMPLY ELEGANT NEW ENGLAND TUDOR LOADED WITH CHARM AND FLEXIBLE FLOOR PLAN ON MAIN
8 FLOOR. BEAUTIFUL BEDROOMS LOADED WITH CHARACTER. ENTICING BREAKFAST ROOM OFF FAMILY ROOM
9 OR FORMAL DINING ROOM. LOWER LEVEL WITH ADDITIONAL BR AND BATH AND FAM. ROOM.
10 THE BEST!

11	L	C	D	Ap Rm Sz	Dir				
12 LR	M			27 x 14	WSO	Heat **FAG**	Mtg $ **PRIVATE**		Type
13 DR	M			INCLUDED	Ext **STUCCO**	AE$	#		ASM
14 ID				AREA	Bsmt **YES (FULL)**	AC **CENT**	W	OD	DV
15 Kit	M			11 x 12	Bsmt Bth **YES**	Fpl **YES**	PI $	R/$ NEW FINANCING	%
16 Fm	M			14 x 15	Mster Bth **YES**	Refrig **YES**	2M/CD$		%D
17 MB	2			20 x 14	G **DBL** Gdo **Y**	R&O **YES**	New Finance Possibilities		
18 BR	2			12 x 13	CW **YES**	DW **YES**			
19 BR	2			12 x 14	CS **YES**	SD	* NEW ROOF (1983-TIMBERLINE)		
20	L			12 x 14	PID		1987- NEW CENTRAL AIR / FURNACE /		
21 DEN	M			8 x 10	SFML/TFF		COMB. WINDOWS		

While efforts have been made to project an accurate market evaluation, it cannot be guaranteed that the information
contained herein is free from errors and omissions.

PICTURE

Suggested List: _309 - 319,000_

Suggested Sell: _290$_
(DEPENDING ON
HOW LONG + THE MARKET)

COMPARABLE "A"   ITEM

photo

LP:	309,000
SP:	299,500
DAYS:	17
BR:	4
BA:	3
TAXES:	4923
BLT:	1937
LOT:	59 x 15
FPLC:	2
EXT:	SHAKE

REMODELED KITCHEN (NEW APPLCS)

NEW FURNACE - CENTRAL AIR - HUMIDIFER

NEW ROOF ++

SUNROOM +   SQ FT: 1263   T

TOTAL OF ITEM

"A"	COMPARABLE PRICE	(+) or (-) Difference	Indicated v of SUBJEC
	$ 309,000	$ 299,500	

	SQ. FEET	GARAGE
SUBJECT PROPERTY	2078 TTL	DBL
COMPARABLE "A"	2661	DBL
COMPARABLE "B"	2550	DBL
COMPARABLE "C"	2500	DBL

	COMPARABLE "B"	ITEM			COMPARABLE "C"	ITEM	
		LP: 282,500				LP: 275,000	
		SP: 275,000				SP: 275,000	
		DAYS: 85				DAYS: 1++	
		BR: 4				BR: 4	
	photo	BATH: 3			photo	BATH: 2	
		TAXES: 4303 ºº				TAXES: 4979 ºº	
		BUILT: 1929				BLT: 1938	
		LOT: 80 x141				LOT: 50 x158	
		FPLC: 2				FPLC: 2	
		EXT: STUCCO				EXT: BRICK/STUCCO	

COMPARABLE "B"
- NEWER KITCHEN - FENCED YARD
- JACUZZI TUB/SAUNA - ATT. DBL GAR.
- (MAIN FAM. ROOM) + DINING ROOM
- NEW BATHROOM UP+   SQ FT: 1170   TTL 2550
  - TOTAL OF ITEMS

COMPARABLE "C"
- MAIN FLOOR SUNROOM
- FINISHED LOWER LEVEL
- APPLC'S INCLUDED - DBL ATT. GAR
- SQ FT 2500 (TTL)
  - TOTAL OF ITEMS

"B" COMPARABLE PRICE	(+) or (-) Difference	Indicated value of SUBJECT	$	"C" COMPARABLE PRICE	(+) or (-) Difference	Indicated value of SUBJECT	$ 5-1-91
$ 282,500	$ 275,000	-7500 ºº		$ 275,000	$ 275,000		0

-9500 ºº

OT SIZE	NO. BRs	BATHS	CENT AIR	FAMILY ROOM	MISCELLANEOUS	BASE TAX	YR. BLT.	LIST TERMS	DAYS MKT.	ASKING PRICE	SALE TERMS	SALE PRICE
x 137	3	3	YES	MAIN 14 x 15	LOVELY MAJESTIC TUDOR - 3 BR - 3 BATH - NEW C.A/FURN/ FPLC -DEN-	5445	1938	SUB	NA	NA	NA	NA
x 158	4	3	YES	9 x 13	2 STORY NEW ENGLAND 4BR- 3 BATH COLONIAL - MASTER SUITE w/ NEW BATH	4927	1937	SUB	17	309,900	CONV	299,500
x 141	4	3	YES	17 x 12	2 STORY - 4 BR - 3 BATH WITH MAIN FLOOR FAM. ROOM + FORMAL DR.	4303	1929	SUB	85	282,500	CONV	275,000
x 138	4	2	NO	SUNROOM	STUCCO 2 STORY ENGLISH TUDOR W/ 4 BR 2 BATH - 1ST FLOOR SUN ROOM	4979	1938	SUB	1	275,000	CONV	275,000

SUBJECT PROPERTY

Prepared for:

Price		Terms		# Bedrooms
				# Baths

1 Add					HS Tax $		Map
2 Mun		Zip		Cty	Tax W/Spec $		Lake
3 Dist	Lt Sz				HS Filed	19	
4 Brk			#		Unpaid Spec $		Poss
5 Of Ph		Apt Ph			Pend Spec $		Yr Blt
6 Agt		Hm Ph			Key	C	T	#

7				
8				
9				
10				

	L	C	D	Ap Rm Sz	Dir					
11										
12 LR					WSO	Heat	Mtg $		Type	
13 DR					Ext	AE$	#			ASM
14 ID					Bsmt	AC	W		OD	DV
15 Kit					Bsmt Bth	Fpl	PI $	R $		%
16 Fm					Mster Bth	Refrig	2M/CD$		%D	
17 MB					G Gdo	R&O	New Finance Possibilities			
18 BR					CW	DW				
19 BR					CS	SD				
20					PID					
21					SFML/TFF					

While efforts have been made to project an accurate market evaluation, it cannot be guaranteed that the information contained herein is free from errors and omissions.

PICTURE

Suggested List: _____

Suggested Sell: _____

COMPARABLE "A"   ITEM

photo

TOTAL OF ITE

"A"	COMPARABLE PRICE	(+) or (−) Difference	Indicated v of SUBJEC
	$_____	$_____	

	SQ. FEET	GARAGE
SUBJECT PROPERTY		
COMPARABLE "A"		
COMPARABLE "B"		
COMPARABLE "C"		

"Sample" Blank Form

		COMPARABLE "B"		ITEM			COMPARABLE "C"		ITEM		
		photo					photo				
				TOTAL OF ITEMS					TOTAL OF ITEMS		

$ **"B"** COMPARABLE PRICE   (+) or (−) Difference $_____ $_____   Indicated value of SUBJECT $ **"C"** COMPARABLE PRICE   (+) or (−) Difference $_____ $_____   Indicated value of SUBJECT $

LOT SIZE	NO. BRs	BATHS	CENT AIR	FAMILY ROOM	MISCELLANEOUS	BASE TAX	YR. BLT.	LIST TERMS	DAYS MKT.	ASKING PRICE	SALE TERMS	SALE PRICE

Comments on CMA

An FSBO owner commented,

"Both my wife and I feel that you really did your homework . . . one agent was so detailed . . . he went on and on and on . . . We had two other agents come in. They had done their presentation and we told them we would get back to them. You came over and we had no intention of listing that evening. However, after looking at your presentation, *we changed our mind.*"

An owner who listed two properties totaling one half million dollars with an agent who called him off of an owner ad in the paper commented,

"First of all, you did your homework."

"It was very well presented."

"You sold us on *you* that evening and you were so *enthusiastic.*"

"You were so *professional* and *thorough* and had such *a history* on the house and did it in a concise, consolidated manner."

"You have a *sense of humor.*"

CHAPTER 6

Computers

big deal
by "Lorayne n' Neil"

Computers

These last few years and going into the twenty-first century will see a revolution in the *real estate industry* regarding the computer and the real estate agent.

A good agent will want to own:

1. a good laptop computer
2. a good printer
3. a fax machine
4. a portable telephone
5. a modem attached to his or her computer
6. various software programs

PURPOSES:

You can use your computer at your open houses to show buyers homes that are currently listed.

You can look up sold properties near and around your open house to be current for clients.

You can access the MLS system from your personal computer and hook up to the qualifying program to quickly qualify clients.

Should you decide to farm a specific area, you can use your laptop computer to set up a geographic farming system and type in the names (alphabetized) and addresses of people listed in the cross reference directory to make a list for your own reference.

You can install a data base program with names and addresses of clients into your computer to mail letters to those that you have visited.

Your computer can also use 8 in 1 software that will enable you to check with people who will be moving in three, six, or twelve months.

You can create a perfect newsletter on your computer in little time without worrying about type-written errors because you can automatically modify.

Your computer calendar can remind you to send clients postcards for anniversaries, birthdays, thank yous or whatever.

There are new PIM (Personal Information Management) programs that allow you to contact up to a hundred or more people a day. You can log when you will call them back and automatically look up their telephone numbers. They will even automatically dial the phone number for you. Some even have time planners to allow you to schedule your entire day and note when to call your prospects back.

On your personal computer you can create a reference chart of all your past clients and when their houses sold and closed.

A computer makes you appear extremely effective and professional when you call on potential clients.

A program connected with Desktop Publishers allows you to create a message to a client and use specific graphics to create any image that you like.

Programs specifically aimed at graphics allow you to specialize in charts, graphs, and special artwork to promote specific listed properties.

Individualized programs enable you to personalize your presentations.

You can obtain a data base program to enable you to keep track of exactly what is required for anywhere from 25 to 100 listings at a time. You may want to write an ad, send a letter, or change a lockbox code. This is important for time management.

Software is available that allows you to inform your seller how the listing is doing and to send him or her a detailed report regarding your advertising marketing plan.

Perhaps you would want to use a spreadsheet to give you an overview look at all your listings and closings on one sheet. This would enable you to see what you have spent for advertising, marketing, and all areas of service to any and all of your listings. You can use your computer to show a potential buyer the pros and cons of refinancing. The computer will compare current rate of interest and payment versus a new, lower interest rate and payment.

A computer will quickly show a client the advantages of owning versus renting and analyze the differences.

You can show your buyer the advantages of a fifteen-year mortgage versus a 30-year mortgage and the amount saved in payments over the years.

Your computer can use a spreadsheet to analyze the best loans at the current rate of interest, including points and origination fees.

What About the Computer and Follow-up?

Going into the twenty-first century it will be essential to have a computerized program setup for the real estate person who wants to be abreast of the market.

The purpose of having a computer is not just to keep up with the Joneses but rather to realize the time savings and the many uses that can be found once you are comfortable with a computer.

Although real estate *is a person to person business*, there are many functions that must be performed by the agent that can be accomplished by a computer to save time and energy. Computer usage can also give a more professional look to the agent representing the seller and the buyer.

Following are abilities that are of the utmost importance to all agents that are available on the computer:

1. tapping into an MLS (Multiple Listing Service) system
2. doing a CMA *(Competitive Market Analysis)*
3. searching the *solds* in the areas of interest
4. searching the *expireds* in the areas of interest
5. searching the *current actives* in the areas of interest
6. *internal phone* for calling other companies
7. internal *calculator*
8. geographic *farming* tool
9. various *mailing* systems
10. sending out a *newsletter* to clients
11. listing *presentation*
12. graphic programs that create charts
13. *filing* system
14. day time *reminder*
15. monthly *calendar* and world clock
16. listing files and escrow/*closing files*
17. tracking *expenses*
18. printing *informative* reports
19. various *financial* help, such as qualifying buyers
20. word processing programs such as *fact sheets* and letters

You may ask yourself how these individual programs can actually help you when you already know how to do all this.

A COMPUTER IS A TIME SAVER!

NOTE THE FOLLOWING:

A good computer financial program:

> can create a CMA (Competitive Market Analysis)
> can create a rent vs. buy program
> can qualify a buyer quickly
> can create a loan rate comparison report
> can show buyers monthly cost breakdown quickly

A good word processor program:

> can produce a *letter or postcard* quickly
>
> can produce a fact/highlight sheet quickly
>
> can produce a newsletter for your farm area quickly
>
> can produce a buyer guide book quickly
>
> can produce a listing presentation book quickly

A good data base program:

> can schedule all listing needs and tasks
>
> adds a listing quickly to your file system
>
> adds a closing quickly to your file/data base system

MLS program:

> searches all printed comparable properties for solds, expireds, actives and also does an area market survey that lets the seller know how long it has taken for similar properties that have been on the market to sell in a given time frame

When you purchase a computer, you may or may not be knowledgeable as to what you should buy.

When I originally walked in the door of the computer sales company, I thought I had suddenly been transported to another country! I had virtually no idea as to what I wanted to buy!

After much trial and error I was able to find the following:

> an IBM compatible computer with a color monitor
>
> a Panasonic 24 pin multimode printer
>
> a modem to go in my hard drive
>
> WordPerfect software
>
> Lotus 1-2-3 software
>
> various books to learn about computers
>
> boxes of computer paper
>
> a mouse, and
>
> an extra phone line brought into my house for the modem on my computer.

Now I was set, or so I thought.

It took me *over a year* and paying the salary of a computer secretary for six months for me to learn some *basic features* and some *basic commands*. *At least* I needed to know how to *enter* my computer and use *some* of the functions! I eventually did learn to prepare a complete program, type out a report to my clients and prepare to print it when . . .

I accidentally pressed the wrong button!

Everything disappeared.

This completely frustrated me and I decided to regroup.

I bought a simple program, and I am now able to save hours of aggravation.

Even though I personally love to sell real estate, I had to be computerized.

Since I am not very mechanical nor take much time to *learn details*, I need things to be simplified for me.

A computer program setup that works for me in a very simplified fashion is the ***Eight In One*** **program.**

I will include all the information for setting yourself up with a computer, the software, the printer, and the modem.

From there all you have to do is:

1. follow directions
2. give your computer business
3. let your computer be your guidebook and your secretary.

If you invest in nothing else in the next decade, try to own the following three items:

1. laptop computer and printer
2. portable compact telephone, and
3. fax machine

These three items *will be able to keep you abreast of a changing market by giving you access to any changing terms and conditions on properties and on purchase agreements.*

A laptop computer and small, good printer (I prefer IBM compatible) should cost you approximately $1,500.

You should be able to purchase a used portable, compact telephone for approximately $200.

Good second-hand FAX machines are available for $300.

Watch for ads in the newspapers under the classified section if you want one that is second hand. Very often people purchase these items and discard them shortly thereafter with hardly any use and at a great savings to you!

Your total dollar amount should not have *exceeded* $2000, and you can usually find a few good software programs to set up on your machine for under a few hundred dollars.

A good program for under $50 that I started on my *laptop* was *Eight In One*.

It functions as a:

1. desktop organizer, tracks appointments and address book outliner, outlines strategy points before you begin.

2. word processor, fully edits and formats all documents.

3. spell checker, 100,000 word dictionary captures 99% of spelling errors.

4. spreadsheet, with 30 functions for all financial analysis.

5. data base, searches any field and creates reports on the information on file.

6. graphics, creates different types of bar charts, line graphs.

7. communications, uses a modem (telephone) for autodialing and full or split screen options.

This is one program that I put on my laptop. I also immediately had a modem put on my laptop to enable me to call the MLS system. Some real estate agents prefer to have a computer *at home* also.

I have a laptop *and* an IBM compatible computer in my home.

The software that is on *my* computer at my home is:

WordPerfect	Approximately $500	WordPerfect Corp. 1-800-225-5000
Instant Recall	Approximately $100	Chronologic Corp. 1-800-848-4970
Qualification	Approximately $250	Command Decisions Commander 1-703-590-8927

Someday I hope to have a better understanding of computers. However, since the majority of my time is for the real estate business, I also have a tendency to do things mechanically, the easy way.

I use my laptop a lot because it is *simple*.

It is *easy* to figure out.

It *adds to my image* as a high-tech professional.

It can *help me save* huge amounts of time and guesswork.

Following is a brief description of computer software on the market to assist the real estate agent.

Name	Price	Company/Phone
Eight In One	$50	Spinnaker Software 617-494-1200

This software has eight functions in one. It enables you to organize, outline, word process, spell correctly, utilize a spread sheet, incorporate a data base system, use graphics, and communicate with other computers.

Real-Term		Moore Data 612-588-7111

This software enables you to communicate with other computers.

Qualifying Keys Program	$139	800-452-5000

With a push of a button the agent can qualify the buyer under any financing plan.

CMA Keys Program	$139	800-452-5000

A computerized CMA that reflects what the market is telling the seller. ". . . has a main list of various amenities . . . formats and lines up comparable properties."

Real Estate Specialist Program/RES	$598	818-592-1000

This program is a planning and tracking program that keeps files with detailed notes, has a word processor and calendar, ties properties, events and items to people, and prints out all the information. There is also an automatic dialer.

Top Producer	$495	800-444-8570

This program has a wide range of features and capabilities. The program enables an agent to store and manage contacts, write letters at a touch of a button, prepare effective mailouts, instantly view all scheduled calls and follow-ups, print daily schedule, control listings and closings, and track clients.

Instant Recall/IR	$99	800-848-4970

This program is a new software program that remembers and finds notes, projects, meetings, deadlines, ideas, tasks, names, phone numbers, everything. It provides instant access to information through a full-featured "personal information" manager.

Qualification Commander	$249	703-590-8927

A complete real estate financial analysis package, this provides a rapid mortgage qualifier, prospect tracking, data base, preprogrammed reports, buyers estimate of closing, buy-vs.-rent information, and mailing labels.

Purchasing a Laptop Computer

When I purchased my laptop computer, I went entirely by *instinct*. This means, I really did not know what to look for. I looked for what I *thought* looked good! Through a lot of trial and error, I realized that I can accomplish all that I wanted to do for my own real estate needs on a *laptop computer*.

You may need to estimate net proceeds quickly. Rather than run to the office to run your figures through a computer, a laptop is at your fingertips.

Your laptop computer can provide you with all the information that you would need at the touch of a button!

Most laptop computers are completely compatible with desktop computers and require the same software and disk drives. They can average in cost from $500 (used) to over $5,000 (new and fully equipped).

There are two types of screens for a laptop computer:

1. liquid crystal display (lcd) screen—gray display
2. gas plasma screen—amber display

The gas plasma screen offers fine resolution, but your investment will be about $1,000 more.

The keyboard of a laptop is a lot smaller than that of a desktop and isn't quite as easy to use. Also the layout of the keyboard will take getting used to. Make sure that when you are looking at keyboards, you try to find a layout that is close to what you are used to using.

The disk drive of a laptop operates the same way that a desktop's would. If you want a larger disk for more memory, it will cost a lot more money (can be thousands more). You might want to purchase a Pentium with a 1 gigabyte hard drive.

Many laptops come with a 3.5 inch floppy disk drive. This allows compatibility with a desktop also.

Probably the best feature of all is the fact that the laptop can be operated on either AC or DC power. You can plug it right into the wall or even use it on batteries. If you buy a laptop with a gas plasma display, you will have to buy a *deluxe* model to get the battery power option.

If you purchase a portable printer (around $200), you can use it anywhere. You also would want to consider a desktop printer as well as a portable printer because the portable printer usually can only print *one at a time* pieces and is much slower.

Printers:

1. Dot matrix printer—approximately $250
2. Laser printer—approximately $1,000

Note: I have a Panasonic 24 pin printer and love it!

In purchasing a laptop, I would suggest that you consider several various models.

A 486 or larger processor will enable you to do mass mailings.

A laptop computer will pay for itself time and time again. It is also a business expense and is entirely deductible!

When you buy a laptop computer and install good software, you will have all you need to stay on top of the business.

A laptop computer can save you endless hours. It will:

1. keep track of your *appointments*. Sound an alarm!
2. print your entire *schedule*, and replace it.
3. provide instant *financial analysis programs* for buyers.
4. *prequalify* buyers.
5. produce professional letters.
6. create *mass mailings* of information to homeowners and purchasers.
7. keep track of all your *farm information*.
8. keep *instant recall* of current clients, listings, etc.
9. send homeowners *letters*.
10. figure instant *net sheets*.

Computer Points of Interest

1. When buying a computer, always find out what the purchase price *does not* include.
2. Buy an *upgraded version* of a computer now rather than later only if the upgrade will amount to saving you at least $400.00.
3. A *complete computer system* includes cpu, ram, keyboard, disk drives, printer, and software.
4. The *advertised price* of a computer does not usually include any of the software for the computer.
5. You will want to have *various kinds of software*, an operating system which teaches the computer how to handle the keyboard, monitor, printer, and disks, as well as a basic application program that includes a word processor.
6. When you buy software, *make backup copies* of the disks. This is in case the original disks get damaged.
7. You are not allowed to give copies of software disks to your friends. This is against the law. *It is called* pirating.
8. A few of the *biggest reputable software companies* are Microsoft, Lotus, WordPerfect, Novell and Ashton-tate.
9. You can phone a program publisher and ask them to send you a demo-disk allowing you to *sample* software before you purchase.
10. There are certain programs (software) for certain computers.
11. Ask a reputable dealer which computer has the most software currently available for it.
12. All information stored in a computer is called *software*.

13. You can buy computer programs on *disk*.

14. The business section of the daily newspaper will tell you anything you need to know about the computer industry today.

15. A weekly newspaper that covers the entire computer industry is called *Computerworld $2.00/issue—508-879-0700 (toll-free) 800-669-1002*.

16. In computer magazines many *discount dealers* that can save you as much as *50%* advertise.

17. Every Tuesday *The New York Times* science section has ads from all of New York's most aggressive discount dealers.

18. There are giant mailorder discount companies for computers. Two of these dealers are Telemart and PC Connection. They mostly sell software and some hardware.

    Telemart   800-426-6659

    PC Connection   800-AID-8088

    Telemart sample pricing:

Area	Program	Price	Telemart Price
Word processing	WordPerfect 5.1	$495	52% off: $239
Integrated	Questions and Answers	$399	38% off: $249
Spreadsheet	Lotus 1-2-3	$495	34% off: $325

Computer Modems

A good modem (that allows your computer to talk with another computer) to buy is a *direct connect internal modem*. It costs under $100. It is cheaper and more reliable than an acoustic coupler. Also, direct connect modems have:

1. automatic dial and

2. automatic answer.

This modem is called SMART

For a high-quality modem at a low price, you can get a modem made by Everex or Practical Peripherals. Zoom makes a modem that costs even less, but is good.

Prices from Telemart in Arizona: Phone 800-426-6659

Style	Manufacturer and Price
Internal	Everex $49; Hayes $135
Internal	Everex $65; Practical Peripherals $120
External	Zoom $75; Practical Peripherals $195

Of all the communication programs available, the easiest to understand is First Choice which costs $89 from Telemart. 800-426-6659

Or there is an even simpler version of First Choice called PFS Easy Start for $36.

Each of these programs handles:

1. word processing,
2. data base,
3. spreadsheets, and
4. telecommunications.

These are very easy to learn!

Computers

Many businesses use IBM PC clones. They are relatively inexpensive and run good software. A typical IBM PC clone will *cost about half as much as a Macintosh.*

IBM PC programs come on CD ROM or floppy disks. *When you buy a software program,* you will get a CD or floppy disk and a manual to explain how to use it.

The very *first software* that you get is the disk operating system (DOS). It will teach your computer how to handle disk drives.

IBM worked with a company called Microsoft to invent Microsoft DOS. This is also called MS-DOS. It is the most popular for the IBM PC and clones. It will come on a pair of disks and you must feed them into the computer before you can use any other disk.

In order to use WordPerfect for MS-DOS (be sure you get the WordPerfect 5.1 version), WordPerfect can be bought from a discount dealer: PC Zone 800-ALT-8088.

In order to use WordPerfect 5.1, you must have at least 512k of ram (memory)

You will want to have a hard disk drive and 3 1/2 inch disks.

Actually, using a computer is not as hard as you think. Here is what I bought when I went into PC Express and purchased my desktop and laptop computers and my printer:

1. Relisys IBM compatible computer desktop
2. VGA color monitor
3. 40 megabytes hard drive/3.5" floppy disk drive
4. internal modem
5. DOS
6. WordPerfect 5.1 (Panasonic KS-PII24 24 pin printer)

The entire package cost approximately $2,000 from

> *PC EXPRESS*
> Bloomington, MN
> 800-937-1100

A Panasonic laptop computer with internal modem costs approximately $1,000 from

> *PC EXPRESS*
> Bloomington, MN
> 800-937-1100

Index of Computer Companies and Numbers

Company	Phone	Comments
Computer Plus	800-343-8124	discounts on merchandise
Digicom Computers	617-536-1888	networking, repairs
Gateway 2000	800-LAD-2000	makes clones
Egghead Discount	800-EGG-HEAD	chain of software stores
National Computer	212-614-0700 800-NAC-OMEX	broker of used computers exchange
New York PC	212-533-NYPC	New York's computer club
PC Connection	800-AID-9088	most all software
Telemart	800-426-6659	most all software
USA Flex	800-USA-FLEX	monitors, printers
WordPerfect Corp.	801-225-5000	publishes WordPerfect

PC Connection has the best reputation of most mail orders.

PHILOSOPHY

Nothing worthy of accomplishment in life comes easy. Success consists of hard work and determination, or it is not worth seeking. I like to work hard, make money, and have fun.

The power of one's belief in oneself is the greatest tool any individual can possess. Believing in yourself helps solve the daily problems that are stepping stones on the pathway to happiness and success.

Finally, it is my belief that any accomplishment in life can be obtained if you: (1) accept your goal as being extremely important to you; (2) constantly visualize yourself reaching that goal; (3) have the sincere desire and will always to be a winner . . .

DREAM—BELIEVE—

PERFORM—ACHIEVE—

Successfully,

Barbara C. Nash-Price

CHAPTER 7

Daily Schedule

Time Management

big deal
by "Lorayne n' Neil"

Daily Schedule

Definition: daily = every day

schedule = a plan allotting work to be done and specifying deadlines

My definition: A daily schedule is imperative to using time management in being successful in the real estate profession.

A daily schedule is essential to success in real estate.

There is no such thing as keeping it all in your head. You must be able to function at a moment's notice, rearrange your schedule, and change appointments depending on your calls. Sometimes the schedule will be totally changed if there is an offer to present or a listing to go on.

The best use of a daily schedule can be accomplished with a daily planner. One that has been extremely useful to me is an $8\frac{1}{2} \times 11''$ daily planner I purchased at:

Office Max
Edina, Minnesota
612-896-0080

They also have an extensive inventory of real estate needs for the professional salesperson to help you keep within a budget.

A large-size daily planner is imperative.

A real estate salesperson must be able to function completely out of a daily planner with all of his or her current needs and inventory in one book. Whether I am in the car, at an appointment, or out of town, my daily planner goes with me. I formerly used the 5" × 7" which appeared to be adequate. I chose the larger size only when I became extremely aware of time management and the importance of carrying certain items with me *at all times*. I advise the *larger* one for real estate business.

In setting up the daily planner, I prefer to keep the following:

Inside front cover:

extra personal brochures
business cards
amortization schedule

Inside back cover:

two copies of purchase agreements and buyer information sheets
two copies of blank listings and seller net sheets

1. yearly appointment book tabbed with each month

2. month in view calendar

3. performance report, including business origination and cost of promotion for your-self

4. buyer section

5. seller section

6. FSBO, expireds, and canceleds section

7. listings

8. current and past five years' transactions

9. plastic business card holder

10. color-coded alphabetized index address section

You are ready to begin planning your schedule. Let's say that your daily schedule starts out with a *blank week.*

You start on Monday morning:

My Monday Schedule

8:00–9:00 A.M.	Check the newspapers for FSBOs. *Circle the ads and call for appointments.* If you get an answering machine, this is all right. Leave your name and company! Tell them you are interested in knowing how they are handling appointments with real estate agents and you would like them to call you back. *75 % will call you back!*
9:00–10:00 A.M.	*Call at least ten* of the expired and canceled listings. Try to get at least three or four appointments. Give your name and company, and ask how they are handling appointments with real estate agents. If they want to talk, listen. They usually have a long, sad story as to why their house hasn't sold and why the agent didn't sell it. Be compassionate, and try not to sell yourself too strong over the telephone. *Just get the appointment and go from there.*
10:00–11:00 A.M.	*Contact at least five companies* that are relatively new in the area. Sunday papers usually list these in the business section. Ask for the personnel office, and see if they would be interested in working with you. Ask to stop by and drop off your personal brochure and/or added information.
11:00–12:00 P.M.	*Call at least five friends, acquaintances, or relatives* and see if they know of anyone who may be interested in buying and/or selling. I usually choose a property that is reasonably priced and that I really like, and oftentimes

refer to this property *first* in calling friends. I might say, "There's a new listing that just came up in our area, and it has a super floor plan. Do you know anyone who may be interested in it?" *Remember that everyone loves to hear about a house.*

12:00–1:00 P.M.	Go to lunch. *Try to have lunch with a potential client* or someone who could assist you in the real estate business. Sometimes if I don't have a client, I *bring my lunch back to the office* or eat at a drivethrough and preview areas and new homes on the market as I eat my lunch.
1:00–2:00 P.M.	*Set up appointments on good candidates to hold open this next Sunday.* Call and ask the agent if you can hold an open house on their property. Set up appointments at other homes in the same neighborhood.
2:00–4:00 P.M.	Xerox each property that you are looking at with the *lock-box combination in the upper corner* and any added information regarding locking doors or animals. *Drive by and go to appointments on at least six properties.* Take notes and keep track of these homes that you have seen in a special folder marked "properties viewed." Rate the home as you would for yourself, and make notes in the margins of the paper on *each* home. When calling friends or relatives, it is a plus to be able to tell them about a property that you have seen yourself.
4:00–5:30 P.M.	*Go back to the office to return calls* and messages that have come in. If you made at least 25 calls today, you should have at least *a few returned calls.* Schedule appointments for the evening hours, and remember to bring your personal brochure and personal promotion book as selling tools when going to clients' homes.
5:00–6:30 P.M.	*Take a break to go home,* have dinner, relax, unwind and freshen up. Hopefully you have one appointment for tonight to preview a property for a buyer. Perhaps you have an appointment to talk to a FSBO. Remember that on the first appointment, only walk through and come back to present the CMA and list the home.
7:00–9:00 P.M.	*Appointment with FSBO to preview* home for a potential listing. This is the best time to catch owners at home, whether expireds, canceleds or referrals. They usually have the evenings free. This is the best time to sit down and talk real estate, or if you are not going on a listing appointment, try to arrange to have buyers meet you at the office. Pre-qualify them and have them look at the MLS properties that they may want to look at.
9:30–10:00 P.M.	*Highlight for tomorrow* what is important, what is first on the agenda, and what you don't want to forget. Record all information, keeping a separate legal pad just for *phone numbers.* I keep these legal pads for years sometimes.

My Tuesday Schedule

8:30–10:00 A.M.	*Office meeting* to share knowledge of new properties.
10:00–12:00 P.M.	*Tour all new properties* in at least two main areas that you are willing to work exclusively. Try to preview at least six to eight homes.
12:00–1:00 P.M.	*Take a break*, but keep track of time. Perhaps wash your car, shop, do errands, or have a bit of lunch. Never spend too much time for lunch unless with a prospect or potential client. Take different people to lunch. *Going to lunch with fellow real estate people* is completely unnecessary!
1:00–3:00 P.M.	*Can I show a buyer?* Do office work; contact FSBO for appointment later in week. Try to get two open houses for this weekend. Send out letters to clients from Sunday's open houses. Send out other letters to potential clients. Try to send out at least five letters to future clients, and perhaps include computer printout material. Include the day on which you will call them back. *Make note* to call on that day.
3:00–5:00 P.M.	Leave this two-hour interval for some kind of business *outside of the office*. Visit a FSBO. Show properties. Meet with any other appointments in this time slot. Take a short walk. If possible, get some exercise.
5:00–7:00 P.M.	Family time, dinner, your own time.

Look at a day in two-hour intervals. These schedules may vary. Yours may be completely different in all respects. What I am trying to show, is how important *balance* is.

You must work hard.

Relax.

Work hard.

Relax.

Find social time with family and friends *each and every day.* I personally favor 7:00 to 9:00 P.M. with my children. Many nights I read to them, do school projects, help with homework, drive to piano or violin lessons, and enjoy quiet time that is just for my family. I try to see that this is done *at least three of the five school days.* It is very rewarding for me and helps me function at my best for my clients and overall business.

You cannot do all things, be everywhere, and want your days to fall into place unless there is a *specified schedule* you have set up for yourself each and every day of the week. If 7:00 to 9:00 does not work, stick with 5:00 to 7:00 and do update work from 8:00 to 10:00.

My Wednesday Schedule

8:30–10:30 A.M. — *Write ads for Sunday open houses.* Make sure you have selected open houses that you feel comfortable with. When writing your ad, try to have three headlines in two cap. (See Chapter 3.)

10:30–12:30 P.M. — *Make appointments with buyers to look at houses.* Preview six to eight properties in two favored areas. Show houses to a buyer who can look midweek. Make appointment with FSBO to bring back competitive market analysis.

12:30–1:20 P.M. — *Take a break!* Wash your car and have lunch.

2:00–4:00 P.M. — *Office work. Send out letters to buyers and other mailings.* Check computer for buyers. Make weekly update. Check computer and send sheets for sellers' comparative listings. Make appointments for Thursday and Saturday.

5:00–7:00 P.M. — *Family or personal time.*

7:00–9:00 P.M. — *Family time or call clients for appointments.* Contact buyer with computer information. Set up appointments for weekend showings and other sellers' appointments.

My Thursday Schedule

8:30–9:30 A.M. — *Set up appointments* for showings. If not showing, preview four to six homes before noon.

10:30–12:30 P.M. — *Show properties. Preview properties.* Keep list of properties that you see along with prices in your daily log book so you always have a reference of reviewed homes. Rate the homes that you see on a one to ten scale so you can reference the best deals for the current market price.

12:30–1:30 P.M. — Take a break! Always take a lunch break somewhere different, and wear a name tag showing that you are a real estate agent. I have met clients grocery shopping.

2:00–3:30 P.M. — On Thursdays, *I preview estate sales and moving sales that are in the paper.* These are usually always worth a good lead or two!

4:00–5:00 P.M. — *Contact a client for an appointment* tonight or Saturday to show homes and a potential listing. Call some expireds. Fill up the remainder of your daily log book.

5:00–7:00 P.M. — Dinner and quiet time alone or with family.

7:00–9:00 P.M. — *Return calls from today* to clients for showing. Contact some FSBOs. Meet with a potential seller to list his or her home. Meet with a buyer at the office. Listen to a positive tape on good attitude. An excellent source is "Insight" which can be ordered through Nightingale-Conant at 800-323-5552.

My Weekend Schedule

FRIDAY	*I try to take Fridays for myself*, especially because on Saturdays I show and Sundays are also busy with *open houses*
SATURDAY	*I divide the day in half.* I either show properties in the early part of the day, perhaps 10:00 to 2:00 P.M. or go after a listing in this time slot. I may also give myself the early part of the day and meet with a buyer in the afternoon (perhaps 1:00 to 5:00 P.M.).
SUNDAY	Mornings are for church and brunch with family.
12:00–2:00 P.M.	First open house.
2:30–4:30 P.M.	Second open house.

Sometimes on Sunday evenings I call on FSBOs from the paper. Also, if I cannot have two open houses on a Sunday, I preview FSBO homes, visit with the owners, and make sure that I leave with another appointment.

This is just a rough draft of my overall schedule. However, basically, it remains the same. *I continuously contact clients* and constantly preview homes.

That is our business. If we don't do it, another agent will.

It is our business to know our inventory.

It is essential that we continuously add new properties to our inventory.

Daily Schedule Fill-ins

If you are at odds about what to do and when to do it, worry no more. After this chapter, you will have a perfect idea of what is expected of you in the real estate business.

You cannot avoid keeping records if you are to be successful. You must learn that the more records and charts that you keep, the more you will see where you are going.

IF YOU DON'T KNOW WHERE YOU ARE GOING, YOU WILL END UP SOMEPLACE ELSE.

Keep track of what you do daily with a chart.

Weekly Chart

	Mon.	Tues.	Wed.	Thur.	Fri.	Sat.	Sun.
Call FSBO							
Call expireds							
Call canceleds							
Send thank you letters							
New listings							
Open houses held							
Open house contacts							
Showed houses							
Relocation referrals received/sent							
Phone canvassing (hours?)							
Door knocking in neighborhoods (hours?)							
Listen to positive motivation tapes (#?)							
Real estate education seminars (#?)							
Listings sold							
Price reductions							

Diary of a Realtor

MONDAY 1/25

7:45 A.M.	See children off to school/start crock pot
8:15 A.M.	Go to office
8:30 A.M.	Review day and start calling clients
8:45 A.M.	Call D. Vesttie - confirm appointment to walk through home at 4609 Beritage
9:00 A.M.	Call two FSBOs: J. Schmidt - 609 Edin Blvd. T. Kent and 671 Samue Rd.
9:30 A.M.	Send two letters to above FSBOs
10:00 A.M.	Walk through on D. Vesttie - 4609 Beritage

10:30 A.M.	Appointments on three houses for D. Bronstrom: 9800 Richy, 9904 Toledo, 9807 Little (meet client at first house)
11:30 A.M.	Appointment on FSBO: 609 Edin Blvd.
12:15 P.M.	Stop for drive-through lunch, take back to office
12:30 P.M.	Start CMA on FSBO on 609 Edin Blvd.
1:30 P.M.	Call buyers: G. Kent (130 + Edin only)
2:00 P.M.	Research houses to show G. Kent in Edin
3:30 P.M.	Finish appointments for G. Kent; make two copies; send letter to new buyer coming into town (referral friend); double check computer and newspaper for new houses to show buyer tomorrow
4:15 P.M.	Walkthrough on FSBO on 671 Samue Road - T. Kent; bring book to show some houses in two areas of interest and personal brochure
5:30 P.M.	Office: check phone messages; call: D. Marsh - 504 Arden (expired list) and G. Owens - 660 Gleason (expired list)
6:15 P.M.	Leave office; drive by two properties for Kent: 4400 Maple and 4600 Brown (new listing)
6:30 P.M.	Home for dinner.
7:45 P.M.	Appointment with D. Sandstrom (church referral) to appraise their home at 6208 Highwood
9:00 P.M.	Home with family, review appointments for tomorrow

MAKE THE MOST OF EACH DAY BY BACKTRACKING AS LITTLE AS POSSIBLE.

PLAN YOUR DAY. When you are driving by houses to preview, this is also the time to stop at the store, to drop off dry cleaning, or to stop by the post office.

When previewing homes, don't forget the estate sales and the garage sales! These people are often cleaning out because they are getting ready to move! Usually the best days for these are Thursday and Friday.

REMEMBER HOW IMPORTANT FIRST IMPRESSIONS ARE. TRY TO GET YOUR CAR WASHED!

EACH DAY	*check the local and suburban newspapers.* Check also for job promotions and new companies.
CHECK	the area that you farm. Your farm area should be your special area of influence. Example: Send mortgage information, new properties for sale.
PLAN	your meals in advance. Try to plan for the evening meal. If you are eating out and entertaining clients, make sure all reservations are made early in the morning. Keep *your telephone daily legal pad with you at all times!* This enables you to remember which calls need to be returned and which calls haven't been returned. Also by *keeping the sheets from each day* to the next (just turn one over the other and fasten with a paper clip), it is *easy to reference* and *double check* for past numbers that have been mislaid or numbers that you have forgotten to record in your daily planner book.

What I Do Daily

8:30 A.M.   *Clip all the FSBO ads from Sunday* and start calling for appointments. (See Chapter 8.) *Contact at least four* good FSBOs.

9:30 A.M.   *Make at least two appointments* for this week.

11:30 A.M.   *Only go to lunch* if I have some appointments made!

1:00 P.M.   *Contact a buyer.*

2:00 P.M.   *Send five* letters to potential clients.

3:30 P.M.   *Contact another buyer* to show houses this weekend. Buyers may have come from opens from last weekend.

Or . . .

Check the computer printout of the area in which I live.

Check the computer printout of the farm area I work.

Check the computer printout of homes I want to see.

Or . . .

Preview homes for my buyer and/or my own portfolio. Do not look at more than seven or eight homes.

Or . . .

Contact a FSBO. Contact expired owner. Contact a potential buyer. Call clients that came through open houses.

Or . . .

Work on CMA (competitive market analysis) for future listing.

4:00 P.M.   *Send five letters* to potential clients.

5:00 P.M.   *Call a friend and ask for a referral.*

Things to Do When the Phone Doesn't Ring

1. *Plan* another open house.

2. *Call someone* you know to say business is appreciated.

3. *Write out* a schedule for tomorrow's activities.

4. *Call to quality a new buyer.*

5. *Check the newspaper* ads for estate sales.

6. *Drive around* areas that are foreign to you or that you wish to know better.

7. *Write a new ad.*

8. *Try to get a price adjustment* on an unsold listing.

9. *Read a good book* that is positive.

10. *Review your last appointment* with a buyer or seller to determine what went right or wrong.

11. *Contact a company* for relocation.

12. *Call a new buyer to suggest homes* as a tax shelter.

13. *Visit the city hall* planning commission to find out what's new in the area.

14. *Call a FSBO.*

15. *Call the owners of your present listings* and give an update on the activity on the property.

16. *Call fellow agents* that have shown your listings to get feedback.

17. *Try a new idea* that you've been putting off until you had time.

18. *Review your sales volume* in the past months and replan.

19. *Send out some notes or postcards* to FSBOs and expireds.

20. *Clean out your desk* drawers and files. *Throw away anything that isn't absolutely necessary to keep.*

Agent Activity Monthly Chart

Make the chart to work off of for a month at a time.

See where the majority of your business is coming from.

What do you like to *do the most* and the least?

Where do you *need strength*?

Real Estate

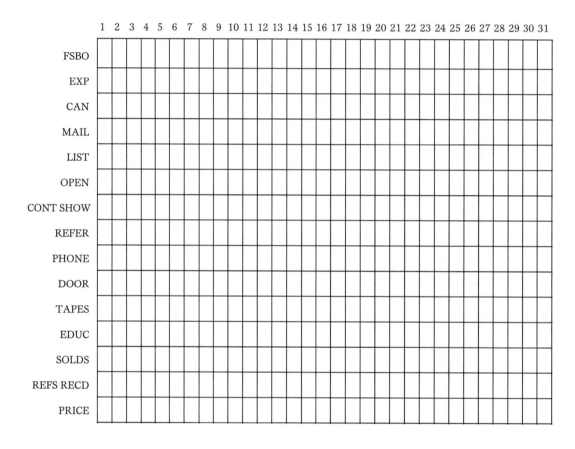

	1	2	3	4	5	6	7	8	9	10	11	12	13	14	15	16	17	18	19	20	21	22	23	24	25	26	27	28	29	30	31
FSBO																															
EXP																															
CAN																															
MAIL																															
LIST																															
OPEN																															
CONT SHOW																															
REFER																															
PHONE																															
DOOR																															
TAPES																															
EDUC																															
SOLDS																															
REFS RECD																															
PRICE																															

FSBOS	*REFERRAL SENT*
EXPIREDS	*PHONE CANVAS*
CANCELEDS	*DOOR KNOCKING*
MAIL THANK YOUS	*LISTEN TAPES/VIDEOS*
NEW LISTINGS	*EDUCATION/SEMINAR*
OPENS	*SOLD HOMES*
CONTACT BUYER FROM OPENS AND SHOWINGS	*REFERRAL RECEIVED*
	PRICE REDUCTION

Ten Business Sources

	Mon.	Tues.	Wed.	Thur.	Fri.	Sat.	Sun.
PERSONAL REFERENCE							
BUSINESS REFERENCE							
NEIGHBOR							
FAMILY							
FSBO/EXP							
AD CALL							
CHURCH							
POLITICAL							
SOCIAL							
VOLUNTEER							

RATING 1–5 (5 THE BEST)

Homes Viewed Pad

* Client	Client Rated	Address	Lockbox Comments	Date

* NO CLIENT NAME IF VIEWING ALONE.

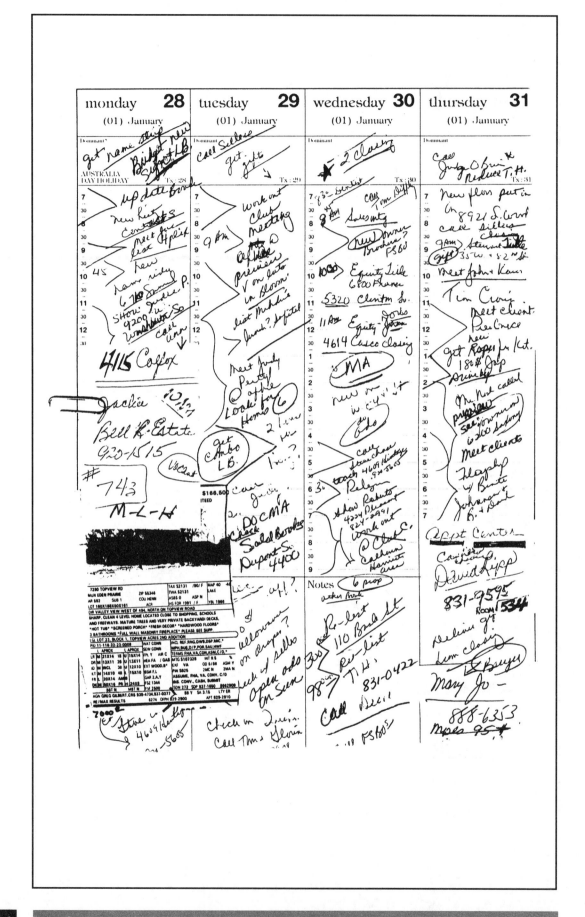

★	Anna Narth	10 AM WED	722-4011
☆	Cori Smith	831-1002	
☆	Wayne Orson	454-1151	
☆	Mary Martin	724-0114	
☆	David Farmer	888-0001	
☆	Paul Herson	224-0411	
☆	Keith Anderson	223-0004	
☆	Don Pate	842-2379	
☆	Dana Price	742-0317	
★	Susan Wallan	921-0336	
☆	Mrs. Jensen	924-0337	
☆	Mr. Dode	831-4222	
☆	Jack Solz	927-8441	
☆	Page Longet	831-4593	
☆	Linda Smatten	(W) 476-3492	Home 831-0043
☆	Lee Orson	(W) 333-0041	
★	Nan Tucket	(H) 223-4091	(W) 435-2497
★	Ed Fresco	441-3902	
★	Nancy Dayes	897-4063	
☆	Pat Sedge	439-2044	
☆	Dave Robbs	(W) 221-9998	(H) 441-2398
☆	Mr. & Mrs. Smith	(H) 439-0019	
☆	Jim Perry	831-1999	
☆	Jenny Camps	398-4016	
☆	Aren Pike	(H) 984-8732	(W) 442-8702
☆	Dede Lotts	891-0413	
☆	Penny Arthur	391-0424	

	MONDAY	TUESDAY	WEDNESDAY
8:00	CALL OWNERS	NETWORK W/AGENTS	CALL CLIENTS
9:00	CALL EXPIRED	TOUR NEW PROP.	COMPUTER TIME
10:00	SET UP OPEN'S	TOUR HOMES	MAILING (EXPIRED)
11:00	PREVIEW HOMES	COMPUTER REFERRALS	WALK THRU
12:00	LUNCH	LUNCH	LUNCH
1:00	CALL BUYERS	CALL ON FSBO	WRITE ADS
2:00	↓	MAIL	SHOW (PREVIEW)
3:00	MAILINGS	FARM MAILINGS	(PREVIEW)
4:00	↓	SHOW	HOUSES
5:00	CALLING	HOUSES	WALK RE-GROUP
6:00	DINNER	DINNER	DINNER
7:00	CALL ON	CALL ON	GO ON LISTING
8:00	FSBO	EXPIRED	PRESENTATION

	THURSDAY	FRIDAY	SATURDAY	SUNDAY
8:00	CALL CLIENTS	CALL CLIENTS		
9:00	COMPUTER TIME	CHECK COMPUTER		
10:00	MAILING	PREVIEW	OFFICE CALLS	CHURCH
11:00	CALL REFERRAL	HOMES CALLS	+ COMPUTER	CHECK ADS
12:00	LUNCH	LUNCH	LUNCH	LUNCH
1:00	CMA FSBO	PREVIEW HOMES	SHOW	OPEN
2:00	↓	CMA FOR	HOLD OPENS	(SHOW HOUSES)
3:00	SEND RELO'S	FSBO	←	→
4:00	CALL ON	MAILINGS	HOUSES	HOUSE
5:00	FSBO	↓	CALL CLIENTS	STOP BY FSBO'S
6:00	DINNER	DINNER	DINNER	DINNER
7:00	MEET BUYER	EXERCISE		FOLLOW-UP CALLS
8:00	BUYERS			CALLS

CHAPTER 8

FSBOs

For Sale By Owners

big deal

by "Lorayne n' Neil"

F.S.B.O.'s

For Sale By Owner

WHAT! CALL THE FOR SALE BY OWNER? I started in the real estate business almost twenty years ago. I had no particular contacts and no real source of referrals. In thinking over ways to bring myself business in a manner that would be profitable for me in a short amount of time, *there was really only one answer:*

Call people who want to sell **NOW!**

"For Sale By Owners" (FSBOs) very much want to sell **right now**.

Contrary to what you may think, FSBOs list.

Look at the following statistics:

95% of most FSBOs list their home.

Almost 90% of all FSBOs are interviewing agents to list their home.

Almost 80% of all FSBOs like to have agents call them.

Nine out of ten FSBOs have business to refer to you later. Every Sunday most FSBOs wait to be called by agents. FSBOs usually have more than enough information already prepared for you before you come to the home. Working on FSBOs can increase your business 75 to 100%!

Now note the following statistic: I have increased my business over 50% consistently by calling on "For Sale By Owners."

What does it hurt? Why not make one phone call to them? *You can't lost anything by trying.*

Almost all FSBOs really are *nice guys*. Just make one call, and change your income for the better.

Ten Best Ways to Get an Appointment with For Sale by Owners

Call them on the phone and say:

> *"Hi, I'm _____, and I'm from _____ Realty. I am calling to see how you are handling appointments with agents in regards to looking at your property."*

If they say "No thank you, I'm not interested," you may want to select one of the following good *foot-in-the-door* statements:

1. *I prefer to concentrate in your area* and like to keep up on *any* property that comes up for sale.

2. *Every day I work with different buyers* and try to keep up on new inventory whether listed through Multiple Listing Services or *For Sale By Owners*. They are all *important* to me.

3. *I try to actively pursue relocation clients* which would be clients transferring in from out of town and they don't always know about *your specific* neighborhood.

4. *I'd like to compare your home to others* that our company has *sold* in your neighborhood and, of course, give you my professional, qualified opinion.

5. *I pride myself on being successful* with other clients *in your* lovely *area*.

6. *I would like to stop over tomorrow* and see your home because I will be in the area looking at another piece of property. I can stop by between the hours of 1:00 and 3:00. When would you prefer?

7. *I feel my usual enthusiasm and experience* helps me sell more homes, especially in your area which is where I prefer to work.

8. I feel that my *unique method of marketing* will most definitely appeal to you. I can show you this method either at 1:00 or 3:00. Which would you prefer?

9. *I will be previewing homes* for clients in your area between 5:00 and 7:00 tomorrow. I can stop by between these hours. When would you prefer?

10. *I am enthusiastic about another home* I have seen in your area, and it would be ideal to compare properties. I will be over by your home tomorrow or Wednesday after 3:00. *What time frame would work* out best for your schedule?

These methods work.

> Be enthusiastic and gentle.
> Pick any one of them.
> I have used them all.
> They will not fail!

Calling the For Sale by Owner

1. *Get the Sunday paper* and circle the owner ads.

2. On Sunday afternoon or night, call the FSBO's number.

3. When the owner answers, say the following:

   "Hi, I'm _____ from _____ Realty. I saw your ad in the paper, and I was interested in knowing how you are handling appointments with real estate agents.

4. The owner will do one of the following three things:

   a. *Ask you* why you want the appointment. See *"Ten Best Ways to Get an Appointment."*

   b. *Set up the appointment for* you to see the house.

   c. *Act genuinely not interested* in you and attempt to hang up. (These owners are a minority and not worth pursuing. *Don't worry.*)

Getting the Appointment

After you have said:	"Hi, I'm Barbara Nash-Price from _____ Realty and I was calling to see how you are handling appointments on your property?"
The owner may say:	"What do you mean?"
At which point you:	Tell them you are available for an appointment. (Never ask them, "can I come over?")
Tell them:	You would like an appointment between (certain hours) and you will be in their area.
Always offer choices:	*"Which time frame is best suited for them?"*

DON'T BE AFRAID OF REJECTION.

They don't bite!

THEY USUALLY SAY YES!!

Be enthusiastic, but gentle.

Be curious, but kind.

Be professional and polite.

And, most of all, *be interested in knowing what their situation really is.* Find out.

TALK to the FSBO.

LISTEN to the FSBO.

Become a *friend* to the FSBO.

Be curious but *kind.*

One FSBO who listed with me had already interviewed over 45 different real estate agents!

Following is a recap of why the owner decided to list with me:

1. She wasn't overly complex and her CMA was *clear* and to the *point*.

2. He was impressed with the fact that I *did* my homework.

3. He said two of the other agents who came in promised to get back with them. *They didn't.*

4. The owner had no intention of listing the night I presented the CMA, *but he listed that evening because* first, the presentation was *thorough* and *complete*, and second *I had sold him on me.*

HE FELT THAT I WAS VERY PROFESSIONAL.

He said that one of the agents from a well known company came with nothing. She had no figures about the house, no history on when it had been sold, nothing. She just walked in as if off the street. He said he had an appointment set up with her. He thought they had a good rapport with her, and she had worked with him many times showing him properties for rehab possibilities. However, she walked in totally cold! She said, "I would really like to list this house for you!" He felt that she was totally unprepared. She expected the listing without doing any work. She did not *appear professional*.

SHE HAD DONE NO HOMEWORK!

The owner was asked if I seemed pushy or if I made him feel uncomfortable in trying to get him to list immediately with me after I presented the CMA. However, he replied, "*Her genuine enthusiasm* and the fact *she had done all her homework* on our house made us feel comfortable. The fact that she had everything right there* made us decide just to sign and *get it over with.*"

*Remember that when you bring your CMA back to the seller for the second appointment, always bring your full-size legal book with:

1. listing agreement

2. seller's statement of condition

3. lockbox

4. net sheet

   Be honest.
   Be enthusiastic.
   Be careful with figures.

Keep the listing agreement right out in front of you on the table.

ASK THE SELLER IF YOU CAN SHOW HIM OR HER HOW THE LOCKBOX WORKS.

After all is explained say, "It's important we get started right away to give you the maximum exposure time on the market. If you just sign right here, I'll explain the tour (other agents that will be coming through next week) to you.

Don't forget!   Try to find a *common interest*.

Try to *get to know* the seller a little.

Try to use a *sense of humor*.

Try *not to be dull*.

I ask the owners to write down why they like their home. I take this back to my office, *rewrite* it on my letterhead, and bring it back to the seller. He insists on having an open house on his own home first so then *I make my second appointment to come back*.

Calling on For Sale By Owners

Pick up the telephone. "Hello, I'm _____ from _____ real estate. I was wondering how you are handling appointments with real estate people?"

Ask the owners for an appointment to come over and look at their home.

Almost every single owner wants the agent to come over and tell them what price they think the home should sell for!

The majority of all FSBOs do list their homes and sell with a real estate company.

In talking with a FSBO, you must do the following:

1. make the phone call,

2. get the appointment, and

3. do a CMA (Competitive Market Analysis).

These three items are essential.

Never talk to a seller in a *negative* tone.

Never ask a question that they can answer "*no*" to.

If a seller says that she is going to try to sell her home for one more week on her own, say,

"Why don't I stop by next Monday, after 5:00 or maybe 7:30 would be better, because I am listing a home earlier. How would later in the evening be?

If a seller says that he wants a couple of weeks to try it on his own, say,

"I understand. After my two open houses next week, and when I finish working with my buyer who is coming into town, why don't we set up an appointment for, say, fifteen days from now. That would make it September 20. I'll call you right before that."

Never leave the house of a FSBO *without another appointment* or something settled regarding a signed listing.

There are a few people who are ornery! If so, you will find it out the *first* time! Don't be upset about this. Those people would go out and beat up a brick wall. This is okay. Leave them alone.

GO ON TO THE NEXT CLIENT!

Remember that on a $100,000 home there could be a 7% commission ($7,000). Do not think that you can just walk into a house and list it, *without* doing your homework and without any questions. You have not convinced the seller that *you are worth it*!

DID YOU TAKE A LOT OF NOTES?

DID YOU ASK A LOT OF QUESTIONS?

Did you prove to them *beyond the shadow of a doubt* that you are worth it?

Did you show them *beyond a shadow of a doubt* that you did your homework on their house?

If you study this manual completely, you can dedicate less than *two hours per* client and have a complete knowledge of the property and 100% better chance of winning the listing.

For Sale by Owner Costs

Without a realtor

(New buyer usually makes an offer *less*)

Minimum of half the commission	$3,500
Newspaper advertising	1,000
Sign expense	300
Legal fees @ $100/hr. for 10 hrs.	1,000
Owner's time @ $100/hr. for 10 hrs. minimum	1,000
Miscellaneous (copying, food and beverages for open houses, supplies) Approx. buyers (points, etc.)	500
Total out of pocket expenses	$7,000

Other Expenses in Selling Your Own Home

Will someone always be able to answer the phone?

Will you know about the latest financing methods?

Will the prospects confide in you about their financial status?

Can you get buyers to sign the purchase agreement? (Remember, once they sleep on it, they seldom sleep in it.)

Who will draft the purchase agreement?

Will you really save money selling your own home?

DESPERATE OWNER NEEDS TO SELL

This type of advertising steers would-be buyers away from owners like yourself! FSBOs have problems pricing!

DANGERS OF OVERPRICING:

Takes longer to sell

Have fewer showings

Receive low, low offers

Helps other properties sell by comparison

Remind the FSBO:

A home must have good location,

Good terms, good price, and

Good condition.

REMIND THE OWNER WHERE BUYERS COME FROM:

40% from real estate company or real estate contact

20% from the for sale sign (real estate company)

18% from a real estate company ad call

8% from an open house ad or sign

7% from a relocation service

3% from an advertised property

1% buy an open house they saw

3% buy for a combination of reasons

OTHER FOR SALE BY OWNERS WEAKEN THE SELLER'S POSITION.

Other owners advertise: *"Bail us out"*

"Foreclosure"

"Owner says, must sell"

"Divorce, must sell"

"Desperate owner needs to sell"

This type of advertising steers would-be buyers away from owners like yourself!

Ask the owner: Are you familiar with contracts?

Recording the deed?

Notarizing documents?

Filling out forms?

Closing costs?

Lien waivers?

Title searches?

Tax certificates?

Warranty deeds?

Earnest money deposits?

TELL THE FOR SALE BY OWNER:

Getting you a buyer is just a third of what my job entails. (See Chapter 10.)

Besides marketing your home,

listing your home,

advertising your home, and

promoting your home,

I ALSO:

Show your home,

arrange the financing on your home,

get an appraiser for your home,

call for the inspection of your home,

get a Truth in Housing Inspection on your home (if required),

do followup on all the mortgage arrangements on your home,

take part in the closing of your home,

and finally help you with any last minute arrangements on your sale!

Prospecting FSBO Dialogue

Door knocking: *"Hi. I saw your sign (ad), may I ask how you are handling appointments with real estate people?"*

By phone: *"Good (day/afternoon/evening) this is _____ from _____ Realty. I saw your ad (sign), and may I ask how you are handling appointments with real estate people?"*

If FSBO says: *"What do you mean?"*

or

"We are not."

You say: *"May I ask one quick question? If we had a qualified buyer willing to pay a price acceptable to you, would you accept an offer through our company?"*

If FSBO says: *"No."*

You say: *"May I ask why?"* (or repeat the question)

If FSBO says: *"Yes" to the first or second question.*

You say: *"Fine. It will take just a few minutes to see enough of your home so I can tell potential buyers about it. May I do that now? or Will 6:30 tonight be okay, or would 8:00 be better?*

6–2–6 System

This system is specifically for *"FOR SALE BY OWNERS."*

1. Make the initial call to the FSBO.
2. Write the name, address and phone down.
3. *Call them two times a week at least!*
4. Do this for six weeks.
5. You should get the FSBO *in one month.*
6. If not converted, replace with another FSBO.

The average agent calls the first week, and the FSBO lists in the fourth week! Average FSBOs say "no" four times before they say "yes."

REMEMBER:

1. WORK WITH SIX OWNERS AT A TIME.

2. CALL THEM TWO TIMES A WEEK.

3. DO THIS FOR SIX WEEKS.

If you keep replacing FSBOs, you will add six to eight new listings to your inventory monthly.

Two things to say to the FSBO:

1. "I can certainly understand that."
2. "I would love to see your house!"

In our city there are thousands of real estate agents, and if fourteen agents called a FSBO today, *my job is to get from 14 to one!* I only work with six *FSBOs at a time. I call them twice a week for six weeks. After that I take them out of my file!*

FSBO Six Week Follow-up

1. It is now your job to stay in touch with the FSBO for *at least six weeks* until they list, sell, or give up.
2. Stop by and drop off some information on today's market, such as rates, point sheet, a pertinent article out of one of our trade magazines.
3. Call and ask how their open house on Sunday went.
4. By selecting only two or three FSBOs to keep in touch with *each week*, you maintain a consistent influx of potential new listings. Two one week, four the next, then six, and so on.

ESTABLISH A LEGAL-SIZE NOTEBOOK

1. Set up your index by district.
2. File your cards by phone number. Most FSBO ads have phone numbers; not all have addresses.
3. Place the phone number in the upper right hand corner with name and address directly below.
4. Down the left hand side, tape their ads to the card and *date the ad*.
5. In the space to the right of the ad, record your conversations.

WHEN THE TIME IS RIGHT

1. In your conversations with the FSBO mention things that *get listings sold* for you.
   a. Many agents in a large office trying to sell the same listing
   b. *Homes* magazine
   c. MLS
   d. Referrals from past clients
   e. Corporate referrals
   f. Any others you can think of, including your market plan, but do not show the plan until you get a commitment

2. An excellent conversation close is, "If you felt that you could actually get more money, a quicker sale, and fewer problems by doing business with our company, would you do so? If the FSBO says "no," say, "May I ask why?" To the FSBO's typical response, "Because I want to try it myself for awhile," say, "Fine, I'll check with you after my open house this next Sunday. I'll stop by to walk through, OK?"

3. That will be *appointment number one*!

THREE KEYS TO LISTING FSBOs

1. Be persistent.

2. Build trust.

3. Be professional. Show them you can get the job done!

WHY SELLING BY FSBOs IS DIFFICULT?

1. Most buyers are just *window shopping*.

2. People will *stop at all hours* of the day and night.

3. A seller *cannot qualify* the buyers comfortably.

4. A seller is letting complete *strangers into his or her home*.

5. It is *difficult for the seller to negotiate* with the buyer.

6. The *seller misses opportunities* to sell when away.

7. Buyers will also want to *save commission* even from an owner.

8. Sellers have only *three ways to attract buyers*: ads, opens and a for sale sign.

9. Sellers *have to give potential buyers the address*: they can *drive by* and not look inside the house!

10. Buyers do not like to *deal directly with the owner*! Many sellers price their home according to what price a home down the street hasn't even sold for yet.

11. Some agents will *promise anything* to get the listing.

12. There are *60 different financing methods* that usually require a real estate agent's help, including FHAs, VAs, discounted notes, amortizations, ARMs, wrap mortgages, points, interest rates, balloons, graduated payment mortgages, and so on.

13. *If the seller isn't familiar with all real estate contracts*, this will really scare a buyer.

14. *Does* the *seller* know that the *four things that make a property sell are* location, price, terms and condition?

15. Does the seller know the *grave danger of overpricing a listing*?

   a. takes four times as long to sell

   b. fewer showings

   c. receives low-ball offers

   d. just helps other homes to sell

Sellers should know that other FSBOs weaken their position with ads such as "foreclosure," "divorce, must sell," "bail us out," "desperate to sell." *Tell them!*

Letter to a For Sale by Owner

It's very hard to sell your home by yourself because most people have their life savings tied up in their home, and buyers and sellers usually want to work with a professional that not only knows the financing part of the home, but is willing to personally represent them.

Most of the buyers calling "for sale by owners" think they can save money because they don't have to pay a commission. They think they can knock the commission off the sale price! It's impossible for the buyer and the seller to save the same commission at the same time. Somebody has to give. If you come down in the price, you lose. Remember, there will be buyers that will *give you ridiculous offers.* Don't get angry.

Nationally, it's been shown *that the* seller *will* make far more money after the commission is subtracted *than if they try to sell the home on their own. There is no standard commission set in the industry, but you really* get what you pay for.

What do we do for our commission that you can't do? Most importantly, we have more buyers coming to us! *We also act as the third party. This is very important when you begin to negotiate. People will be more candid with a real estate agent than they will with the owner. You may become offended by something the buyer says from the beginning.*

We will use all professional tools and utilize the Multiple Listing Service system which helps establish the highest market value possible for you.

Probably a real estate agent's most important function is that we can qualify the buyers. *This will be very uncomfortable for you to do! Can you ask them about what they make, if they have declared bankruptcy, and how much indebtedness they have without feeling uneasy?*

The only reason that properties fail to sell is either overpricing or poor marketing. After looking at a good Competitive Market Analysis, *you would know exactly what range your home falls into.* I would do this for you at no extra charge.

I want to caution you, however, that many agents will tell you anything *you want to hear just to get your listing.* I won't do this. *I am a professional with many years experience and referrals. Please call me for additional information.*

And, good luck!

Twenty Questions to Give to the For Sale by Owner

1. Do I have the time to sell my house by myself? _____

2. Do I know where my buyers come from? _____

3. Do I know how to make my home show the best? _____

4. If I list with a real estate company, will I be bothered by people all the time? _____

5. Do I know the questions I should ask buyers? _____

6. Do I know the information to give to the buyers? _____

7. Do I know what to say when I show my home? _____

8. Do I know how to qualify my buyers? _____

9. Do I know the latest financing methods? _____

10. Do I have ways of attracting buyers other than my ad and sign? _____

11. Do I know what my closing costs and obligations are? _____

12. Do I know how to write out a contract on the spot? _____

13. Do I know how to negotiate and compromise with a buyer? _____

14. Do I know what to do during the showings? _____

15. Do I have the time to invest in follow up on a buyer? _____

16. Do I know what is involved in title examination? _____

17. Do I know different and unique marketing techniques? _____

18. Do I know the key questions to ask the buyer? _____

19. Do I know how to close? _____

20. Do I know if FSBOs list with agents? (Yes—95%) _____

If you answered "no" to most of the questions, you probably should be seeking competent real estate advice!

90% of expired listings relist too!

I WANT YOU TO KNOW THAT GIVING YOU THE SECRETS I'M GIVING YOU TODAY IS SIMILAR TO GIVING YOU THE RECIPE FOR COCA COLA!

I've been selling real estate for twenty years now and credit at least $1/3$ to $1/2$ of my business to FSBOs.

In the beginning I did not have referral business, nor did I have any solid leads. I tried expired listings and found them somewhat successful. However, it was harder to convince sellers who were already soured in one way or another by other agents. So I decided most FSBOs wanted to move and if I could list their home it would mean three things:

1. *automatic buyers*
2. *a secured listing,* and
3. If sold, *money in my pocket!*

I also decided to go after a goal that I knew I could fulfill within a six to twelve month time period, such as a new stove, trip to Florida, new car. Every owner I listed would put me that much closer to my goal. Before I called each one, I would focus first on my goal, which always gave me enough confidence to get through the phone call whether positive or negative. I discovered something very interesting: *most FSBOs really wanted to talk and talk and talk!* I'd call FSBOs when idle, sitting in the sun, waiting at the club, before working out, from a friend's home, and in front of the TV! I found it really fun to take a moment and feel as though I had accomplished something. A day that seemed somewhat unproductive became a *day with an appointment made.*

In one of my first years in real estate, I earned $62, 752. I attribute $25,104 of that to FSBOs. Taking into account the fact that this was a twelve month period, I took a month off in the summer to be with my children at our lake home as well as a winter vacation. That leaves the ten and a half months of actively working the real estate market. I found that in order to maintain the lifestyle that I was accustomed to:

I HAD TO CALL ON FSBOs!

At any rate, I have decided to walk you through some individual FSBOs that I have called on in one year to let you see how I handled the situation.

Try to remember that whenever you call on a FSBO, do not deviate from the initial statement and question:

> **BNP:** *"Hi, I'm Barbara Nash-Price from _____ real estate company. I follow the ads closely in the paper and just noted your home for sale. Could I make an appointment to see it?"*
>
> **Seller:** *"No!"*
>
> **BNP:** *"Oh, I see. I was wondering if you could tell me how you are handling appointments with agents on the property?"*
>
> **Seller:** *"Well, I guess just setting up an appointment with us, why?"*
>
> **BNP:** I then go on to secure the appointment and go to the house.

Case Study 1

AUDREY AND BUD GALLAHANLY
650 PARN RD—$179,500

BNP:	*"Hi, Mr. Gallahanly. This is Barbara Nash-Price from _____ Realty."*
Seller:	*"I'm not interested in listing my house, and I'm sick of all the agents calling on me. I'm fed up to here with it!*
BNP:	"Do you have a second to tell me what happened? I'm really curious to ask one thing. How could *one* real estate agent make you *so upset*?"
Seller:	"Do you have ten or fifteen minutes?"
BNP:	*"I certainly do!"*
Seller:	*"Agents have called to try to get the listing by bringing people over, getting here two to three hours late. They brought the people in, raced through the house,* never called back to tell me if they liked it, took off ahead of me, talked too fast and too loud, woke up my wife who was napping, made promises that I never asked for, told the seller the decorating was tacky and to take out all the carpeting, and told me my ad was cheap-looking."

By the time Mr. Gallahanly finished talking, he felt much better *because I agreed with him.* He was also growing more curious to meet me. Mr. Gallahanly and I made an appointment for Friday at 2:00 P.M.

Case Study 2

JULIE AND BILL DORNFELD
740 GLEA RD

BNP:	*"Hi, I'm Barbara Nash-Price from _____ Realty. May I ask how you are handling appointments to sell your home?"*
Mrs. D:	*"Right now we're letting anyone come that wants to, but not real estate agents!"*
BNP:	*"Oh, not Real Estate agents. I see. How are you handling real estate agents then?"*
Mrs. D:	*"No! no! We have a real estate agent if we want to use her, and that's who we will list with."*
BNP:	*"Oh, shall I call her for an appointment?"*
Mrs. D:	*"No! no!* We're not listed with anyone now! *We are really trying to* sell it ourselves! But, oh, I don't know how to handle it. *It's so new and we do want to sell. Did you really want to look at it?* Do you have someone?"
BNP:	*"Not right now, but it's the area I work heavily! I could have a buyer tomorrow. I would very much like to compare it to others. I also work with relocation buyers and new clients every day."*

Mrs. D:	*"Well, maybe. I guess you could come to see it. After all, we don't owe anything to anyone, and someone my husband knew told us to list with her. We really don't want to move for months, and it's such a bother already with calls, and we're leaving on vacation in two weeks."*
BNP:	*"Oh, by the way, I haven't even asked your name."*
Mrs. D:	*"Julie Dornfeld"*
BNP:	*"And what is your address?"* (The ad was a blind ad, no address.)
Mrs. D:	*"It's 740 Glea Road. I've known June Black from _____ Realty Company for a long time, but like I said, I haven't told her she'll get the listing."* (Owners are often contradictory.) *"You can come over and look if you want."*
BNP:	*"Well, perhaps I could stop by since I'm already going to be over in that area tomorrow. What time do you think would be best? I have 11:00 to 2:00 open and 3:00 or after."*
Mrs. D:	*"Three thirty is perfect!"*

Case Study 3

This owner was a young couple transferring out of the state. I was the first real estate agent to ask to come over. When I got there, all the lights were on, even in all the closets! The house had just been vacuumed, and Keith and Rhonda Smith asked me to come back Friday. They said that this was the first time they'd advertised, and they expected to get their real estate agent this way. Some friends had told them to pick one of the real estate agents that called off their ad if they got tired of advertising on their own!

Keith and Rhonda had me come back Thursday night at 7:00 P.M. I listed their home for $96,900.

IT TOOK 43 DAYS TO SELL THEIR HOME.

I spent $187 in advertising.

I had two open houses.

The buyer for their home came to my open house. This was the ad:

JUST LISTED
OPEN 2–4
"BEAUTIFUL ENGLISH . . . "

Bungalow . . . this 3 br. 1 3/4 bath beauty boasts hardwood floors—formal dining room — handsome brick hearth — full dormer—finished 2nd floor—amuse.rm. down—plus dbl. garage . . . 2 blks. to Lake Harriet—hurry! Mid-90s—won't last!! 490 Morgan Rd—920-0000 Barbara Nash-Price

The buyers for the home paid $95,400 \times 7\% = \$6678.00$

Commission:	$6678	30 % list: $2003
List commission:	$2003	30 % sell: $2003
Sell commission:	$2003	
My total commission:	$4006	

I MADE $4006 FROM AN AD IN THE PAPER.

I BELIEVE FSBOs WANT TO SELL!

Calling the FSBO

1. Sunday night pick up the telephone and dial the number.

2. When the owner answers, say the following:

   "Hello - I'm June Summer from _____ Realty. I saw your ad in the paper and I am interested in knowing how you are handling appointments with agents?"

3. *The owner will do one of the following three things:*

   a. *"Not interested"* and hang up. (Note: this very, very, small minority is truly not interested and not worth pursuing.)

   b. Ask you *"WHY"* you want an appointment.

   c. *Set up an appointment* for you to see the house.

I make sure of 3 things on the first appointment with the owner:

1. *Take* lots of *notes*

2. *Ask* lots of *questions*

3. *Don't leave without* another appointment to bring back your "CMA"

The easiest part and the *hardest* part is *picking up the telephone* and making yourself known!

Another favorite activity of mine is going to house sales and estate sales. One FSBO that I sold for $223,000 was having a moving sale! I stopped by early one morning. I started asking a lot of questions. After calling on FSBOs and before going to their home if you have not secured an appointment, you can drop a letter in the mail and make a note to send various newsworthy articles or just a handwritten note *twice weekly* as well as *phoning*.

Remember that 88 % of all FSBOs list

When you call FSBOs, you must *follow up as well*. If they take a long time to decide, one thing is for sure. They won't forget you. Calling on FSBOs can be fun if you make up your mind not to *fear failing*.

Letters to Send

Sample Letters for Every Client

big deal

by "Lorayne n' Neil"

Prospective Buyer Letter

Mr. and Mrs. Jordan
500 Arthur Street
Minneapolis, Minnesota

Dear Mr. and Mrs. Jordan:

My name is Barbara Nash-Price, and I am associated with _____ Realty.

Investment opportunities come and go. Most people in this time have difficulty in being able to depend on any sure thing.

Real estate continues to outlast any long term investment.

There has never been a better time to buy a home than now.

I am a specialist in the metropolitan area. With our computer services now available, I can show you the latest for sale properties almost immediately.

I look forward to your call, and hopefully we can set up an appointment in the very near future to see some great homes!

Sincerely,

Barbara Nash-Price

Expired Listing Letters

Mr. and Mrs. Jack James
3000 West Street
Minneapolis, Minnesota

Dear Mr. and Mrs. James:

My name is Barbara Nash-Price, and I am associated with _____ Realty.

I have specialized in your area for a long time and have enjoyed helping with the marketing of many properties in your neighborhood.

I recently noticed that your property has been deleted from the active file in our multiple listing books and computer.

I drove by your property, and this puzzles me a great deal.

I am currently involved with a client but will try to arrange an appointment with you the first part of next week.

Looking forward to meeting and talking with you soon.

Sincerely,

Barbara Nash-Price

Mr. and Mrs. Jack James
3000 West Street
Minneapolis, Minnesota

Dear Mr. and Mrs. James:

I understand, from looking over the computer printout of current multiple listings that your home is not listed at this time.

I drove past your property today.

This really puzzles me!

I would very much like to meet with you and talk with you about what the problem may have been and how the right remedies could expedite a swift sale for you.

Looking forward to meeting with you soon.

Have a nice day.

    Sincerely,

    Barbara Nash-Price

Letter to Seller When [Your] Listing Is Ready to Expire

Mr. and Mrs. Grand
1005 North West Street
Minneapolis, Minnesota

Dear Mr. and Mrs. Grand:

I understand from looking at my records that your listing is getting ready to expire in a few weeks.

It's time to get together to go over a summary of all the activity on your property.

I have come up with an additional marketing strategy and feel that it would be beneficial to the sale.

I have enclosed a new listing contract. Please feel free to sign it and return it to me in the enclosed self-addressed envelope, and we will also set up an appointment to review the information that I am concerned about.

    Sincerely,

    Barbara Nash-Price

Just Listed Letter

Mr. and Mrs. North
400 West Avenue
Minneapolis, Minnesota

Dear Mr. and Mrs. North:

Thank you for the opportunity to market your home. Following are a few suggestions that would help enhance the desirability of your property.

1. *Put yourself in the place of a prospective buyer. Look critically all around your home, both inside and out.*

2. *Make sure that every part of your home is clean and in top-notch condition. Replace light bulbs, clean closets and anything else you feel would help.*

3. *Do something extra to make the home look "homey." Get some flowers, air freshener, wash rugs . . . anything to spruce it up!*

Let's do our job together, so we will make a swift sale on your home.

Thank you for the opportunity to serve you.

Sincerely,

Barbara Nash-Price

For Sale by Owner Letters

Mr. and Mrs. Johnson
300 State Street
Minneapolis, Minnesota

Dear Mr. and Mrs. Johnson:

My name is Barbara Nash-Price, and I am associated with _____ Realty.

I have specialized in your area for a long time and have enjoyed participating in the marketing of many properties in your neighborhood.

I recently drove by your property for sale. I very much would like the opportunity to have an appointment to walk through your home as soon as possible.

I am currently involved with a client but will try to set up an appointment with you the first part of next week.

Looking forward to talking with you.

Sincerely,

Barbara Nash-Price

Mr. and Mrs. Johnson
300 State Street
Minneapolis, Minnesota

Dear Mr. and Mrs. Johnson:

I understand and respect your decision not to use a Real Estate agent at this time.

During the time you are working on your property though, you will be needing certain information in regard to the selling of your home. Please find enclosed a purchase agreement, a buyer information sheet, information on financing and the costs you will be asked to pay. I hope this helps.

I will be contacting you in the near future to see how you are progressing. In the meanwhile, good luck!

Sincerely,

Barbara Nash-Price

Mr. and Mrs. Johnson
300 State Street
Minneapolis, Minnesota

Dear Mr. and Mrs. Johnson:

I drove past your home today. It is really a nice property.

I have enclosed my brochure and my business card.

I have done a lot of business in your neighborhood, but I will talk with you later when you have a moment.

Looking forward to meeting with you, and good luck!

Sincerely,

Barbara Nash-Price

Farming Letters

Mr. and Mrs. Johnson
300 State Street
Minneapolis, Minnesota

Dear Mr. and Mrs. Johnson:

I noticed your "For Sale By Owner" sign today, and I am curious about what activity it has generated for you.

Your home is a property I would like to have in my inventory to market. However, I pride myself on the fact that I personally maintain only twelve listings for sale at a time. I feel that is the maximum number any agent can handle if he or she is to be fair to, and is to do an effective job for the home sellers that the agent is representing.

Since I have an abundance of listings now, it is really premature for me to discuss representing you, but when one of my current listings sells, I will contact you. Good luck.

Sincerely,

Barbara Nash-Price

Mr. and Mrs. Smith
1000 South Street
Minneapolis, Minnesota

Dear Mr. and Mrs. Smith:

The following information is a market update for homes sold in your area from the following dates: _____, 19__, _____, 19__, _____, 19__.

During this time, frame two-bedroom homes have sold for an average of $_____. Three-bedroom homes have sold for an average of $_____. Four-bedroom homes have sold for an average of $_____.

Should you have any questions about the value of your home at the present time, I would be happy to give you a free market analysis.

If you have any other real estate questions, please feel free to call.

Sincerely,

Barbara Nash-Price

Mr. and Mrs. Olson
1000 South Street
Minneapolis, Minnesota

Dear Mr. and Mrs. Olson:

My name is Barbara Nash-Price, and I am associated with _____ Realty.

I have currently been working with some buyers who prefer only the area of _____.

Currently there have been few properties to show to them, and at the present I am appealing to individual homeowners.

If you would consider selling your own home or know of anyone in your area or surrounding area who is thinking of selling, could you call me today? I would appreciate it very much.

Thank you for your time and attention to this matter.

I look forward to hearing from you soon.

    Sincerely,

    Barbara Nash-Price

Mr. and Mrs. Smith
1000 South Street
Minneapolis, Minnesota

Dear Mr. and Mrs. Smith:

My name is Barbara Nash-Price and I am associated with _____ Realty.

I have enjoyed working and specializing in your particular area for quite some time now.

I especially prefer to work with relocation clients and corporate referrals, clients that are particularly stable in today's market.

If you are considering a move in the near future, I very likely could have a buyer for your home and/or help you with the marketing of your property.

Please feel free to contact me at your earliest convenience.

I look forward to our getting together soon.

    Sincerely,

    Barbara Nash-Price

Mr. and Mrs. Smith
1000 South Street
Minneapolis, Minnesota

Dear Mr. and Mrs. Smith:

My name is Barbara Nash-Price and I am associated with _____ Realty.

I have specialized in your area for a long time and have enjoyed helping with the marketing of many properties in your neighborhood.

At the moment I am carrying more buyers than I have homes for.

I very much would like to talk to you about the possibility that you may want to consider selling your home.

I am involved with a client for the remainder of this week, but I will try to contact you the first part of next week for an appointment.

If this does not work out, please feel free to call me, and we will arrange a time we can get together.

Looking forward to talking with you.

Sincerely,

Barbara Nash-Price

Mr. and Mrs. Smith
1000 South Street
Minneapolis, Minnesota

Dear Mr. and Mrs. Smith:

We pride ourselves in offering real estate services in all areas. Our company also concentrates on a few specific areas where we have been most successful.

These areas are _____ and _____.

Some of our recent sales in your area have been:

_____

_____

_____

Our company is constantly working in these areas, and should you be thinking of buying or selling we would appreciate the opportunity to talk with you before you consider anyone else.

Sincerely,

Barbara Nash-Price

Dear Homeowner:

The exposure your home has to the market of buyers that are looking is unbelievable.

Did you know that nearly 70% of all homes sold are to out-of-town buyers? They never read or even get the local paper. They usually come into town over the weekend. They are pushed to look at homes for two or three days straight, and then they must decide quickly!

The majority of the time they seek out a real estate agent. They know that the agent can tell them about the market value in various areas, what the best interest rates are, what schools are available, and what lender to use.

Please feel free to call me, and I would be happy to give you a free estimate on selling your home.

Sincerely,

Barbara Nash-Price

Open House Letters to Potential Buyers

Dr. and Mrs. John Graham
5813 Harris Avenue
Minneapolis, Minnesota

Dear Dr. and Mrs. Graham:

It was so nice to meet you and talk with you at the listing I held open last Sunday located at: _____

Thank you very much for taking the time to tell me of your real estate needs in the near future.

I have taken the liberty of enclosing a few properties that I feel meet some of the qualifications that we discussed.

If you have any interest in any of these or would wish to look at additional homes, please feel free to contact me.

This week I am currently with a client. Next week I look forward to contacting you to arrange a time we can get together to review some properties.

Sincerely,

Barbara Nash-Price

Dr. and Mrs. John Graham
5813 Harris Avenue
Minneapolis, Minnesota

Dear John and Karen:

Thank you for coming through my open house yesterday and looking at the property on 213 Duncraig. It was sold this morning, and we have a closing set for April 30, 1997.

I have enclosed various listing sheets in the Edin area that are currently listed for sale. I think it will help you to get a good feel for the market in Edin at the present time.

Please feel free to call me regarding an appointment on any of the listings that I have enclosed. I look forward to hearing from you and would be happy to come over and give you a free estimate on your own property and go over what I think you would be able to realize from it. I will wait to hear from you.

Have a good day.

Sincerely,

Barbara Nash-Price

Dr. and Mrs. John Graham
5813 Harris Avenue
Minneapolis, Minnesota

Dear Dr. and Mrs. Graham:

Thank you for coming through my open house last Sunday. The property that I held open at _____ happens to be one of my favorite homes in this price range.

I feel that the market is excellent now for investing in real estate. Interest rates are very competitive.

I would like very much to work with you to service your real estate needs. My specialty is working with buyers in the metropolitan area.

I pride myself on keeping up to date on the new methods of this area's use of computerization and being able to put you on my computerized mailing list featuring all the homes in the areas that you desire.

Please feel free to call me, and we can set up an appointment to get together to look at some properties.

I will also contact you the first part of the week to arrange any and all appointments.

Thank you for your time and consideration.

Sincerely,

Barbara Nash-Price

Holiday Letters

Dear Friends:

At this very special time of year, I like to look back, reflect and give thanks for all of the wonderful things that have happened to me over the past year.

I want to take a special moment and wish you and your family a very happy holiday season, and may God bless you in the new year.

I look forward to helping you with any of your future real estate needs and hopefully servicing you in the years ahead.

My very best wishes for happiness.

    Sincerely,

    Barbara Nash-Price

Mr. and Mrs. Cooper
4003 Oak Street
Minneapolis, Minnesota

Dear Mr. and Mrs. Cooper:

With the end of the year upon us and the dawn of a new one in sight, I want to express my gratitude to you for your business and having had the pleasure of representing you in the past.

Last year I had excellent results in my business, and I want to thank each and every one of my valued clients.

Referrals from you and other friends are the most important asset in my growth as a real estate salesperson.

I really appreciate your thoughtfulness and your loyalty.

My responsibility to you lies beyond just selling you a home. Please feel free to contact me at any time if I can be of service to you for any and all real estate needs.

Have a wonderful new year and feel free to call me anytime!

    Sincerely,

    Barbara Nash-Price

Mr. and Mrs. Cooper
4003 Oak Street
Minneapolis, Minnesota

Dear Mr. and Mrs. Cooper:

Somehow, during the scurrying hustle and bustle of the year and through the holiday season, we just don't seem to find the time to call on our friends and clients as often as we would like to.

A new year has come again with all its hope and aspirations, a chance to look ahead and a chance to review the many things done and left undone over the past year. But most of all it gives us a chance to pause and reflect.

As I look back over the past year, it comes to mind that I may not have expressed adequately my appreciation for our relationship and what you have done for me over the year. I would sincerely like to do it now, gratefully and sincerely!

My very best wishes for abundant health, happiness and all the success possible in the coming year and the years ahead.

> Sincerely,

> Barbara Nash-Price

Just Listed Letters to a Neighbor

Mr. and Mrs. Peterson
1002 Sun Road
Minneapolis, Minnesota

Dear Mr. and Mrs. Peterson:

We have recently listed your neighbor's home. They have asked for our help in trying to sell the property.

I am currently trying to find people who may know of someone who would be interested in viewing this property. It is located at _____ .

Perhaps you have a friend or a relative who would be interested in seeing this lovely home. Please feel free to call me for the price and the particulars on the residence.

Should you have any specific real estate questions, I would be happy to help you with them.

Have a good day.

> Sincerely,

> Barbara Nash-Price

Mr. and Mrs. Peterson
1002 Sun Road
Minneapolis, Minnesota

Dear Mr. and Mrs. Peterson:

As you may or may not have noticed, we have recently listed the property at
_____ *with our company.*

I pride myself on enjoying selling properties in your area and would welcome you to come through any of the open houses that I will be holding on the home. Feel free to call me with any questions that I may be helpful in answering and any friends or relatives who you may care to recommend the property to.

Looking forward to talking with you.

    Sincerely,

Barbara Nash-Price

Just Sold to a Neighbor Letter

Mr. and Mrs. Jacobs
1563 Trellis Road
Minneapolis, Minnesota

Dear Mr. and Mrs. Jacobs:

I am very happy to inform you that I have just sold the listing located at _____ and that Mr. and Mrs. _____ will be your new neighbors.

I have completed many successful sales in and around your vicinity.

During this year I am pleased to tell you that the real estate market has been excellent. Should you have any real estate questions about your own property, please do not hesitate to call me. I would be happy to help answer them.

Have a good day.

    Sincerely,

Barbara Nash-Price

Price Reduction Letters

Mr. and Mrs. Hanby
247 Parley Street
Minneapolis, Minnesota

Dear Mr. and Mrs. Hanby:

We have now had your home listed for _____ days.

There have been _____ showings on the property. The following agents gave these responses:

_____

_____

_____

In your area there are presently _____ homes for sale.

In comparing your home to others in your area with comparable square footage and like amenities, your home should be currently listed at $ _____.

I we continue to market the home at the current price without a reduction, we will only help the others in your area to sell faster!

Thank you for your immediate attention to this matter.

    Sincerely,

    Barbara Nash-Price

Mr. and Mrs. Hanby
247 Parley Street
Minneapolis, Minnesota

Dear Mr. and Mrs. Hanby:

We have had _____ open houses on your property so far to date.

There have been _____ offers made on your property.

I feel that we should sit down and talk about a price reduction that you are comfortable with and some additional marketing tools that may be advisable at this point.

I look forward to meeting with you within the next few days to go over the information that I think is important in getting your home sold as soon as possible.

    Sincerely,

    Barbara Nash-Price

Mr. and Mrs. Realistic
247 Parley Street
Minneapolis, Minnesota

Dear Mr. and Mrs. Realistic:

We currently have been marketing your home at a price and terms that you have decided upon.

Since we have had it on the market for _____ days, there have been _____ offers on the property.

THIS IS NOT GOING TO GET US A FAST SALE.

It is important that we realize that a lender will not put a mortgage on a property that does not appraise for a certain price either.

I think you have a good property, and with a realistic adjustment of $ _____, we should be able to activate a swift sale for you.

I look forward to your response. I will call you in the next day or so to set up an appointment to get together.

      Sincerely,

      Barbara Nash-Price

Staying in Touch with Seller Letters

Mr. and Mrs. John Doe
3003 Windsor Avenue
Minneapolis, Minnesota

Dear Mr. and Mrs. Doe:

Now that I have had the opportunity to list your property for a while (actually _____ days), it has become apparent to me, based upon comments from different real estate agents and people who have come through the home, that we may want to consider dealing with the following points:

1. *The roof needs repair.*
2. *The exterior should be touched up and painted.*
3. *The lawn should be mowed.*
4. *The kitchen should be completely cleaned out and all papers tacked to the refrigerator taken down.*
5. *The draperies should come off.*
6. *The old lawn furniture should be discarded and the lawn picked up.*

Let's get together or give me a call to discuss how many of these things are workable in your time frame.

There is always some kind of solution and we do want to get the highest price possible for your home without letting small annoyances get in the way.

Looking forward to talking with you this week.

      Sincerely,

      Barbara Nash-Price

Mr. and Mrs. John Doe
3003 Windsor Avenue
Minneapolis, Minnesota

Dear Mr. and Mrs. Doe:

I know that it has been over six months from the date we first listed your property. However, rest assured that because of the situation we initially addressed in regard to the fact that the home is located [on a busy street, high hill, close to freeway], we did take into consideration that it would be a bit longer for the property to sell.

Rest assured that we are using every conceivable marketing strategy necessary and will keep you posted as to when we get an offer.

Within the next 30 days we will address a price reduction that will help us to realize an offer faster if there is no purchase agreement presented prior to that time frame.

Sincerely,

Barbara Nash-Price

Thank You to the Buyer Letter

Mr. and Mrs. Buyright
2006 Right Street
Minneapolis, Minnesota

Dear Mr. and Mrs. Buyright:

Thank you for the opportunity to help you relocate. I sincerely enjoyed working with you.

Now that you have moved, and life is back to normal (almost), I hope that I can stop by to see how you are doing.

Please keep in mind that I will be happy to help if you have any concerns about real estate or any questions or problems.

Thank you again for your business, and should you have any friends or acquaintances who may be looking for a home or interested in selling, feel free to give them my name.

Best wishes in your new home!

Sincerely,

Barbara Nash-Price

Thank You to the Seller Letters

Mr. and Mrs. Sold
1005 Date Street
Minneapolis, Minnesota

Dear Mr. and Mrs. Sold:

Now that we finally have your home sold and all the details have been taken care of, I want to extend my sincere thanks for the opportunity to have been of service to you.

I am most thankful for your satisfaction and hope that my service has met with your approval.

Feel free to call me regarding any and all future real estate questions you may have.

Should you have any friends or relatives that may be thinking of buying or selling, feel free to have them give me a call. I always love to get a referral!

Sincerely,

Barbara Nash-Price

Mr. and Mrs. Sold
1008 Date Street
Minneapolis, Minnesota

Dear Mr. and Mrs. Sold:

I recently have received word that all has progressed well on the transaction of your home.

I thoroughly enjoyed working with you in the marketing of your property.

Be assured that I will keep you abreast of any news in the real estate industry that I feel you may wish to know of.

Should you have any friends or acquaintances that you feel I may be able to help, feel free to give them my name, and I will certainly be appreciative.

My very best wishes to you, and congratulations on the sale of your home.

Sincerely,

Barbara Nash-Price

Thank You for the Listing Letter

Mr. and Mrs. Tucker
47 Roper Street
Minneapolis, Minnesota

Dear Mr. and Mrs. Tucker:

I want to take the time to personally thank you for listing your home with _____ Realty and me.

Be assured that we will make every conceivable effort to market the home to the best of our ability and bring you the best offer possible in the current market.

You will continue to be updated and notified as to the showings and comments that are given to us regarding your home.

Together, you and I will be able, with a meeting of the minds, to bring a swift and smooth sale on your home.

Thank you for entrusting your property with us.

Have a good day.

Sincerely,

Barbara Nash-Price

CHAPTER 16

Listings

Getting, Keeping, and Selling Them

big deal

by "Lorayne n' Neil"

Listings

When I first started selling real estate, I *quickly* became aware that you are never really *in the business* until you have your *own listings*.

THERE IS NO QUICK SHORTCUT TO HARD WORK.

There is a shortcut for doing it the long way, however.

When going to a client's home for the first time, *bring three things with you*:

1. large, legal-size notebook and pen,
2. lockbox and blank listing (just in case), and
3. your appointment book.

IT IS IMPORTANT TO START OFF RIGHT.

Throughout this chapter I will give you an account of:

1. what I do to *get a listing*,
2. what I do to *service a listing*, and
3. what I do to *market a listing*.

Once a salesperson has a *format* down, knows what is expected of him or her, and realizes what his or her chances are, things always look better than starting out in the dark!

GOOD LISTINGS ARE LIKE GOLD. THEY ARE WORTH A LOT AND THE BENEFITS LAST A LONG TIME.

Whether you are new to the business or have been in the real estate business for a long time, I feel that in order to *just make ends meet* you must:

list two to four homes and sell two to four homes monthly.

This is extremely, extremely, *CONSERVATIVE*!

If you are not doing *at least this much business*, something is wrong. Something is not working for you to become *successful* in selling real estate.

No one but you (and your sales manager) know the truth.

Start by trying to better yourself.

If you are listing two homes a month, try to list four homes!
If you are selling one to two homes a month, try to sell three to five homes.

WATCH YOUR LISTINGS GROW FROM THIS CHAPTER'S APPROACH, AND WATCH HOW MUCH BETTER YOUR REAL ESTATE OUTLOOK BECOMES!

You do not have to "go bananas." Just try one new way.

Try to do one more CMA for one more seller.

Watch what happens to your business!

What to Do to Get a Listing

Whether it is a *for sale by owner*, a referral, an expired, or a canceled, *they are the same in this regard*:

1. They *want* to sell their home.

2. They are investigating different alternatives, one being you!

3. You'd better know what to do if you want the listing.

In Going to a Seller's House

Bring five things with you for a new listing:

1. your partially filled out listing agreement,

2. your measuring tape,

3. your net sheet,

4. your promotional brochure, and

5. a lockbox.

Two characteristics guarantee a listing:

1. honesty and

2. enthusiasm.

TAKE A PICTURE WHEN YOU ARRIVE.

Make the *first appointment* short. Bring a nice notebook with a cover to take notes from! Tour the property, *take lots of notes*, and *don't leave without another appointment* to come back!

UPON FIRST ARRIVING AT THE HOME, ASK THE SELLER THE FOLLOWING QUESTIONS:

1. **When did you purchase the home and for how much?**

2. **What is the remaining mortgage on the property?**

3. **Has the city sent you a card with the Estimated Market Value? If so, how much is it?**

4. **What is the amount of the taxes assessed against the property?**

5. Have you *made any improvements* to the property since you have owned it? What is the approximate dollar amount of the improvements?

6. If you were to get an offer to buy your home today, *where would you want to move and when?*

7. Have you personally come up with a figure that *you thought your home would sell for?*

8. Do you happen to have a floorplan *on the property* with the dimensions, room sizes and so forth? Often a seller has already prepared extensive highlight sheets on his or her home, thereby saving the agent time in doing a CMA.

9. Is there anything in your home that you are *specifically including or excluding* in the sale?

10. What is the *best phone number* to reach you at during the day?

11. How do the next few days look to *schedule an appointment for me to stop back* with the information that I have formulated into a market analysis on your home?

12. I have either the afternoon or the evening of _____. *Which is better for you?*

All of these questions are essential.

All of these questions should be written down and answered *while you are at the property* for the *first* time!

DON'T LEAVE THE SELLER'S HOUSE without scheduling an appointment to come back and present your competitive market analysis (CMA) to them. As you leave the *first* appointment, make sure that you have given the seller *a brochure on you and one on your company.*

In touring the home with the seller the first time, make sure that you not only ask lots of questions about the home, but also remember to get to know the sellers. Notice as you tour through the rooms any plaques or trophies that might have been given out for a certain hobby or merit. Also notice any unusual collections that they might have acquired. Take an interest in them as people. *Become a friend. Ask lots of questions.*

THE KEY TO SUCCESSFULLY OBTAINING THE LISTING IS *BALANCE.*

1. *Do your homework* on their house.

2. *Do your best* to learn about those who live in the house and their housing needs.

3. *Be sincere.*

4. *Look professional.*

WHEN YOU LEAVE THE PROPERTY FOR THE FIRST TIME:

1. Go back to the office and start pulling comparable properties for the home that you just saw.

2. *Finalize the homes* that you are comparing to the subject property by eliminating all but *three*.

3. *Do a computerized competitive market analysis* (CMA) of the subject home, including the neighborhood (*get the map coordinates*), the solds, current actives, and all *homes that "expired."*

4. *Consolidate your notes* by completing a listing that is ready to go with the information that you obtained from the seller as well as the highlight part of the listing (the verbage that describes the home).

5. *Write an ad* on the home.

6. *Get a lockbox* ready to take back to the property.

7. *Start a legal-size folder* on the subject property with the listing, statement of condition, and any other pertinent data.

8. Partly fill out a seller *net sheet* to put into the above file.

9. Get a *glossy 8″ × 11″ file folder* and insert information about your company, yourself, moving information, school information, computer information, and your CMA.

10. *Insert three pictures* of the comparable sold properties into your CMA folder, finish and complete.

NOW YOU ARE READY TO BEGIN.

If you did not *make your next appointment with the seller*, do so as soon as possible (within the next few days).

SECOND APPOINTMENT

1. Keep the listing agreement out in front of all.

2. The biggest hurdle to overcome with the sellers is *getting to know them* and *having a sense of humor*. Go over your marketing plan (sample at the end of the chapter). Stop real estate talk for awhile, and find something to discuss that will create a common bond.

3. The best way to break the ice with a seller is to:

   a. follow through

   b. *be concise and accurate with the CMA*

   c. *discuss the net sheet and dollar amounts*

   d. *take time out to relax the seller*

   e. *spend a few minutes on them, not real estate*

   f. *go back and ask for the listing*

   g. *open the next sentence of real estate with,* "May I show you how the lockbox works on the door?"

Don't assume that just because a potential client has a friend in the business that you don't have a chance. *You always have a chance.*

One seller said that *forty agents* had been to his home *prior to me*. I said, "You have not met *me* yet, and you haven't seen how I work."

The majority of agents who come through a house to see it for a seller *will not ask outright for the listing.*

Listing Luggage

TO GET A LISTING THE RIGHT WAY:

1. The *first appointment* must be made. *Telephone and ask for it.*

2. Go to the property and *walk through the home.*

    a. Take lots of notes.

    b. Ask lots of questions.

    c. Write down everything.

    d. Take a *picture* of the home.

3. Don't leave the property without first having made the *second appointment* to come back.

4. Go back to the office and start a CMA on the property while it is fresh in your mind.

5. If you can't do the CMA right away, at least try to find three properties that compare to the home, and jot down some added notes about the home. In this case, work on the CMA as soon as possible.

6. At the *second appointment* bring the following:

    a. *legal-size listing folder* with seller's name typed on it. The folder includes:

        (1) seller's net sheet

        (2) partially filled out multiple listing

        (3) home condition statement

        (4) written ad on the property

        (5) computer printout of solds, expireds and currents

        (6) notes taken on the property

        (7) any mortgage or tax information accumulated

        (8) latest thank you letter from a past client

    b. seller's folder (see sample)

    c. personal presentation manual (manual on yourself with past listings, thank you letters, information about your company and your real estate achievements)

    d. legal pad

    e. lockbox

f. measuring tape

g. calculator

h. highlight sheet about the neighborhood

7. Sit down with the sellers and start your conversation with a smile. I tell them "I have enjoyed spending *a great deal of time* preparing this market analysis for you on your property." Then carefully go through the listing folder.

8. "*I will start with the CMA* that I have prepared for you and explain how each of the three properties compare to your home."

9. "*Now that we have gone over the CMA* and the net sheet, you have a fair idea of what you can realize from the sale of this home."

10. "*Thank you for putting your signature at the bottom of this listing.* I am going to show you how the lockbox works on the front door and ask you what inclusions you will be leaving with the house."

11. *As you leave the home with the signed listing*, remember to give the seller a copy of everything that he or she has signed. If there is not a lockbox, *get a key to the house.*

12. *You will probably have to come back to measure.* Don't get caught up in measuring before getting the listing signed. The seller can find ways to stall then. Come back the next day if you have to. At the end of the listing presentation,

13. Put your lockbox on the front door if it's not already.

14. You have a signed listing agreement on the property.

15. It's not as hard as you think. *You have done your homework.*

16. Call the listing in to the office *immediately* or go to the office and turn it in depending on the time of day.

17. Turn in the ad that you have already written for the home. Make sure that it is open on *the very next Sunday*.

18. Make a *highlight* sheet on the property, and have copies made up as soon as possible to leave at the home. Until the highlight sheet is finished, xerox the listing and leave 30 copies at the house.

19. Call any and all buyers that you think may be interested in this property. Tell your friends about it. Tell your relatives.

20. Write many "just listed" cards to send to as many of the surrounding neighbors to this new listing as possible.

Twelve Tough Questions Before Seller Lists

1. **How long have you been in real estate?**

   In the beginning this was a very difficult question. I answer it by saying, "I've been selling real estate for quite some time now."

2. **What is the average number of days on the market for your listings?**

   Your listings also mean your company listings. I would make sure I take this right off of the computer under AMs (area market survey) or in the beginning of the MLS book.

3. **What is the average listing price to selling price ratio?**

   "It usually varies from a winter market to a spring market and depends on the condition of the property and the price, compared to others like it that have sold."

4. **Can I have a copy of your marketing plan?**

   "Yes, I have included one for you in the CMA that I have prepared along with some other pertinent information."

5. **What do you know about our area?**

   "I have made sure that I researched all the homes in your area that have been sold, expired or are currently on the market, and I have included them in my CMA brochure for you."

6. **What is your professional fee?**

   "I am pleased to tell you that although homes have gone up over the years, our fee has stayed extremely competitive and will help the majority of real estate agents that are looking in this area to show your home."

7. **Have you sold any homes in our area?**

   "I was hoping we could touch upon that point. I have brought along various homes that our company has sold in or around your surrounding area, and I have included these in my CMA brochure."

8. **What is the standard length of listing?**

   "I have seen agents take listings from 120 days to six months. I feel that although we would market the home with these parameters, we would be happy to insert a clause in which you could cancel within a 24 hour notice if for any reason you were displeased with my service." (Remember that you can't make a seller sell if he doesn't want to.)

9. **Does our home need anything major that you can see?**

   "I have brought along a great helpful hints sheet that agents like myself use in selling homes. Hopefully, it should answer any and all of your questions."

10. **What price range would you market our home at, just off the top of your head?**

    You sell real estate, so you should just know these things!

    "I enjoy selling real estate, and I have always found that it's difficult to eat your words, so . . . I always try to do my homework, and you will see, as we go over the CMA that I

have prepared for you today, that I have arrived at a price range that I feel would best represent your type of home. I never like to guess."

11. **Do you have any references?**

    "I have made a point of keeping records of all my past clients after their successful closings and stay in touch by word and mail. I would be happy to have you talk with any one of them." (Make sure that there are a couple of references that you really do feel comfortable using just for this situation. You call them before giving out their names. If you just started in the business, use a good friend.)

12. **Why do you think that you could sell our home?**

    "I love working in your neighborhood and this area. I feel comfortable telling buyers about the various advantages to living here, and our company enjoys a great deal of success here." (Remember only to say this if you really do mean it.)

Masterpiece Market Plan

A detailed market plan has always been the *finishing touch* to getting any listing that I have gone after. Following is an excerpt from my personal promotion book and my market plan:

1. Prepare an *in-depth CMA* on the property for solds, expireds, and current listings available.

2. Take a *color picture* of the subject property from its best angle.

3. Prepare a *journalistically approached* highlight sheet on the property with color picture and mass copy for potential buyers' viewing. Leave 150 at the property.

4. Place a *for sale sign with name rider on the property* with a brochure box attached so that people driving by can familiarize themselves with the home.

5. Utilize a *lockbox* installed on the door to facilitate easy access for showings.

6. Enroll the property in the *multiple listing service* with an additional supplement sheet (if needed) with picture and exposure.

7. Hold an *open house* for agents of my company and multiple listing companies on the first Tuesday after the listing is initiated.

8. Place *special feature cards* at the property to point out highlights to prospects.

9. Send *highlight sheets* to surrounding *neighbors* who may have friends or relatives moving into the area.

10. *Place an ad* in the first Sunday paper with "just listed" and bold stand-out lettering to bring attention to the property.

11. Give sellers all *follow-ups on showings* with comments and suggestions.

12. Insert a *picture ad* in our company's exclusive magazine promoting the property.

13. *Review property biweekly* and suggest remedies for selling.

14. Offer continuous service and *follow-up* to ad calls with two separate home lines, home answering service, office secretary and carphone.

15. Carefully calculate *seller's net* on any and all offer presentations.

16. Complete *follow-up on all buyers* applying for loans and prequalify if buyer origination is through listing agent.

17. *Promote property weekly* to other agents at meetings and office.

18. Complete new CMA if necessary after *30 day checkup*.

19. Provide the homeowner with *helpful home selling hints* brochure to help home sell quickly (sample at end of this chapter).

20. *Help sellers* with locating a moving company, and/or relocation company if out-of-state, and all necessary information. Provide free out-of-state newspaper from city seller is moving to.

This specific marketing plan will give a real estate agent credibility, especially to those sellers who think the real estate person does not do that much. It also adds a certain amount of professionalism and causes the seller to wonder when and how you will ever have the time to do all these things that you are promising.

ACTUALLY, IT'S NOT THAT HARD!

As you read through each chapter of this book, you are given samples and examples of how to do everything that I speak of in the listing presentation and in the individual marketing plan.

Try to see if you can incorporate this plan in *each and every CMA* that you prepare to present to your seller.

Checklist for a New Listing

1. *Make a seller's file.* Use legal size folder (8½″ × 14″). Type seller's name in capitals. Ex: JONES, JOHN E. 444-3333 555 ELM ST. Fax: ____ Listed: ____ Sold: ____

2. *Turn in the listing* at the office and enter it into the MLS.

3. *Get a brochure* box for the property.

4. *Find out* and record on file the utility amounts.

5. *Note* any exclusions on the outside of the file.

6. Put the property on *office tour*.

7. *Write an ad* for Sunday and put in newspaper.

8. *Place the ad in* local homes or city magazines.

9. Make sure the *lockbox is on* the property.

10. Make a *listing entry on the listing sheet* in your daily planner book with the seller's name, address, phone (work and home), date listed and lockbox combination.

11. *Take a color picture of the property.* Have at least 100 made up at a local photomat.

12. *Prepare a home highlight sheet* on the property (8½″ × 11″). Have at least 40–75 made up and left at the home and in the brochure box outside of the home.

13. *Type up just listed cards* for the neighbors around the subject property (100 to 300 families).

14. Find out *where the seller's mortgage* is, and record the loan number and the amount owed at payoff on the outside of the file.

15. Find out *if the property is "torrens" or "abstract"* and where the deed to the home is. Make sure this is written on the file!

Filling Out a Listing

This may appear to be elementary once you understand how to fill a listing out. However, *if you are not completely accurate and careful in putting in only the correct information:*

1. There can be a *lawsuit*!

2. You can *lose large amounts* of money!

3. A fellow agent can cause you *tremendous problems*!

Example   A particular agent listed a home for sale and turned the listing in at 6%, but the computer printout of the listing showed 7%. The listing was on the market for quite a few months. When it finally sold and the listing agent was filling out the closing information papers, she realized with hindsight what had happened. She wound up having to make up the difference (well over $1100 in order for the other agent to be paid, based on a 7% commission)!

This was a sad situation that *could have been avoided* had the listing agent checked and double-checked her listing before the offer came in from another company.

Many, many more problems can develop at the buyers' end if they feel they have been *grossly misrepresented* and seek legal advice.

BE VERY, VERY CAREFUL.

Fill out the listing carefully, and when you have completely finished it, go back over and check it all out again.

Try not to leave any part of the listing blank. The computer has a problem with this.

To help fill out a listing:

1. Keep handy a *reference guide* for local school numbers.

2. Check in advance for *tax information* and assessments.

3. Bring a checklist on *home information* with you the first time you go to the property.

Servicing a Listing

After I secure the listing, this is how I service my listings:

1. When I turn the listing in, I:

   a. put the listing *on tour* immediately,

   b. *send copies* of the new listing to as many other offices as are in the surrounding areas, and

   c. *type up a highlight sheet*, and take a *color picture* of the home. (When developing the film, use the best picture of the house; have 150 pictures made.) Put one color picture on each highlight sheet. This is an economical way of having a professional-looking information sheet at the property almost immediately.

2. I put the secretary on call that *"I wish to be notified of all showings."* Therefore I can immediately follow up on the showing. I contact the agent and put his or her comments on the back of the showing card. At the end of each week, I contact the sellers and tell them of the progress in showings and the positive and negative comments that are made. *Never forget to call* a seller to tell him or her about *every single appointment.*

3. I keep a *30-60-90 chart on all my listings.* Every 30 days I review the listing price, condition, and terms with my seller as well as keeping them abreast of competition in their neighborhood by giving them a computer printout sheet of all the homes that are in a comparable price range in their eight- to twelve-block radius.

4. I normally try to take a *six-month listing minimum.* I tell the seller that *if the home is priced correctly, it should sell within the first 30 days.* We continue to discuss the marketing, weekly, after that period. I also tell them that if the home has not sold after 30 days, there is a greater opportunity of selling the home with *a price reduction* and change of format to put the home out as a *new listing*! At this time, perhaps we extend the listing agreement, depending on whether it is 60 or 90 days yet.

5. If there has been a price reduction, I make sure there are new highlight sheets at the property. I always try to give the impression that the home is not stale.

Highlight Sheet

I use an $8\frac{1}{2}'' \times 11''$ sheet of paper that *always has my picture at the top corner.* This is usually a piece of my real estate stationery. I center the address of the property and list in short sentences the main attractions the home has to offer. I make sure that I start out with the room dimensions, the year built, the square footage, the lot size, the taxes, and if there is any assumable financing on the property. I then go on to highlight advantages of the neighborhood and proximity to schools and bus. I especially tell about any fireplaces, finished lower level, extra family rooms, and special decorating or updating in major rooms such as the kitchen and bedrooms. I also include any special comments that the sellers made regarding *why* they chose the home to begin with. If I cannot or do not have a printer accessible, a copy machine will do temporarily after all of the above has been typed.

THESE HIGHLIGHT SHEETS ARE ESPECIALLY APPRECIATED BY THE SELLERS WHEN YOU CAN HAVE THEM AT THE PROPERTY ALMOST IMMEDIATELY.

Helpful Home Selling Hints

I am pleased to help in the marketing of your home. These suggestions may expedite a successful sale for you.

1. *First impressions are crucial!* Mow the lawn. Trim the hedges. Weed a garden and/or rake the leaves and shovel snow. Replace any burned out light bulbs outside, and polish up brass door knobs and/or light fixtures.

2. *Try to replace* any missing tiles in a bathroom or any broken windows, railings and/or leaking pipes.

3. If paint is totally peeling off the walls, a *room should be repainted*, or if there are badly damaged water spots from a roof repair, paint is needed.

4. *If carpeting is totally worn out*, consideration should be made for replacement if possible, otherwise the marketing price should be adjusted.

5. *Clean out the garage and basement!* Getting rid of all junk makes the house look much larger.

6. *Straighten closets* and storage spaces to create a larger overall look.

7. *Clean all stains* off of sinks, and check faucets for new washers.

8. *Check all windows* for sticking and broken glass. Replace sash chords and remove old drapes or broken window shades.

9. *Clean the house from top to bottom!* Nothing is more offensive to a buyer than clutter. Polish the windows, scrub the floors, vacuum dust and wash curtains.

10. *Straighten up the house!* Get rid of old newspapers and magazines. Put out the garbage. Make sure the litter box is emptied! Make sure the kitchen counters are as clear as possible.

11. *Make sure all pets are confined* to definite inconspicuous areas. Many buyers are afraid of or allergic to animals.

12. *Make sure the house looks cheerful and bright!* All the window shades should be up for showings. Leave some soft music on in the background. If nighttime, turn all the lights on. Have flowers on the table. Light a fire.

13. When showing the house, if possible, *leave for awhile*. If not, you and the children should try to be in one room that is out of the way for the duration of the showing.

14. Make sure that you have left any *written comments that you feel* are an extra bonus as to why you have enjoyed living in the house and the area. Also consider leaving a list of children and babysitters in the neighborhood. Leave helpful hints as to who your neighbors are.

    Sample buyer questions:

    What school will our kids go to?

    Where does the bus run from here?

    Who is a good dentist/doctor here?

    Are there babysitters around here?

    What are the neighbors like on either side of this house?

    How close is the grocery store?

15. *Try to be flexible* in your schedule. Some buyers can only see the home at certain times. If you can't be home to show the home, make arrangements for a lockbox. It would be wise to have a lockbox on from the beginning.

Sellers' Questions: After We Have Listed, Now What?

1. *All appointments on your property* will come from our sales secretary. Real estate agents will be asked with whom they are affiliated, and a record of their showing your home will be kept at our office and given to the listing agent for follow-up.

2. There will also be times when sales agents will call to request an appointment to *preview the property*. You will be called in advance for these appointments also.

3. *Our office only will be making appointments on your home.* The appointments will always be for a specific time frame, and you will be asked if this meets with your schedule.

4. *The secretary may call to make the appointment* for the same day or for a few days in advance. The secretary will always tell you who the agent is and what company the agent represents. A typical time frame could be from 3:00 to 4:00, for example.

5. In the event that you cannot be reached by the secretary to establish an appointment that is within a short period of time from the initial call *we will use the lockbox* if you give your approval. If it is quite a few hours off, we will continue to try to reach you and/or the listing agent before showing the home.

6. If you are planning on being away for a time period of more than a day and a night, it is wise to *let your listing agent know of this, and leave a key* (if no lockbox) and any forwarding numbers that would enable him or her to reach you for an offer.

7. If you have *any specific instructions regarding an animal* being confined, cards left by agents in specific places, or special notes of interest, please inform your listing agent, and he or she will make special note on the appointment book and on the listing agreement.

8. Most *real estate agents try to be punctual.* However, there will be times when, because of previous appointments running overtime, they may be late. We hope it will not happen, but we want to prepare you for this, if on a rare occasion, it does happen.

9. Once in a while *an agent may have to cancel an appointment.* This does not happen very often. However, if a buyer is late or has changed appointments, it becomes necessary. We always request that our secretary call you and inform you as quickly as possible to avoid putting you out in any way.

10. At times there will be *sales associates who will preview your home* after calling for an appointment. This is because the agent may have a client coming into town or working with him in the near future, and he or she wants to be prepared.

11. If at times a *stranger comes to your door* and asks to see the home (either from an ad and/or the yard sign), I would suggest that you not let anyone in without first calling your real estate agent and referring this person to him or her.

12. *All real estate agents should have business cards.* If you are having showings and do not know if they have been there (at times they may forget), please feel free to leave a note with a dish into which agents could deposit their business cards.

13. Because of high technology taking over the industry, *more and more real estate agents have car phones.* Occasionally they may phone for an appointment and be right in front of your house! If possible, try to be as accommodating as you can. The buyers may be from out-of-town and cannot come back to see your home again.

14. *Talk to your agent about any special instructions* regarding security systems, lights left on, or pets left out. Your listing agent should know all of this, and the secretary will be informed.

15. You have selected us so that we may obtain a sale for you as quickly as possible. *Our ultimate goal is a sold sign.* We ask for your patience and understanding as we attempt to proceed and accomplish this goal.

Thank you for listing your home with me and our company.

Monthly Listing Update

Dear Seller:

This is a monthly update to familiarize you with the market today.

There are currently: _____ *homes for sale in your area.*

There are currently: _____ *homes sold in your area.*

There are currently: _____ *homes expired in your area.*

There have been: _____ *showings on your home.*

Other agent comments:

Price high: _____   *Number of agents:* _____

Price low: _____   *Number of agents:* _____

Price OK: _____   *Number of agents:* _____

Agents' comments: (number of agents) _____

Interior condition: *poor:* _____ *average:* _____ *excellent:* _____

Exterior condition: *poor:* _____ *average:* _____ *excellent:* _____

Seller's comments: _____

_____

_____

_____

Please return in the self-addressed envelope as soon as possible.

Thank you for your cooperation.

    Sincerely,

    Barbara Nash-Price
    Real Estate Agent

Monthly Review Listing Sheet

Agent's name _____

Company _____

Phone _____

Property address: _____ Phone: _____

Date property listed: _____ Expires: _____

Today's date reviewed: _____

Summary of activity:

Toured by agents: _____

Agent's comments: (tour)

_____

_____

Agent's feeling toward price:

_____

_____

Listing agent's comments:

_____

_____

Price reductions:

_____

_____

Open Houses:

Date: _____ Date: _____

Date: _____ Date: _____

Showings: _____ _____

_____ _____

_____ _____

Sixty Day Listing Action Plan

I have designed this plan so as to help you establish a more definite plan of action in selling your home quickly. Please respond by checking either yes or no in the appropriate sections and returning this to me as soon as possible.

	YES	NO
Have we presented an offer in writing to you in the last 60 days or less?	☐	☐
Have homes sold in your area in the last 60 days that you are aware of?	☐	☐
If so, has your agent made you aware of these?	☐	☐
Do you know of, or has your agent made you aware of any qualified buyers that can make an offer on your home at the present time?	☐	☐
Have you made the terms or conditions to buy more favorable in the last 60 days?	☐	☐
Have you changed the condition or the appearance of your home in any way in the last 60 days?	☐	☐
Have you adjusted the price significantly lower in the last 60 days?	☐	☐

If the majority of these questions have been answered by "no," it is time for us to meet to make an appropriate adjustment in the marketing strategy for your property.

Please return this to me in the *self-addressed enclosed envelope* with any and all additional comments you may feel are important.

Thank you for your time in responding to my questions.

Seller Net Sheet

SELLER'S NAME: _____

Address of property: _____

Date of presented offer: _____

Offering price: $ _____

Mortgage balance: $ _____

Any interest adjustment: $ _____

Contract for deed balance: $ _____

Interest adjustment on contract for deed $ _____

Home improvement loans: $ _____

Taxes owed: $ _____

Special assessments: $ _____

Deed tax owed: $ _____

Abstract extension: $ _____

Recording fees: $ _____

New mtg. points: $ _____

Real estate fee: $ _____

Water/sewage connection fee: $ _____

VA/FHA fees: $ _____

Soil test: $ _____

Inspection fee: $ _____

Approximate selling fees: $ _____

Final equity to seller: $ _____

Seller's Folder Contents
Bring to Listing Presentation

1. Company brochure

2. Any newsworthy information about your Company

3. Your brochure

4. Your city map

5. School information in seller's area

6. Moving information from any moving company

7. Helpful home selling hints sheet

8. Marked map book sheet of home location and other homes for sale with red X marked

9. Computer printout of CMA on property

10. Subject property's picture on folder exterior

11. Marketing plan for the seller

12. "Promotional ad" of yourself (from newspaper)

Listing Service Record

Property Address: _____

_____

Owner: _____   Phone: _____

Date	Time	Prev	Agent Name	Company	Office No	L.B. Given	Canc	Comments
5/17	10–11		L WASSEN	C/B	924–1111	X		OWNER CALLED AG. WILL MEET ME
5/20	12–1		J AMES	E/R	921–0001	X		MEET AGENT THERE ANS. SVC.
5/21	10:45		TOM NESS	R/H	828–0001	X		MEETING AGENT
6/2	11 AM		GEO NOO	HH	920–1111	X		OWNER WILL BE GONE
6/2	2:45		MARY ANE	B/R	832–4441			ANS. MACHINE
6/5	3–4		JEFF MARK	HH	920–2222	X		
6/11	7–8		MINNIE POOL	E/R	824–0411			OK-OWNER HOME
6/11	4–5		SETH JONES	R/H	924–3014		X	BUYER CAN'T MAKE IT
6/12	2–3		GEORGE NOOB	C/B	332–0401	X		
6/15	10–11	X	JANE JONES	HH	338–7928	X		MEET THERE ANSWER MACH.
6/20	11:30 –2:15		TOM JOHNS	E/R	224–9178	X		OWNER MAY BE HOME
6/25	2–3	X	MAY ALICE	HH	824–3701	X		DON'T LET CAT OUT DAUGHTER HOME

Seller's Acknowledgment Statement of Home Condition

Property Address:_____

Date Listed: _____

When did you buy the home? _____

How long have you lived here?_____

Have you ever had a fire, flood, or disaster at this property?   YES ☐   NO ☐

Comments: _____

Details:_____

What is the age and condition of your roof?

Age: _____ Condition: _____

Has there ever been ice buildup?   YES ☐   NO ☐

Have you ever replaced/repaired the roof?   YES ☐   NO ☐

Details:_____

Comments on heat, plumbing, electrical systems:

Are they and will they be in working order at closing?

	YES	NO		YES	NO		YES	NO
OVEN	☐	☐	ELEC. SYSTEM	☐	☐	VENT FANS	☐	☐
HOOD	☐	☐	HOT WATER HEAT	☐	☐	SUMP PUMP	☐	☐
MICRO-OVEN	☐	☐	GAR DISPOSAL	☐	☐	PLBG SYS	☐	☐
DISHWASHER	☐	☐	SPRINK SYSTEM	☐	☐	PRIV WELL	☐	☐
CENTRAL HEAT	☐	☐	FURN HUMID	☐	☐	PRIV SEW	☐	☐
SUPP HEAT	☐	☐	WATER SOFT	☐	☐	T.V. ANT.	☐	☐
CENT. AIR	☐	☐	ELECT PURIF	☐	☐	INTERCOM	☐	☐
WALL AIR	☐	☐	GAR OPENER	☐	☐	FIREPLACE	☐	☐
			ALL CONTROLS	☐	☐			

Comments: _____

Condition of trees: any infected, diseased, etc.   YES ☐   NO ☐   Explain: _____

_____

Insulation:

Does insulation contain urea formaldehyde foam?   YES ☐   NO ☐

Date insulation installed:_____   Company: _____

Known defects in home: _____

_____

Seller's signature_____   Dated: _____

Buyer's signature _____   Dated: _____

New Listing Property Information
7326 West 14th Street Circle

"Quail Ridge" is an exceptionally quiet, quaint and friendly neighborhood.

There is a neighborhood directory, neighborhood crime watch, neighborhood fun days and picnics at the park with the neighborhood children and parents.

There are outstanding schools, such as Olson Elementary which was nominated as an "honorary school of excellence" and Jefferson High School.

The home sits back nestled on a lot abundant with wildlife, ducks in the pond, and deer in the backyard. The home backs up to park and trails.

There are six neighborhood working babysitters.

This home is on the "Sedqwick Blue Plan" and has the furnace and the air conditioning checked twice a year. The home is wired for music, cable television and VCR in most every room.

The exterior of the home is maintenance free, upgraded in "dryvit outsulation." There is no fading, no staining and no cracking.

There is a central vacuum system.

New Listing Property Information
7326 West 14th Street Circle

The builder of this home was Ace Construction, a top builder in the metropolitan area.

Some of the upgrades include beautiful Princeton trim on the door and windows.

The formal living room and dining room have sensational skylights.

Some of the neighborhood children are as follows:

Boys	Girls
1 baby	2 six year olds
2 three year olds	2 seven year olds
1 four year old	1 eight year old
1 five year old	3 nine year olds
2 six year olds	4 eleven year olds
3 seven year olds	2 thirteen year olds
1 eight year old	2 fourteen year olds
1 ten year old	1 sixteen year old
1 eleven year old	3 seventeen year olds
2 fourteen year olds	1 nineteen year old

Several kids in college and senior high

Seldom has there been a home offered with so many upgrades, additional built-ins, and the best in quality workmanship available.

Highlight Sheet

PHOTO

1. WHEN TYPING UP A HIGHLIGHT SHEET FOR A NEW LISTING:

   a. BE AS DESCRIPTIVE AS POSSIBLE.

   b. WRITE ABOUT THE HOME WITH ENTHUSIASM.

   c. MAKE A POINT OF SHOWING WHERE THE HOME IS LOCATED.

   d. MAKE SURE THAT YOU TELL ABOUT THE HIGHLIGHTS.

   e. TAKE A COLOR PICTURE OF THE PROPERTY AND SEND IT IN WITH A PRINTER TO HAVE THE HIGHLIGHT SHEETS MADE.

   f. TAKE THE REST OF THE COLOR PICTURES YOU HAVE DEVELOPED (ABOUT 75 AT LEAST) AND GLUE THEM ON THE HIGHLIGHT SHEETS.

2. a. MAKE SURE THAT *THE TOP AGENTS IN THE OFFICE GET ONE OF YOUR HIGHLIGHT SHEETS* ON THE HOME.

   b. *PUT YOUR HIGHLIGHT SHEET IN THE MAIL* TO OTHER TOP AGENTS AT COMPETING COMPANIES.

   c. PUT THE HIGHLIGHT SHEET IN THE MAIL TO SOME GOOD BUYERS THAT YOU THINK MAY LIKE THE HOME.

3. PUT AT LEAST 40 TO 50 HIGHLIGHT SHEETS AT THE PROPERTY IN THE HOUSE AND IN THE BROCHURE BOX OUTSIDE OF THE HOUSE.

4. TOTAL EXPENSE SHOULD BE APPROXIMATELY $50 INVESTMENT FROM YOU.

Home Profile $289,000

Offered by ——

Barb Nash-Price

Bus. (612) #_____
Res. (612) #_____

Information deemed reliable
but not guaranteed.

PHOTO

Highlights ——

Welcome to this custom built 2-story executive home adjacent to 1000-acre Hyland Park Preserve, Hyland Hills Ski area and Mt. Normandale Lake. Enjoy the deer in your backyard as they walk through the woods!

This home, located on a quiet cul de sac, is within 15 minutes of the airport and 20 minutes to downtown, yet feels like a country location with the park that has walking and cross country ski trails and the lake with its public beach.

Enjoy the wooded backyard and private setting with the 38 × 17 inground pool and 6-person hot tub surrounded by 900 + sq. feet of decking and low voltage lighting. Extensive landscaping, a security system, and underground sprinkling system add to the amenities of this fine home. Also enjoy downtown skyline views from the *MASTER BATH* jacuzzi!

Home ——

Approximate room sizes in this fine home include:

- Living Room   16.5×12.5
- Dining Room   14×11.6
- Kitchen   13.7×10.3
- Eating Area   15.7×9.6
- Family Room   20.7×15.5
- Screened Porch   16×12
- Master Bedroom   17×16
- Bedroom #2   14×11.7
- Bedroom #3   13.6×10.6
- Bedroom #4   16.6×13
- Game Room   32×13.6
- Amusement Room
                       20.7×15.5
- 1989 Homestead Taxes: $6,746.48
- Lot size: 81×155×120×173
- Year Built: 1980
- Main floor sq. footage: 1712 approx.
- Total finished sq. footage: 4000 approx.

Property ——

Special features of this home include:

- Country Kitchen with center island Jenn Air and large eating area overlooking pool
- Master bedroom suite has remodeled bath with jacuzzi tub and the largest walk-in closet you have ever seen with maximum space organized!
- Family room with brick fireplace and built-in bookcases
- Oak pegged hardwood floor in dining room
- Lower level ideal for entertaining with game room and 2nd family room with another fireplace and daylight windows—perfect for children!
- 4th bedroom on lower level ideal for live-in help with its own full bath
- Large main floor laundry—loads of storage throughout!
- Panoramic views of Hyland Hills ski area from many rooms!

Home Profile

$152,900

Offered by ———

Barb Nash-Price

Bus. (612) #_____

Res. (612) #_____

Information deemed reliable
but not guaranteed.

PHOTO

Highlights ———

Welcome to this beautiful custom built split-foyer home at
the foothills of Indian Hills.
The property is adjacent to the
most conveniently located area
of Edina between Highway 18
and Gleason Road. There is a
lovely floor plan that flows
from the moment you enter to
view neutral decorator tones
throughout and excellent carpeting. Absolutely perfect floor
plan to include formal dining
and eat-in kitchen with separate planning desk and all built-
in appliances! A feeling of
warmth and pride are reflected
throughout every spacious
room showing care and concern for home ownership.

Home ———

APPROXIMATE ROOM
SIZES IN THIS FINE HOME
INCLUDE:

- Living Room   22×13
- Dining Room   12×10
- Kitchen   12×8
- Eating Area   9×8
- Family Room   20×13
- Bedroom   13×12
- Bedroom   12×11
- Bedroom   11×10
- Fam. Rm. (lower)   18×12
- Addn. Room   13×12
- Taxes: $6,746.48 (1991 HS)
- Lot size: 132×130
- Year Built: 1965
- Square feet: 1700
- Total square feet: 2310

Property ———

SPECIAL FEATURES OF
THIS HOME INCLUDE:

- Beautiful first floor family
  room with lovely window
  treatment and walkout to
  delightful private rear yard
- Two beautiful brick
  fireplaces. One is located in
  formal living room and one
  is located in lower level
  family room
- Lower level is ideal for
  entertaining with separate
  area for small game table
  and additional area for
  larger furniture placement
  around beautiful brick
  fireplace—lovely daylight
  windows perfect for
  children!
- A tremendous opportunity
  for fine family living at its
  best!

Home Profile

$309,000

Offered by —————

Barb Nash-Price

Bus. (612) #_____
Res. (612) #_____

Information deemed reliable
but not guaranteed.

PHOTO

Highlights —————

Absolutely exceptional New England Tudor loaded with charm and character throughout! There is a main floor family room with handsome hardwood floors off front foyer. Perfect breakfast room accents delightful kitchen with an abundance of cupboard space and work area. Huge formal living room boasts full-wall picture window and beautiful fireplace, plus quiet den is the highlight room adjacent to living room/dining room. The second floor features three lovely bedrooms, each with a character and flavor of its own—two bathrooms and separate exit to huge full-size deck above the garage which is double and attached to the property. This very unique home is situated on a quiet, corner lot in prime country club location.

Home —————

APPROXIMATE ROOM SIZES IN THIS FINE HOME INCLUDE:

- Living Room   14×27
- Dining Room   Included
- Kitchen   18×19
- Family Room   15×14
- Main Den   8×10
- Master Suite   14×19
- 2nd Bedroom   12×14
- 3rd Bedroom   12×13
- Amusement Room   13×26
- Lower Bedroom   12×14
- Taxes: $5,445
- Lot size: 81×155×120×173
- Year Built: 1938
- Main Square Feet: 1,115
- Total Square Feet: 2,078

Property —————

SPECIAL FEATURES OF THIS HOME INCLUDE:

This property is located in one of the most sought-after areas of country club. It is within blocks of the Edina shopping, theatre and library. There are exceptional upper bracket quality homes that surround the property. The home is nestled back on a prestigious corner lot, exemplifying pride of ownership throughout. The amenities are too numerous to name, and there are extra quality improvements made by the present owners that reflect definite care and upgrading within the interior of this fine home.

Home Profile $279,900

Offered by ——

Barb Nash-Price

PHOTO

Bus. (612) #_____
Res. (612) #_____

Information deemed reliable
but not guaranteed.

Highlights ——

WELCOME TO AN INCRED-
IBLE HOME! This property is
located in the heart of the Brae-
mar area near the base of Indian Hills. THE BEST LOCA-
TION . . . The property was
originally custom built with the
finest quality and has been
COMPLETELY RENOVAT-
ED. THERE IS A BRAND
NEW KITCHEN with custom
cabinetry, new ceramic floor,
new appliances and beautiful
decorator wall coverings.
CLASSIC LINES prevail in the
extraordinary FAMILY ROOM
with vaulted ceilings and floor
to ceiling glass accented by oak
pegged floor completely RE-
FINISHED. EVERY bathroom
is COMPLETELY NEW. The
entire interior reflects WON-
DERFUL WHITE tones com-
plimented by wonderful window placement. There is a
gorgeous lower level featuring
upgraded OFFICE WITH
BUILT-INS galore and two
BR's.

Home ——

APPROXIMATE ROOM
SIZES IN THIS FINE HOME
INCLUDE:

- Living Room   13×18
- Family Room   18×18
- Kitchen   12×9
- Formal DR   10×11
- Master Bedroom   12×18
- 2nd Bedroom   11×13
- 3rd Bedroom   10×11
- Office   12×14
- Amusement Room   16×31
- Lower BR   11×11
- Lower BR   11×15
- Built: 1967
- Taxes 1990: $4,347.00
- Fireplaces: 3

Property ——

HIGHLIGHTS OF THIS FINE
HOME INCLUDE THE FOL-
LOWING: This custom-built
beautiful home has been totally renovated, including every
room on every floor! THERE
IS gorgeous new carpeting
throughout the main level with
upgraded NEW BERBER CAR-
PET IN THE LOWER LEVEL.
BRAND NEW CEDAR SPLIT-
SHAKE ROOF, BRAND NEW
FURNACE. ALL WALL COV-
ERINGS AND WALLS HAVE
BEEN FRESHLY PAINTED
AND COVERED. The lower
level also features a beautiful
eight person sauna, plus two
additional bedrooms and office
as well as storage room, utility
room, and wonderful lower
level entertainment room with
BRICK FIREPLACE. THERE
IS ALSO AN INTERCOM
SYSTEM. This unique proper-
ty backs up to SOLID WOODS
and is nestled on a prestigious
quiet CUL-DE-SAC location. It
is a property that is TRULY
DISTINGUISHED, loaded
with amenities and class.
THERE IS ABSOLUTELY
NOTHING TO DO EXCEPT
MOVE IN!

Home Profile $69,900

Offered by ———

Barb Nash-Price

Bus. (612) #_____
Res. (612) #_____

Information deemed reliable
but not guaranteed.

PHOTO

Highlights ———

Exceptional townhome in
Cedar Trails with the land included! Wonderful floor plan
with floor to ceiling windows
in living room accented by
white brick fireplace, new carpeting, and wonderful window
treatments. New wallpaper in
great kitchen with planning
desk and perfect eating area.
The second floor has very large
bedrooms with huge walk-in
closet in the master bedroom,
plus access to full bathroom.
There is a second floor laundry room and additional storage closets! A once in a lifetime
opportunity for privacy and
maintenance free living. Association dues: $90

Home ———

Approximate room sizes in this
fine home include:

- Living Room   13×9
- Dining Room   9×11
- Master Bedroom   10×18
- Bedroom (2nd)   11×12
- Taxes: $583.00
- Square Footage: 1,232
- Assoc. Dues: $90.00/mo.
- BBQ: owned by seller

Property ———

This property is located in one
of the most sought-after areas
of St. Louis Park. It is within
close proximity of shopping,
restaurants, and five minutes
from downtown exits. There
are exceptional homes, and the
townhome maintenance is outstanding. The amenities are too
numerous to name with a lovely private deck accenting a double garage. All appliances con-
vey with the property. The
present owner has reflected
definite care and upgrading
within the interior of this fine
townhome.

Feedback Fax on Showings

Agent picture

Company name _____

Company # _____   333-3333

Kindly inform us as to

Your opinion & your

customer's opinion of

The home at:

_____

_____

Opinion:

_____

_____

Price: ok: _____ high: _____ low: _____

Showing agent

Name & Phone _____

_____

_____

CHAPTER 11

Open Houses

big deal
by "Lorayne n' Neil"

How Important Are Open Houses?

OPEN HOUSES ARE A KEY FACTOR IN HAVING GREAT BUSINESS.

From the onset of my career to the present time, I have consistently tried to have a standing rule:

TWO OPEN HOUSES EVERY WEEK
(unless a major holiday)

By keeping this type of schedule, I am able to maintain an active business that keeps giving me:

1. *adequate qualified buyers*
2. *my own listings to sell*
3. *generated fast sales*

My Sunday *schedule* is usually similar to the following:

First open:	12:00 to 2:00 P.M.
Second open:	2:30 to 4:30 P.M.
or	
First open:	1:00 to 3:00 P.M.
Second open:	3:30 to 5:30 P.M.

OPENS ARE BIG BUSINESS. Open Houses are very big business if you know what to do.

You must be prepared to have a certain *plan of action* before going over to the house that is to be held open.

OPEN HOUSES REALLY DO KEEP YOU IN BUSINESS.

Open houses enable you to really select good buyers and sellers to work with if you know how to qualify them!

I maintain that many of the people coming through open houses have interest in relocating.

How to pick a house to hold open:

1. It should be *PRICED TO SELL.*
2. It should be in an *AREA THAT YOU KNOW WELL.*
3. It should *GENERATE BUSINESS* automatically.
4. It should be in *GOOD CONDITION.*
5. It should be *EASILY ACCESSIBLE.*
6. It should be *FAIRLY NEW TO THE MARKET.*

Open houses will make you a lot of money if you do your homework first, preview the home before you hold it open, and know the area.

Open House Plan of Action

1. Preview the home.

2. Drive the neighborhood and look for other homes for sale.

3. Check the computer for solds in the neighborhood and also any expired listings that you may be able to call on.

4. Make highlight sheets from the computer listing if there are none at the property. Add a copy of your business card to this.

5. Bring at least 25 to 30 extra brochures on yourself to the home.

6. Bring your open house legal pad.

7. Make a computer printout (CMA) of the neighborhood using the map coordinates. This will give you all the active, sold and expired listings in the area.

8. Do an AMS (Area Market Survey) of the neighborhood. This will tell you how long the properties take to sell and the average, high, and low selling prices in the neighborhood.

9. Decide where you will need to place signs . . . you may need extras. Perhaps put out a sign telling the home will be open (ex: "home will be open next Sunday afternoon).

10. Work on a good catchy ad, not too long, but specific and enthusiastic. Example: just listed—1st open—none like it.

11. Try to memorize what has sold in the neighborhood and know the home. People like to work with knowledgeable agents.

12. Go over the highlight sheet and the listing sheet on the subject property being held open. Know pertinent information such as taxes, square footage, year built, lot size, and so on.

13. Wear a name tag if possible.

14. Do not forget the name of the person once they give it to you! Stand at the door with pen, pad, and home information in left hand. When the people come, extend right hand and say, "Hi, I'm from _____ Real Estate Company and you are?" As they tell you their name, repeat it to them, "Oh, it's nice to meet you Mr. and Mrs. _____. Now write it down, otherwise you will **forget it**.

15. Try to spend a little time showing them part of the house and give them a little space to look alone.

Questions to Ask at an Open House

First and foremost, start the question with their name, either their last name or their first name, whichever you feel most comfortable using.

1. Did you just *START LOOKING* for homes?
2. Do you *LIVE* in this area?
3. Are you *FAMILIAR WITH* this neighborhood?
4. What part of the city are you *COMING FROM*?
5. *HOW LONG* have you been looking at properties for sale?
6. Are you working with *ANOTHER AGENT* at this time?
7. *ARE YOU SATISFIED* with your present home?
8. How does this *HOME COMPARE* to your home?
9. *WHAT FEATURES DO YOU LIKE*/dislike about this home?
10. *WHAT ARE THE FEATURES THAT YOU* like/dislike about your present home?
11. *WHAT ARE THE DRAWBACKS* of your present home?
12. *WHAT IS THE PRESENT MORTGAGE* on the home you own now?
13. *DO YOU HAVE A SPECIFIC TIME* frame that you want to move in?
14. *ARE YOU LEAVING YOUR HOME* because of a financial situation?
15. *DO YOU NEED A LOWER*/higher *HOUSE PAYMENT*?
16. *WHAT IS YOUR FAVORITE STYLE* of home?
17. *WHAT STYLE OF HOME DO YOU LEAST* prefer?
18. *HAVE YOU SEEN A HOME* that you could move into tomorrow?
19. *HAVE YOU MADE ANY OFFERS* on any homes as yet?
20. *HAS YOUR HOME EVER BEEN LISTED?*

What to Do at an Open House

1. Make sure that *every light is turned on* in the house.

2. Make sure that all draperies, curtains and blinds are *completely open.*

3. Make sure that the *kitchen is spotless*, dishes are out of sight and towels are discreetly put away.

4. Perhaps put a *little vanilla* on the burner to give the hint of bread baking in the oven.

5. *Air freshener or potpourri* is refreshing. Cloves in an orange are also a nice twist.

6. *Some agents like to have cookies* and juice and some mints out on the table. This entices the people to spend a bit more time talking, and if there are children, it seems to appease them a bit.

7. *Stay by the front door* and *greet each person* as he or she enters.

8. *Do not have the television on.*

9. *Have some soft, soothing music on* in the background.

10. *Make sure your brochures are out* and they have to ask you for a highlight sheet on the property. I prefer to give them the information, and then, if the interest persists, I hand them a highlight sheet.

11. *Ask all potential clients* if you can take a *look at their home.*

12. Ask *them if you could meet them tomorrow* at your office to talk about other properties for sale in the area.

13. Ask *them if you could come over later* in the week to see their home and give them an idea of what it is worth.

14. *Try to make some kind of appointment* with potential clients who appear to be qualified buyers before they leave.

15. *Try to be relaxed*, friendly, professional, and interested in asking a few questions about their life in order to familiarize you with their particular situation.

What to Do If an Open House is Slow

What if no people come through?

What if you have two and a half hours of just sitting and looking out of the window?

DON'T DO THIS!

THERE ARE AT LEAST A DOZEN DIFFERENT PRODUCTIVE THINGS TO DO.

1. *Work on your schedule* for the next week.
2. *Call and talk to a prospective buyer* while you are looking at the MLS book.
3. *Call and talk to a prospective seller*, and set up an appointment to appraise his or her house.
4. *Go through the newspaper* and *clip the for sale by owner* (FSBO) ads.
5. *Call the FSBOs* that are closest to the listing you are at. Try to make an appointment following your open.
6. *Call other FSBOs*, and set up appointments for the rest of the week. (You should have your schedule in front of you.)
7. *Go through your daily planner* from the previous week or month, and see if there are appointments or people that you have forgotten or overlooked.
8. Go through your *buyer list and update it.*
9. *Go through your seller list and update it.*
10. *Work on a competitive market analysis* (CMA) for a seller.
11. *Balance* your *checkbook.*
12. *Pay* important *bills.*

. . . *And if you are in a real slump*, bring an inspirational book to read like *Power of Positive Thinking.*

Ways to Achieve the Best Open House

1. *Try to call the neighbors* ahead of time to invite them over to see the property and to introduce yourself.

2. *Distribute door-hangers* about the subject property being held open about three to five days before the open house to surrounding neighbors in the four to six block radius.

3. Make sure that you *put out at least four open house* signs.

4. *Have with you your MLS book*, your laptop computer, if possible, and a computer printout of the area's for sales and solds.

5. *Keep your legal pad for open houses* in your hand while greeting clients.

6. *Bring brochures* on yourself and your company with you to give out to prospective clients.

7. *Know the properties that have sold* in the neighborhood of the home that you are holding open.

8. *Know all the properties that are for sale* in the neighborhood of the home that you are holding open.

9. *Be sincerely interested* in each and every client that comes through your open house by *asking them what their needs are.*

10. *Ask each and every person coming through* if you could stop by and see their home, or if they would want to come in this week to your office to talk about their real estate needs.

    Keep on hand:

    a. calculator

    b. amortization schedule

    c. loan officer's name and work and home phone numbers

    d. current mortgage rates

12. Look professional! Go to your open house dressed for success with a tailored, sleek, polished look that will give a new client a feeling of being with a professional.

Every open house has the potential for giving you a new listing and a new buyer or both in one client! Be prepared to acclimate yourself to whatever needs the potential client states.

REMEMBER: DON'T LET THEM LEAVE WITHOUT AN APPOINTMENT.

How to Get the Right Names and Numbers at Open Houses

WHEN YOU ARE AT AN OPEN HOUSE TRY TO:

1. *Keep your legal pad* with you at all times.

2. *You will be spontaneously meeting people.* One or two people may come to the door, and as you are greeting them, another couple may come right behind them. *Do not let the first couple pass by* without asking for and writing down their name. Let them pass and go on to the next couple.

3. When you are with the next couple, ask them the same information: *WHAT IS YOUR NAME, AND WHERE ARE YOU PRESENTLY LIVING?* Most people will give you this information without having to think about it.

4. *I do not use a guest register sign-in* because many people have not written down their correct name. This is up to you, however.

5. While people are walking through the home, try to catch up with them in the latter part of their tour. *ASK THEM THE FOLLOWING QUESTIONS:*

   a. How do you *like* the house so far?

   b. How does this home *compare* to your own home?

   c. Is this the *area* that you feel you would move to?

   d. Have you had an *estimate* on your own home as yet?

   e. *How many* homes have you seen already?

   f. Would this afternoon work out if I were to *stop by* after my open house to look at your property?

   g. *I'll be in your area* tomorrow or Tuesday, which would work better for me to stop by and see your home?

   h. Do you think you and your family could *enjoy living here*?

   i. Have you had anyone give you a brief idea of how you *would qualify*?

   j. Why don't we sit down for a minute so I could give you a brief idea of *how you qualify* for this property?

6. Ask all the people who come through the open house to give you their name, address and phone number. *Most of them will.*

7. Repeat their name as they give it to you so that you will have the spelling correct from the very start.

8. *Ask them up front* if they are just looking at homes or are really very serious.

9. Always, always, smile, be pleasant, and show that you do *enjoy selling real estate.*

Letter to Seller/Selling Agent

THANK YOU SO VERY MUCH!
IT WAS A PLEASURE SHOWING YOUR HOME TODAY!

_____ Held property open

_____ Showed client

_____ I previewed home

My feelings: _____

_____

My client's feelings: _____

_____

If my client decides to write an offer on your home, or if I have any questions, I will call your agent. Again, thank you.

Barbara Nash-Price

Open House

Date:	Name:
Address:	Phone:
Time:	Combo:
Client #1	
Client #2	
Client #3	
Client #4	

SAMPLE NOTES FROM OPEN HOUSE LEGAL PAD

4-6-92   Ad Copy:

4515 Morexal

Open 2:00 to 4:00 P.M.

65 people came through (five buyers, three sellers), five letters to send, three call backs next Monday morning.

Opinions on house: priced right, should sell, "as is" condition, lovely decorating throughout

Seven dialogues with clients. Passed out all brochures (ran out of highlight sheets), lots of neighbors through. Two people through listing with another agent. E. Doon will list on Chappel Lane 4/25 - approx. $200,000 walkout rambler.

One lady, single - working with Mary H.

Open House: Sunday 3/1/92 (2:00 to 4:00)

4515 Morexal South

4br - 3 bath

2500 square feet

$339,900

People through the Open: _____

Lisa and Rod Benson live on Williamsburg, just like to look, bought a Cape Cod three years ago

Andy and Ellen Tugar No. Riverside Drive apartment E New York, NY 10020 phone: _____. Write to them. Husband just took job here, just sold apt. in New York, no children, highly motivated, send sheets immed. for +$325,000 suburbs

Diane and John Pittapold renting, no home to sell, working with Babette B. of this company, very, very interested, will probably write offer, call Babette

Kathy Maertner 500 Arden 620-6493 likes house a lot, not quite right, call to look at her house

Kent and Lyn Gregory 450 Casco Rd 920-0000, young couple renting. Told to drive by 532 Wood Drive.

OPEN HOUSES MAKE THE DIFFERENCE

* ALWAYS HOLD TWO TO FOUR OPEN HOUSES EVERY WEEK.

* PROMISE YOURSELF NEW CLIENTS AT EVERY OPEN.

* CALL THE PEOPLE BACK THAT EVENING AFTER THE OPEN.

* MAKE APPOINTMENTS AT OPEN HOUSES WITH PEOPLE.

Open House Dialogue

NOW YOU ARE SET . . .

The lights are on, the music is soft, the aroma in the air is fresh and clean, and your signs are strategically placed. *IT'S THAT TIME!*

A couple pulls up in front of the open house, and you watch as a man and a woman get out of the car and come up to the door.

1. You are standing at the door to *greet them*.

2. You have your *legal pad* in your left hand with a pen clipped to it.

3. There is also the *highlight sheet* on top of the legal pad for you to refer to.

4. You now *extend your right hand* and say to them:

   "Hi, I'm Barbara Nash-Price from _____ Real Estate company, and you are?"

5. As they tell you their name, repeat it and *write it down*.

NOW TELL THEM *FIVE BRIEF FACTS* ABOUT THE PROPERTY . . .

1. *The price of this home is _____.*

2. *It was built in _____ and has _____ square feet.*

3. *These owners are very motivated to sell because _____.*

4. *The taxes on this property are _____.*

5. *The improvements that have been made are _____. OR The improvements that need to be made are _____.*

   Why don't you look around a bit, and I will be right here to answer any questions you may have when you are finished?

The potential buyers will proceed to walk through the home, enabling you to do **two things:**

1. *Get ready for the next people* who are either coming up to the door or have arrived.

2. *Position yourself with the needed information* when they have finished looking.

Let's assume that these are the only potential clients at the property for the moment. They have finished walking through the home. Never go down to a basement with a client! Let them look on their own. Now they have come back and are about to . . .

. . . WALK OUT THE FRONT DOOR!

You see that this is not the home for these people. Now what?

You walk over to them and ask them the *following questions:*

1. *Is this the type of home that you are looking for?*

2. *Have you been looking* in this area for a long time?

3. *Do you know* of all the *good properties that are available* around this location?

4. *Which would be better for you,* tomorrow or the next day, for me to stop over to show you a few things and to take a look at your property?

5. *Why don't I stop over* after my open house, and we could go through some numbers on which home could work for you?

6. *Why don't you come into my office* either tomorrow after 5:00 or would after 7:00 be better for you?

7. *Let's get together* at my office, and we could see how you would qualify for a home that I think might be just perfect for both of you, then we could run over and look at it.

At one point you will see just *how serious* these people are. Most people will not want you to come over or set up any appointment with them if they do not have any intention of buying something. You will be able to sort out the good buyers early on if you can decipher *when to ask for an appointment* and how to narrow down whether or not the people you have just met really do indeed want to buy a home *from you!*

IT IS VERY IMPORTANT TO LEARN TO CLOSE AT AN OPEN HOUSE.

Closing at an open house is asking for an appointment for:

1. getting together to *qualify* potential buyers,

2. *looking* at the buyer's existing property, and

3. Obtaining *loyalty* from the buyers.

On a busy open house day a potential client will go right from your open house to the next. Unless you have established some sort of relationship, you will lose these people to the next agent soliciting them.

ASK FOR AN APPOINTMENT BEFORE THEY LEAVE THE OPEN HOUSE!

**OPEN HOUSE
NOTE
ON FRONT DOOR:**

"Everyone Is Welcome
to View This Home!
However,
If You Are Currently
Working with Another
Agent, Please Notify Me
As You Enter.

Thank You.
Barbara Nash-Price

Open House Profile $324,900

Hosted by ——

Barb Nash-Price
Bus. (612) #_____

Res. (612) #_____

Information deemed reliable
but not guaranteed.

PHOTO

Highlights ——

Welcome to an incredible home! This property is located in the heart of QUAIL RIDGE WHICH IS AN UPPER BRACKET EXCLUSIVE WOODED NEIGHBORHOOD KNOWN FOR FRIENDLY NEIGHBORS SELDOM MOVING UNLESS TRANSFERRED! The owners have meticulously maintained this fine home from the fabulous family room on the first floor to the beautiful master bedroom suite on the second floor and throughout the entire decorator's interior boasting classic eclectic lines.

The home offers very private wooded views of nature, deer, and wildlife. Every window overlooks beauty and scenery not often viewed in most home sites. This incredible QUAIL RIDGE location has easy access to both downtown Minneapolis as well as the airport, both of which are within 20 minutes driving time. Quail Ridge is an exclusive upper bracket area boasting pride of ownership and upper bracket properties.

Home ——

Approximate room sizes in this beautiful home:

- LIVING ROOM   16×18
- FAMILY ROOM   19×19
- KITCHEN   10×18
- INFORMAL DINING   9×13
- FORMAL DINING   11×13
- MASTER BEDROOM
  SUITE   18×19
- BEDROOM #1   16×11
- BEDROOM #2   13×14
- LOWER BEDROOM   16×14
- OFFICE   15×15
- PORCH   15×15
- WALKOUT FAMILY
  ROOM   19×18
- Taxes: 6000
- SQ. FEET: 1500 main floor
- TOTAL SQ. FT.: 3600
- YEAR BUILT: 1985
- LOT SIZE: APPROX. ½ ac.

Property ——

HIGHLIGHTS OF THIS FINE HOME INCLUDE: INCREDIBLE FIRST FLOOR FAMILY ROOM WITH CORNER BRICK FIREPLACE AND WALKOUT TO DECK O'LOOKING WOODS. BEAUTIFUL BUILT-IN WET BAR WITH CUSTOM SHELVING. WIRED FOR STEREO. WONDERFUL WINDOW TREATMENTS. THE CLASSIC KITCHEN IS A JULIA CHILD'S DELIGHT WITH A SENSATIONAL CENTER ISLAND. PLANNING DESK, INVERTED INFORMAL DINING AND EVERY CONCEIVABLE APPLIANCE PLUS FIRST FLOOR LAUNDRY ROOM. ACCENTED BY PERFECT PORCH, FULL LENGTH DECK ALL OVERLOOKING WOODED VIEWS PLUS BEAUTIFUL PARKLANDS AND TREMENDOUS TRAILS!! THE LOWER LEVEL IS A PARADISE IN PLEASURE. THE ACCENT IS ON FOUR-PERSON CUSTOM STEAM ROOM WITH PIPED IN MUSIC, SEPARATE GUEST QUARTERS, AND FANTASTIC WALKOUT FAMILY ROOM WITH ADJACENT LIBRARY HALL. IT'S A BEAUTY.

Open House Register

Name	Address	Phone	Comments

Open House Registration Card

To help me serve you better, please fill in the appropriate information below, and leave this card in the box provided. Thank you!

—BNP

Name: _____

Address: _____

Phone: _____

Children: _____ Boys, ages: _____

_____ Girls, ages: _____

Please give your comments on this home:

_____

_____

_____

_____

Are you:

☐ looking to move to this area?

☐ planning to buy a home soon?

☐ currently working with an agent?

Agent's name: _____

Agent's Phone: _____

☐ looking for something in this price range?

Desired range: _____

Please answer all that apply:

Is this the kind of home you are looking for? _____

_____

Are you selling your present home? _____

_____

How many homes have you seen already? _____

_____

Why are you moving at this time? _____

_____

When would be a good time to discuss your move in more detail? _____

_____

Comments: _____

_____

_____

_____

_____

Thank you for your time!

CHAPTER 12

Self-Marketing

Personal Brochure, Farming, Mailers

big deal
by "Lorayne n' Neil"

Self-Marketing

Self-marketing is extremely important. The way you sell yourself will be the deciding factor in how successful you will become.

You should have a brochure, card, and mailing system that enables a person who has no idea of who you are *to want you for who you are* by looking at your promotional items.

MANY REAL ESTATE AGENTS FEEL THAT A CARD IS ENOUGH.

A REAL ESTATE CARD REPRESENTING AN AGENT IS NOT ENOUGH.

Anybody and everybody has business cards made up telling who and what they are. As fast as they are given away, they are thrown away!

MAKE YOURSELF STAND OUT AND BE SET APART!

THE FOLLOWING ITEMS ARE ABSOLUTELY ESSENTIAL FOR ME:

1. *dignified business card* with picture (Dignified means *NOT* having a flashy card.)
2. *personal brochure* (single page or two-fold depending on layout)
3. *personal logo* (identification mark personalized to represent me)
4. *personalized stationery* with envelopes
5. personalized *postcards*
6. personalized *calendars*
7. personalized *notepads*
8. personalized market plan (see chapter on listings)
9. personalized *pencils* (could have a slogan on them such as: *"JUST SAY NO TO DRUGS."* Pencils are inexpensive, and adults can use and give them to their children.)
10. personalized *stamp* for my mapbook, MLS books, files, folders, and other real estate transactions

Have Everything Personalized

1. Business cards
2. Stationery
3. Envelopes
4. Newsletters
5. Calendars
6. Open House signs
7. Name riders for signs
8. Newspaper ads
9. Mailouts to farming areas
10. Thank you letters
11. Expired listing letters
12. For Sale By Owner letters
13. Grocery list handouts
14. Postcards
15. Personal brochure
16. Personal promotion book
17. Just listed cards
18. Just sold cards
19. Closing gift thank you cards
20. Personal notepads

Self-Marketing

This type of promotion involves *five* things.

1. Your business *card*
2. Your personal *brochure*
3. Your *notepads*
4. Your *stationery* and envelopes
5. Your *logo*

IT IS SO VERY IMPORTANT THAT YOU DEVELOP A STYLE THAT DEFINITELY SETS YOU APART FROM OTHER AGENTS.

You can find a niche that instantly tells others how good you are. Buyers and sellers will want to *seek you out*. Looking, reading, and surmising the information on one of the above items (numbers 1 through 4) and from the unique logo specifically designed for you will get you many buyers.

By implementing a *total design* for yourself by choosing a *logo* and *imprinting* it on your business card, brochure, *personal stationery*, envelopes and on all your notepads, you will set yourself apart with *distinction*.

People don't care how much you know until they realize how much you care about yourself and your business.

You must show that you are a professional with integrity, you are serious about getting results, yet you are unique and *creative in your image*.

THERE ARE MANY IDEAS FOR NOTEPADS.

1. Logo *at the top* with your name in block letters and phone only
2. Logo *centered* at top with block initials and phone only
3. Logo *off-centered* with your name and "to do today" slogan
4. Logo *off right center* and your name and phone with "must do" slogan
5. Name, logo, phone on *top three lines* and fourth line down, centered, "my personal list" slogan
6. Name, logo, phone, and "and so today . . ." slogan

Some agents feel that they would like a slogan *on their business card*. This is fine if you specialize in a specific area that enhances your real estate image overall. Be careful, though, **not to limit yourself!**

Sample:

BILL JONES
"SPECIALIST IN LAKE PROPERTIES"

JANE JONES
"VINTAGE HOMES SPECIALTY"

This can work for and against you. You must decide what *image* you want to create and put across.

I chose to work five surrounding, close in, areas. This enables me to have my office *centrally located* and near my home. When I receive referrals and business that bring me into an area that I normally do not work, I simply *call another office* that I am associated with, refer the client to another agent, and *ask for a referral fee*. In the long run, this will save much time, energy, and gas in learning an area that you are not comfortable with. The buyer can usually tell. A seller can tell also, if you do not know the convenient stores, parks and other points of interest close to the seller's home, not to mention properties that have sold and are active. It is best to create a plan, work the plan and refer business that you are not well versed in to another, more experienced agent. In the long run, you will receive *more referrals* and be able to continue to promote yourself in the areas of concentration that you know well.

Clues for Promoting Yourself

1. *MAKE A VIDEO OF YOURSELF.* Tell clients exactly what you are prepared to do for them and how you service your listings. Tell clients how you work with buyers. This is extremely effective in getting both buyers and sellers.

2. *HAVE A HIGH INVOLVEMENT* with the National Association. Join various organizations. Better yourself educationally. Keep a loose-leaf notebook with all the classes you have attended. This provides added credibility for your potential clients.

3. *SECURE AND KEEP TESTIMONIAL LETTERS* on yourself and the way you have done business. Use these letters as added insurance to give you a better image. Secure letters from clients who have enjoyed working with you. Keep them in an $8\frac{1}{2} \times 11$ loose-leaf notebook.

4. *MAT AND FRAME ALL AWARDS AND CERTIFICATES* that you obtain, and display them in your office. You may wish to put them in clear sheet protectors into a binder to use in securing a buyer or getting a listing.

5. *COPY* promotional ads that you have run, and keep in clear sheet protectors to use as listing tools.

6. *KEEP TRACK OF VARIOUS UNIQUE OPEN HOUSE DISPLAY ADS* and other tour ads that you have run. Use these to promote yourself. Keep in clear plastic in a separate loose-leaf binder.

7. *KEEP A SEPARATE PROMOTIONAL IDEAS BOOK.* This book would include different ways that you have promoted property, yourself, and your company.

8. *KEEP YOUR CAR WELL SUPPLIED* with all promotional items on yourself and your company at all times.

9. *Keep your briefcase and DAILY SCHEDULE BOOK UP TO DATE WEEKLY.* Make sure promotional tools on yourself, such as extra brochures, cards and highlight sheets are also included in your briefcase and daily schedule book.

10. *ON COMPANY LETTERHEAD COPY ANY NEWS ARTICLES* pertinent to your real estate area of expertise to use as a listing tool.

11. Stand at a mirror before you leave home each day and say *ONE NICE STATEMENT ABOUT YOURSELF.*

12. Plan a specific amount of money from your commissions that is to be used to *PROMOTE YOURSELF.* This is very important.

Twenty Ways to Promote Yourself

1. *Call specific neighbors* and tell the people that you have a client interested in their neighborhood. Ask if they happen to know of anyone selling.

2. *Promote your relocation service* by calling people and telling them that you have a free service to put people personally in touch with an agent in the neighboring state.

3. If you just listed a property, *call the neighbors* and tell them all about it. Ask if they know of anyone wanting to move into the neighborhood.

4. Pick a certain day of the week to *promote yourself* and make a certain number of *cold calls* in a select area of town. Tell them that you would be happy to come out to give them an idea of the value of their home at no charge whatsoever.

5. If you just sold a home, *call the neighbors* to tell them all about the property and ask them if they know of anyone wanting to move into the area.

6. *Hold an open house.* Call surrounding neighbors, using the reverse directory to tell them the time you are going to be there, and ask if they might know of anyone buying or selling.

7. *Call a FSBO.* Tell him or her that you work the area, specialize in the neighborhood, and very much would want to see his or her home.

8. *Call an expired listing.* Tell the owners that you are frustrated from trying to figure out why their home did not sell. Could you come over to see their home and give them your price opinion at no charge?

9. *Make up a newsletter* and send it to a *designated area*. Do this *four times* a year.

10. *Make use of the holidays* to express the holiday wishes to specific people in areas that you would want business.

11. *Cold call tenants in apartment buildings* in which the rent could be similar to the amount of a monthly mortgage payment with these explanations.

12. *Call your church parsonage* and ask if there have been any members who are new or are thinking of leaving.

13. *Talk to your mailman* and ask him if there have been any requests for change of addresses.

14. *Join a neighborhood* organization.

15. *Join a school* organization.

16. *Find a specific volunteer program* that would interest you. Always wear your name plate.

17. *Join a local health club* and ask if you could advertise in their newsletter.

18. *Join a specific church* and advertise in the roster.

19. *Advertise in your local neighborhood* newspaper.

20. *Send flyers out about yourself* to all your surrounding neighbors.

The more that you personally promote yourself, the more one person will talk to another person, and so on and so on, ABOUT YOU!

It is imperative that while in the real estate business you can and will and do eat, sleep and talk real estate to as many people as you meet.

Educational Ways to Promote Yourself

Once you have joined your local association, there are many different ***educational designations*** that you can acquire through the National Association of REAL ESTATE agents.

By acquiring additional knowledge beyond the necessary information that is needed to pass the real estate test, you become more and more professional and believable in the industry.

FOLLOWING ARE DEFINITIONS OF A FEW OF THE TITLES YOU CAN ACQUIRE:

GRI (GRADUATE REAL ESTATE INSTITUTE)

———— concentrated four day program
———— must pass an examination
———— completing the initial level of education

CCIM (CERTIFIED COMMERCIAL INVESTMENT MEMBER)

———— successful completion of *240 hours* of graduate level study
———— submission of a resume of qualified consummated transactions and/or
———— completing *eight hours* of comprehensive examination

CRE (AMERICAN SOCIETY OF REAL ESTATE COUNSELORS)

———— best source of knowledge to give home owners, investment people and those *developing*
———— CRE designation recognizes good judgment in all real estate matters, including integrity, experience, plus good client service
———— membership must be sponsored and/or membership by *invitation only*

IREM (INSTITUTE OF REAL ESTATE MANAGEMENT)

———— insures high standards of professional practice in property management
———— membership consists mostly of property managers and real estate managers
The CPM @ designation is achieved by conforming to the specific code of ethics and meeting all requirements for property management. This organization gives two award designations
1. AMO @ (Accredited Management Organization)
2. ARM @ (Accredited Residential Manager Recognition)

SIOR (SOCIETY OF INDUSTRIAL AND OFFICE REAL ESTATE AGENTS)

———— for people specializing in all phases of industrial and office real estate
———— offers full range of courses in office, industrial, and marketing
———— must complete course work for designation
———— also offers PRE (professional real estate executive) designation

Educational Organizations

REAL ESTATE AGENTS LAND INSTITUTE

——— helps members improve their image in marketing and all areas of land brokerage, agricultural and urban and recreational properties

——— this institute offers two programs:

1. The RLI (Land University), a designation program with monthly publications
2. The ALC (Accredited Land Consultant) earned by members who meet the standards and complete requirements

WOMEN'S COUNCIL OF REAL ESTATE AGENTS

——— the symbol is WCR

——— has referral and relocation programs (RRC)

——— gives award of LTG (Leadership Training Graduate) after completing four training courses and meeting the requirements

REAL ESTATE APPRAISAL SECTION

——— for real estate appraisers

——— newsletter and three national meetings

——— annual fee

——— CIPS (Certified International Property Specialist) for members with international interests

——— must complete several courses

——— must submit a resume

——— must have at least 100 elective points

——— can take courses at reduced tuition

——— listed in international directory

——— international newsletter

All of the above "distinctions" enable a real estate professional to show that he or she is constantly seeking to promote him- or herself not only through advertising in self-marketing, but in advertising in educational attributes also.

Postcard Promotional Ideas

"PEOPLE SPREAD GOOD RUMORS ABOUT ME"
(Take picture of yourself and have slogan under the picture on front.)

"OUTSTANDING IN HER/HIS FIELD"
(Take picture of yourself standing in a corn field.)

"I LOVE TO SELL HOMES"
(Take picture of yourself in front of a sold sign at the Capitol.)

"I MAKE THINGS HAPPEN"
(Take picture of you and sold sign in front of a house.)

"TOPS IN HIS/HER FIELD"
(Take picture of you standing in a corn field.)

"NOT JUST ANOTHER PRETTY FACE"
(Take six to eight various expressions of yourself. Shrink these down so as to have lots of little different pictures on the front of the postcard with the caption off to the side. You could also take enough pictures for the months of the year. For example, for January you could hold a Happy New Year sign, for February hold a valentine, for March hold a four-leaf clover, for April hold an Easter egg, and so on.)

"BARBARA'S BACK AND BETTER THAN EVER"
(Take picture of yourself looking over your shoulder and pointing to your back with caption below picture.)

"HOME IS WHERE THE HEART IS"
(Take a picture of a beautiful home and your picture with the caption below.)

"LET ME INTRODUCE MYSELF"
(Take a picture of yourself with the caption below it.)

"EXPERIENCE = RESULTS!"
(Divide the postcard in half. Make half with you holding a for sale sign and the other half with you holding a sold sign. Back of postcard can say, "Is your house too big? Too small? Let me know." Or the back can say "Why isn't your *For Sale By Owner* home selling? Call me today!"

"GOOD AT HIS/HER GAME . . . REAL ESTATE!"
(Picture of yourself on front of postcard and the above inscription on half of the back. Also say, "Whatever your game . . . when it comes to real estate call _____.")

"ALL STAR SERVICE"
(Picture of yourself on front of postcard with five stars.)

"BARBARA SELLS SERVICE"
(Picture of yourself on front of postcard holding a for sale sign with a sold sign on it plus your personalized name strip and phone numbers.)

If you are working as a husband and wife team

"SPOUSES SELLING HOUSES"
(This goes on the front of the card with both your pictures on half of the back. Also say, "Let us put a 'Sold' sign in your yard!")

"WHY WAIT ANY LONGER TO SELL YOUR HOME?"
(Picture of yourself in front of a home with a sold sign.)

"IF YOU'RE THINKING OF BUYING OR SELLING . . . NOW IS THE TIME!"
(Picture of yourself on front of postcard with above caption.)

"MAKE THE RIGHT MOVE!"
(Picture of yourself on front of postcard.)

"I FIND YOUR WAY HOME"
(Picture of yourself on front of postcard with caption below.)

"TOGETHER WE CAN DO IT"
(Picture of yourself on front with a for sale sign and sold on it.)

"PEOPLE ARE TALKING ABOUT"
(Picture of yourself with the above caption below it.)

"THE REASON PEOPLE ARE SATISFIED WITH BARBARA'S SERVICE IS . . . BECAUSE SHE IS NOT"
(Picture of yourself with above caption below it and next caption below that on the back.)

"BARBARA RISES TO EVERY REAL ESTATE OCCASION"
(Picture of yourself with above caption below.)

"WHEN IT COMES TO SELLING REAL ESTATE . . . I MAKE A STATEMENT!"
(Picture of yourself with above caption below it.)

"YOUR SEARCH IS OVER"
(Picture of yourself with above caption below picture.)

"I'M HERE FOR THE MOST IMPORTANT MOVE OF ALL . . . YOURS!"
(Picture of yourself with above caption below picture.)

"I'LL TEND TO DETAILS . . . YOU TEND TO PACKING"
(Picture of yourself with above caption below picture.)

"TO INCREASE YOUR HOME VALUE . . . MAY I SUGGEST AN ATTRACTIVE LAWN ORNAMENT . . ."
(Picture of yourself holding a for sale sign of your company.)

"A TOP PRODUCER IS ALWAYS TOO BUSY TO POSE FOR PICTURES . . ."
(Picture of an empty chair with a sold sign and your name rider.)

Do a Postcard with the *"Take Time"* Poem (Author Unknown)

Take time to think,
*   it is the source of power.*
Take time to play,
*   it is the secret of perpetual youth.*
Take time to read,
*   it is the fountain of wisdom.*
Take time to pray,
*   it is the greatest power on earth.*
Take time to love and be loved,
*   it is a God-given privilege.*
Take time to be friendly,
*   it is the road to happiness.*
Take time to laugh,
*   it is the music of the soul.*
Take time to give,
*   it is too short a day to be selfish.*
TAKE TIME TO WORK,
*   it is the PRICE OF SUCCESS.*

Self-Promoting with a Farm

Farming can be more profitable than most agents think and is often completely overlooked and forgotten.

Once an agent sets up his or her farm and develops a newsletter, the farm pretty much runs on automatic pilot.

A FARM CONSISTS OF THE FOLLOWING:

1. an area of homes that you would like to *WORK*

2. an area that has a consistent *turn over*

3. an area that has from 200 to 300 *homes* in it

4. includes 50 of your *closest neighbors*

5. an area that is *convenient* to both the office and home

TYPICAL SURVEY CONVERSATION OF A GEOGRAPHICAL FARM:

1. *"Hello Mr. Jones. I am from _____ Real Estate Company. I am doing a survey and am wondering if you plan on moving sometime within the next few years."*

2. *"May I ask when and if you are staying in the area?"*

3. Make specific notes to call back at a future time.

4. This will give you *leads for later*.

5. You can *use the CMA function* on your computer to find out the actives, solds and expireds in your farm.

How to Set Up a Farm

1. *Narrow down the area* that you want to work in and get the names and addresses of 200 to 300 people and phone them.

2. *Make up an introductory letter* that you will send out on your personalized stationery with your personalized logo.

3. *Make up a newsletter that is either:*

   — real estate information

   — garden and home information

   — food and recipe information

4. *Have holiday cards made up for:*

   Happy New Year
   St. Patrick's Day
   Valentines Day
   Mothers Day
   Lawn Care Calendar
   Back to School
   Fourth of July
   Halloween
   Thanksgiving
   Happy Holidays

5. *Start a farm book to:*

   — keep a list of all the homes that you have in your farm in the book

   — keep track of all the *mailers* that you send

   — keep track of every house you *list* in your farm

   — keep track of every house you *sell* in your farm

   — keep track of all *solds* in your farm

   — keep track of all *actives* in your farm

   — keep track of all *expireds* in your farm

6. *Send out mailers* at least *four times* a year to your farm.

7. *Send an update on the market* at least *three times* a year to your farm.

8. *Send out a community directory* to each homeowner in your farm with your picture on the front of it.

9. *Give grocery list pads* to homeowners in your farm.

10. *Give out handy service organizations for* spring cleanup, carpet cleaning, winter cleanup, window washing, and so on.

Fantastic Farming Ideas

1. Find a farm where there is at least a 5% *turnover yearly*.
2. *Buy a bulk rate stamp.*
3. Send out at least *twelve mailings a year*.
4. *Use gum labels.*
5. Send at least 300 to 500 *newsletters*, postcards or whatever when you mail.
6. *Go door to door* only if you have to.
7. Deliver at least *four doorhangers* a year.
8. *Call every home* in your farm at least three times a year.
9. *Personalize every piece of information* you send out.
10. *Go to* the community association *meetings* in your farm.
11. *Sponsor* a holiday *event* for your farm area.
12. *Give* people *gifts* whenever possible.
13. *Mail* your farm *just listed* and *just sold* cards.
14. *Send an annual letter* about yourself to your farm.
15. Keep a complete and *up-to-date farm book*.

Suggested Mailings

JANUARY	CALENDARS, PENCILS, PENS
FEBRUARY	VALENTINES, POSTCARDS
MARCH	ST. PATRICK'S DAY
APRIL	EASTER, SPRING, "FLOWER SEEDS"
MAY	MOTHERS DAY, CARNATIONS, FLAGS, MEMORIAL DAY
JUNE	DOORHANGERS, FATHERS DAY, PENS
JULY	FLAGS, BALLOONS, COUPONS FOR FREE MARKET ANALYSIS
AUGUST	LABOR DAY, BACK TO SCHOOL, MEMOS, MAGNETS
SEPTEMBER	BACK TO SCHOOL, PENCILS, PENS, NOTEPADS
OCTOBER	PUMPKINS, HALLOWEEN, LAWN BAGS
NOVEMBER	THANKSGIVING, TURKEYS, DRAWINGS
DECEMBER	FRUIT BASKETS, POINSETTIAS, MAGNETS

Magnet can say:

Trust your doctor: _____

         phone: _____

Confer with your lawyer: _____

         phone: _____

Rely on your accountant: _____

         phone: _____

Consult your
REAL ESTATE AGENT: _____

         phone: _____

Five-Star Promotional Ideas

1. *Send out color envelopes* with your photo imprinted in the top left hand corner.

2. *Get a stamp printed* with your signature written out.

3. *Use personal stationery* imprinted with odd-size envelopes.

4. *Type or write* short come-on *statements* such as:

   "Your home could be worth more than you know."
   "Are you sitting on a goldmine?"
   "You wouldn't believe the interest rates."
   "Do I have news for you!"

5. *Send* out *recipe postcards.*

   An excellent source is: **LESLIE NELSON**
                                 "SENDSATIONAL" CARDS
                                 801-225-9511

6. *Have a sticky label made up* with your logo, name, address, and a catchy slogan on it.

7. After a buyer's purchase, *send a scrapbook* with the picture of the home, school information, neighbors, and other useful information.

8. During the holidays, *buy a beautiful holiday music tape*, wrap it nicely, and bring to clients.

9. *Make up a brochure of favorite restaurants* at a glance, and put name, type of menu and phone number on $8^{1}/_{2} \times 11$ sheet with your picture and phone number.

10. Set up a five-star plan of action for yourself. Promote yourself in this fashion:

Five Stars:	super selling experience
Four Stars:	best value for your home
Three Stars:	accurate preparation of all documents
Two Stars:	perfectly professional
One Star:	unbelievable service

11. Sample of *yearly give-a-ways*:

> refrigerator magnets
>
> telephone pens and pencils
>
> notepads
>
> thank you notes
>
> litter bags
>
> lawn bags
>
> pumpkins, turkeys, fruits, nuts

12. *Unique mailers* are:

PUZZLE PIECES	Contact:	CHUCK BODE 16227 ELM ST. OMAHA, NE 68130 402-334-9156
BASEBALL CARDS	Contact:	B.L.C. ORDER FORMS P.O. BOX C TEANECK, NJ 07666 201-692-8228
SUPERSTAR PERSONAL PROMOTION IDEAS (hundreds of marketing ideas)	Contact:	MARKETING YOUR SCRAPBOOK HOWARD BRINTON SEMINARS 3013 NORTH 67TH PLACE DEPT. O SCOTTSDALE, AZ 85251 602-994-9874
MAGICARD (magnetic backing for cards)	Contact:	M.C. ENTERPRISES P.O. BOX 406 BUSINESS OWINGS MILLS, MD 21117 800-634-5523

Ways to Promote Yourself to Get Sellers

1. *Call your friends.*

2. *Give your business cards* and brochures out everywhere you go.

3. *Wear a lapel pin* with your name and company everywhere.

4. *Use a name rider* on all of your signs.

5. *Utilize walk-in office business.*

6. *Hold opens* at new subdivisions of homes being built.

7. *Get referrals* from other companies out of town.

8. *Get referrals* from business management.

9. *Get bank referrals* from foreclosures.

10. *Hold open houses.*

11. *Relist properties* that have expired with other companies.

12. *Ask other agents* if they want to split any business that they either can't keep up with or don't want to work.

13. *Call* on *FSBOs.*

14. *Get and work a farm* area.

15. *Get a referral service* started through networking with friends, church, organizations, and other places.

16. *Send newsletters*, postcards, and so on.

Ways to Promote Yourself to Get Buyers

1. *Call your friends.*

2. *Give your business cards* and brochures out everywhere you go.

3. *Wear a lapel pin* with your name and company everywhere you go.

4. *Call past clients* from any other business.

5. *Try to secure walk-in* business.

6. *Work with a new subdivision.*

7. *Get referrals* from personal contacts.

8. *Ask for referrals* from management.

9. *Utilize multiple listing service* and know your inventory for others that ask. Keep track of homes for sale.

10. *Hold open houses* and try to qualify good buyers to work with.

11. *Get a farm area* going and work it.

12. *Write good ads* with name, phone, and price of the property!

13. *Call tenants* in good apartment buildings.

14. *Send newsletters* and postcards out.

Perfect Prospecting

REAL ESTATE IS PROSPECTING!

From the day you begin to sell to the day you stop selling, *you are always prospecting.* The ways to find prospects are endless. However, here is a short list of some *great possibilities* for obtaining clients.

1. **Family contacts:** classmates, classmates' parents and relatives, teachers at school, husband's or wife's friends and colleagues at work

2. **Business contacts:** customers, clients, past and present employees, competition

3. **Personal contacts:** friends and their friends, their friends, and so on

4. **School contacts:** classmates, teachers, past and present fraternity and sorority kids

5. **Hobby contacts:** members of church clubs, men's and women's golf and other clubs, farm organizations, military organizations, hunting, fishing, bowling and photography

6. **Service contacts:** dry cleaner, grocer, butcher, druggist, mailman, newspaper man, plumber, dentist, physician

7. **Neighbor contacts:** this person knows this person who knows this person who knows this person

An important fact to remember here is that *prospecting is a lot like building a bridge.* You need certain things before you can cross over. In this case, you need *good, qualified* clients who will stay with you, thereby *bridging the gap* between the lookers and the buyers.

Personal Logo

HOW IMPORTANT IS A PERSONAL LOGO?

IT MAY VERY WELL BE THE ONLY THING THAT SETS YOU APART!

Real estate has become extremely technological. With all of the various roles the computer plays and all of the competition, being able to "one up" the other agent, sometimes when you have only that 30 to 60 second contact with a buyer and/or future seller at your open house, it will be your brochure and business card that may convince them to call you rather than someone else.

PERSONAL LOGOS DO NOT HAVE TO BE THAT EXPENSIVE.

EVERYONE HAS A DIFFERENT FLAIR AND A WAY ABOUT THEM THAT WOULD APPEAL TO DIFFERENT PEOPLE.

LEARN TO MAKE A STATEMENT WITH A PERSONAL LOGO.

If you golf, a golf logo may be the opener in a conversation with someone you just met. Maybe if antique cars are your hobby, find a picture of an antique car that you like and take it to a printer. You would be surprised at how economically you can design your own brochure and card.

Put the logo in the corner of your business card, brochure, and every mailer that you intend to send out from here on in.

Maybe as a woman you love fashion and design and clothing. Have a classic woman drawn by a print shop. The minimal expense for this is surprising.

Perhaps you play a favorite instrument or have a favorite sport. Even a caricature of yourself is very unique.

Choose something that is a conversation opener and allows another person to get an inside "peek" of you.

A chess knight is a great symbol for a "move ahead."

A top hat and gloves suggest "top drawer" service. A symbol of the sun shows that you have a sunny disposition.

Maybe you have a pretty picture of your city or your own home or something that interests you that sets you apart. Or even choose something that you have always wanted to have as a part of you.

> **SEE IT**
>
> **DESIGN IT**
>
> **MAKE IT HAPPEN**

Write your name differently, and let that be your signature.

Spend a little extra time in *looking at yourself from outside of yourself.*

Would you buy a home from you based on your personal promotion?

Finally, *consider having your picture taken beside something that is meaningful to you*, perhaps an antique car, perhaps a favorite pet. You may want a picture taken of you all dressed up and then have a cartoon or caricature made from that.

LOGOS LEAVE LASTING IMPRESSIONS.

Look at department stores. Look around your city now. How many different companies, restaurants, and businesses have added logos to their identity?

It is important to try to incorporate a logo into your look as the best professional in real estate.

A Promotion Idea . . .
Important Numbers Not to Forget

EMERGENCY _____

DRUG INFORMATION CENTER _____

FBI _____

POISON CONTROL _____

POLICE DEPARTMENT _____

Personal

DOCTOR _____

DENTIST _____

BABYSITTER: NAME: _____   PHONE: _____

                NAME: _____   PHONE: _____

NEIGHBORS: NAME: _____   PHONE: _____

                NAME: _____   PHONE: _____

Utility Service
CABLE TV   _____

ELECTRIC CO   _____

GAS CO   _____

RECYCLING   _____

WATER CO   _____

TELEPHONE   _____

GARBAGE   _____

County Numbers
PUBLIC SCHOOLS   _____

PUBLIC LIBRARY   _____

ANIMAL SHELTER   _____

COMMUNITY COLL.   _____

State Numbers
GOVERNMENT INFO   _____

TRAVEL & TOUR   _____

DRIVERS LICENSE   _____

FARMERS MARKET   _____

MUSEUM OF ART   _____

MUSEUM OF HIST   _____

VEHICLE REG   _____

Other
WEATHER BUREAU   _____

BETTER BUS. BUR   _____

GOODWILL IND   _____

RED CROSS   _____

SALVATION ARMY   _____

YMCA   _____

YWCA   _____

REAL ESTATE AGENT   _____

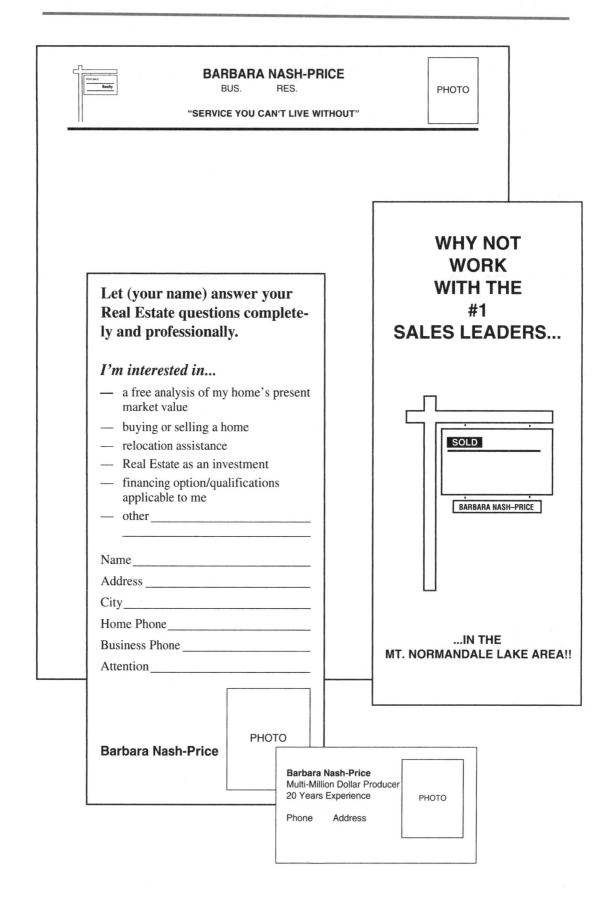

BARBARA NASH-PRICE

BUS.   RES.

"SERVICE YOU CAN'T LIVE WITHOUT"

PHOTO

**WHY NOT
WORK
WITH THE
#1
SALES LEADERS...**

SOLD

BARBARA NASH–PRICE

**...IN THE
MT. NORMANDALE LAKE AREA!!**

Let (your name) answer your Real Estate questions completely and professionally.

I'm interested in...

— a free analysis of my home's present market value

— buying or selling a home

— relocation assistance

— Real Estate as an investment

— financing option/qualifications applicable to me

— other_____

_____

Name_____

Address_____

City_____

Home Phone_____

Business Phone_____

Attention_____

PHOTO

Barbara Nash-Price

Barbara Nash-Price
Multi-Million Dollar Producer
20 Years Experience

Phone   Address

PHOTO

Put your name or initials on a special marking that represents you.

Put these on stationery, business cards, postcards, monthly mailers, thank you notes, birthday cards, etc. . .

Everyone becomes familiar with your "look" . . .

Testimonials...

"...Barbara is tops in her field, she goes that extra mile every time..."

"...We worked with Barbara after talking to 20 other agents, she was able to sum it all up and show us results fast..."

"...We needed an agent that was the best all the way way around. Barbara kept us up on everything, we had a great partnership. She's the best agent in the field..."

Barbara Nash-Price

PHOTO

Bus. (612) 000-0000
Res. (612) 000-0000
Car (612) 000-0000

Outside of Brochure

Barbara Nash-Price

The Professional...

- Seventeen (17) years full-time experience
- "Multi-Million" Dollar Producer
- Member of Minneapolis Board of REALTORS
- Top Outgoing Referral Associate from 1979 through 1989
- Specialist in Edina-Bloomington-Mpls. Lakes Areas

The Person...

- Empathetic/Understanding...Barbara has experienced the drama/trauma of moving families and helping them establish a new life. She fully analyzes and shows how your home and neighborhood will meet the physical and emotional needs of the buyer.

- Supportive...Barbara was Co-Chairman of St. Joseph Home for Abused Children and received an award for community involvement. She volunteers for her childrens' schools and was the first woman to change legislation for Victims Rights in the Sate of Minnesota. She has also been Secretary of her Home Owners Asssociation in Forest Haven.

- Knowledgeable...Barbara continually updates her skills through courses, seminars, and synergistic interaction with other REALTORS. For seventeen years she has been a Twin Cities tour guide—she know the cities.

The Company

BNP Realty has fantastic financial and legal resources. It is large enough and small enough to respond to your needs now. Its new four-color Photo Trieve will dramatically and quickly expose your home to hundreds of buyers.

And YOU...

PARTNERS...you and Barbara share joint responsibility. Barbara works with "Only Qualified" people throughout the year–in the joint decision to be client and agent, you and she agree to communicate honestly. Barbara's success in selling has been marked in large part through what is known in the trade as **"REFERRALS"**...

Inside of Brochure

CHAPTER 13

Time to Close
Listing and Selling

big deal
by "Lorayne n' Neil"

Time to Close

There are three types of closings:

1. Closing on a *buyer to buy*

2. Closing on a *seller to sell*

3. *Closing time* (close in escrow or settlement time)

All *three types of closings* require the agent to remember that:

1. the buyer needs a home,

2. the seller needs his money, and

3. the closing must go smoothly for the agent to get his or her money.

I have learned *three very important things* in the real estate business.

1. *Be ready to close* all the time.

2. Every person is *ready to buy* if they are looking.

3. *Be ready to list* and sell a house on any given day.

Regardless of whether or not it is a buyer you are closing on or a seller that you are closing on, or the actual closing (some people prefer to say "close in escrow") that you are *going to,* you always need one main ingredient:

BALANCE.

You should try to have good timing in knowing when to "talk it up" and when to "clam up." No transaction is ever complete until the buyer and seller mutually agree to *sign on the dotted line,* the keys are exchanged, and everyone has shaken hands.

When they can't buy that house right now because "THEY JUST HAVE TO THINK ABOUT IT A LITTLE WHILE LONGER"

KNOW WHEN TO CLOSE.

Thesaurus of Stall Phrases and How to Handle Them

CLOSING = OVERCOMING ALL OBJECTIONS

CLOSING ON A LISTING

"WE DON'T LIKE SIGNS IN OUR FRONT YARD."

"That's fine. We can market the home through MLS and eliminate the sign for now." (Check in a few weeks for a sign.)

"WE DON'T WANT TO GIVE OUT A KEY."

"That's understandable. We can set up appointments for now if you are both home at different times, and I'll make a note to tell the secretary."

"WE HAVE SOMEONE OF OUR OWN WHO IS INTERESTED."

"Fine, let's put his or her name as an exclusion at the top of this listing contract for ten days."

"WE DON'T JUMP INTO THINGS."

"I understand that, and I feel that we should spend a little more time discussing your objections and how important the timing is now."

"WE HAVE A FRIEND IN THE BUSINESS WHO IS GOING TO GIVE US SOME ADVICE."

"*I realize how easy it sounds sometimes*, however timing is everything, and when you have an interested buyer he or she needs an agent who will get the contract signed immediately."

"WE DON'T WANT TO PAY A BROKERAGE FEE."

"*I can see from your point of view* that it is a lot of money. However, when you are selling probably one of the most expensive investments in your life, you would want a professional to help handle offers that are coming in. Most times the brokerage fee can be absorbed. Many buyers, knowing that the seller is marketing his own home, automatically take the commission off too."

"MY ATTORNEY WILL HANDLE THE PAPERWORK FOR US."

"*An attorneys is a very valuable asset.* However, sometimes in getting all the paperwork to the attorney and waiting, you wind up waiting for the buyer to just plain change his mind. Timing is everything in the real estate business. If a buyer sleeps on it, he may not sleep in it."

"WE HAVE A FRIEND IN THE BUSINESS WHO IS GIVING US SOME ADVICE."

"*It's wonderful to have people who you can fall back on.* However, when an offer is coming in from a buyer, there are many considerations that go into deciding if the buyer is *even qualified* to make an offer. An agent that is representing you knows, on the spot, how to handle difficult situations while a friend would have to be called. In this time, the buyer might also cool on the property."

"WE'RE NOT GOING AHEAD UNTIL WE TALK IT OVER TOGETHER TONIGHT."

"That is perfectly understandable. I meant to show you this ad that I have written up for this Sunday's open house if that agrees with you. And I would like to show you how this lockbox works on your front door." (At this point you try to change the subject, yet become more and more involved in getting the listing signed tonight.) "You see, Mr. and Mrs. Seller, if we get our ad in by tomorrow morning, we have a good chance at getting the best buyers that are in *the market today*."

"WE CAN SELL THE HOME OURSELVES AND SAVE THE COMMISSION."

"*Yes, it certainly appears that no one would better represent a home* than the owners themselves, but sometimes it is likened to "not seeing the forest for the trees." You become too close to the situation. I know as an agent I tried to sell my own home and had to turn it over to another agent when I became incensed over a potential buyer's dislike for my kitchen wallpaper. The buyer wound up leaving my house in a huff. It is very difficult to put distance between the would-be buyer and yourself. It also is uncomfortable for you to ask a would-be buyer how much money he makes and if he has ever claimed bankruptcy. This would be difficult to ask a buyer up front."

"WE ENJOY TALKING WITH YOU, HOWEVER, WE FEEL WE SHOULD GIVE ANOTHER COMPANY THE CHANCE TO SELL IT FIRST."

"*I understand this completely and feel that they are a fine firm.* I wanted to show you the highlight description that I am going to put on the supplement sheet. How do you feel about having a tour for all of our agents to come through. And I might serve a light lunch; this usually attracts many of the top producers in our company who have clients and relocation referrals coming up."

"WE DON'T WANT ANYTHING TO DO WITH REAL ESTATE PEOPLE!"

(*These people have probably been burned by a company before.* They need to talk it through.) "I understand completely how you feel and have had situations before in which the sellers have been hesitant until meeting with me and seeing how they can benefit from my presentation program and my techniques. Do you like the ad that I have written on your property?"

"I DON'T CARE IF THE HOUSE ISN'T WORTH IT. I NEED MORE MONEY."

"*It's important to realize all the dollars that we can save for you,* and in doing this we try to price the property for the best market price possible without overpricing it and helping other homes to sell rather than yours. It's a fact that buyers are more likely to make full-price offers on homes priced right before making low offers on homes too high-priced."

"WE DON'T WANT TO BE TIED UP WITH ANY REAL ESTATE COMPANY FOR A LONG TIME."

"*We understand this completely* and feel that we should write into the listing agreement that the seller has the option of terminating this contract at any given time with 24 hours notification."

"WE ARE THINKING OF LISTING WITH ANOTHER COMPANY THAT HAS A MUCH LOWER COMMISSION THAN YOUR COMPANY."

"*That's perfectly understandable* to think that way as a seller. However, in the real estate business, the homes that are sold from the Multiple Listing books are most often the ones with competitive commissions . . ."

"THERE IS NOTHING YOU CAN DO FOR ME THAT I CAN'T DO TO SELL THE HOUSE MYSELF."

"*I can see how most of it may appear to be simple.* However, getting a qualified buyer to pay top price for your home is a very hard part of the transaction, not to mention the tremendous amount of follow-up that is entailed. Then there is the fact that most prospects calling on owners are usually investors or bargain hunters."

"WE JUST WANT TO THINK IT OVER ANYWAY."

"*There really isn't anything that you would know differently tomorrow* than you know tonight. However, there might be that one buyer coming into town tomorrow that this home would be perfect for, and we would miss out. By letting me get started, you would get a good night's sleep."

"ANOTHER AGENT SAID THAT WE CAN GET A LOT MORE FOR OUR HOME."

"*Whatever you do in regard to listing, make sure that you look at all the credentials* rather than just who will price your home for the most money. Too often in our industry an agent will "buy a listing," which means he or she will list an unrealistic price just to get the listing.

"I DON'T REALLY NEED YOUR SERVICES, I ALREADY HAVE A BUYER."

"Unless the buyer has given you an earnest money check and signed a purchase agreement, you still would want to market the home. *We can exclude that buyer for a period of ten days.*"

"LOTS OF AGENTS ARE WITH MULTIPLE LISTING SERVICE. WHY SHOULD I JUST LIST WITH YOU?"

"Because the chance for a successful sale relatively soon is determined, in large part, by the agent's know-how, success in the business, and dealing with *a successful company that knows and works your area.*"

"WE STILL PLAN ON LISTING WITH ANOTHER FIRM."

"That's fine. I want to take this opportunity to show you my *personal promotion book.* It has all the information about my successes in your area and those surrounding. I also have some fine samples of my advertising here that I think would interest you."

"WE ARE TOO BUSY TO TALK WITH YOU ABOUT LISTING."

"*I would very much like to help you* in that area so that you can get on with your own interests and I can absorb the real estate problems for you."

"YOUR COMMISSION IS WAY TOO HIGH!"

"*I would want to be fair with you* in explaining that if there were two properties that I was showing and I had the opportunity of showing either, I would show the one with the most competitive fee rather than a low-cut fee."

"THIS IS A BAD TIME TO SELL PROPERTY"

"*There really is no bad time to buy and sell property.* No one is inventing more land and real estate will always be a steady, good investment. We only need one buyer."

"I KNOW AS MUCH ABOUT REAL ESTATE AS YOU DO."

"It's refreshing to see someone with knowledge of real estate. However, you would want to have the greatest exposure possible for your home, and multiple listing service can provide that for you. Along with that fact, all *my time is dedicated to finding buyers,* and that's just what you want."

"I DON'T TRUST REAL ESTATE PEOPLE."

"I agree with you that there are some unethical people in the real estate business. Like any profession there is good and bad. However, I am sure you have heard of *our firm and the fine reputation we have.* I would be happy to provide you with clients I have that have been extremely happy with the service I have provided."

"I WANT TO BUY A HOME FIRST BEFORE WE LIST."

"For most people not in real estate that probably sounds like the best method. However, it is far easier sometimes to find a new home before selling the old. We can achieve both objectives by *putting a clause in the listing* giving you the option of finding a property within the next 60 days while the listing is in effect. We call this a contingency clause."

"WHY DOESN'T YOUR COMPANY SHOW MY HOME AS MUCH AS OTHER COMPANIES?"

"I can see how you might be confused, however, I expect to give you overall marketing through listing with me rather than showings. I appeal to *all markets for total exposure.*"

"WE DIDN'T PLAN ON BUYING A HOME SO FAST . . . WE WANTED TO LOOK AROUND."

"I understand how you feel. Are you aware of the fact that most people find the home they like fairly quickly? Then they have a problem finding fault with it. I wouldn't want you to miss this one and then *compare it to all the others we continue to look at.*"

"WE DIDN'T BRING OUR CHECKBOOK WITH US."

"That is easy to remedy. We always have *blank notes* just for this situation. We can redeem your check upon acceptance of the offer."

"THE ONE BEDROOM IS JUST TOO SMALL."

"*Let's take another look at the property* and see that overall, for the most part, everything is workable. I think a few feet in the bedroom can probably be dealt with."

"IT'S FIVE THOUSAND DOLLARS MORE THAN WE WANTED TO GO."

"If you look at the fact that most people take a vacation once a year and spend five thousand dollars . . . but whether you vacation or not, the difference amounts to about $1.50 a day. This way you can have the home you want and perhaps save the difference in another minor area."

"WE WANT TO KEEP LOOKING; THIS IS HAPPENING TOO FAST."

"*I understand the feeling.* Most buyers get a little jittery when they find a perfect home so quickly. The nice feature about finding a home right away is that you can start planning, placing your furniture, and making arrangements for moving now rather than having that worry in the future."

"WE WENT THROUGH THE HOME SO FAST THAT WE CAN'T REMEMBER . . ."

"*That can be easily remedied.* We can go back, look at the house again, and go slowly through it."

"WE WANT OUR FAMILY TO SEE IT BEFORE WE DO ANYTHING."

"That's understandable, and we can put a clause in the contract that would say 'this offer is subject to inspection and approval of buyer's parent on or before _____.' " (Try very hard not to have it in writing though. It's best just to say that you will *arrange to show the parents* the home within the next few days as soon as everything is consummated.)

"IT'S EXACTLY WHAT WE WANT EXCEPT IT NEEDS DECORATING, AND WE DON'T REALLY WANT TO DO THAT."

"*Sometimes it's important to see the value in a property 'before the after'.* You can realize a greater profit by purchasing a property when you, yourself, can participate in the improvements rather than paying for them."

Presenting the Offer

When calling a seller to present a purchase agreement, the presentation is the key to a successful closing. *Never tell the seller what the offer is on the phone.*

Most agents like to have an ideal setting. Some agents feel that it is best to have the sellers come to the office and conference there with both agents present and a professional feel to the presentation.

This is not always possible. Often the sellers want the agent or agents present at their own home, and as is the case for many sellers they are set on a certain price, then the scenario becomes more difficult from the onset.

Presenting a purchase agreement has always been the ultimate challenge for me. I prefer a good challenge, and I prefer to have all my bases covered so to speak from the beginning.

If the above is the case, and you must deal from the onset with a difficult seller and go to a home where you know there is a large family, dog and noise, *I try to do the following:*

I ask if it is all right that we use a table that we could all sit around. I know there are little children at home, before I come, so I make sure to bring coloring books, which our company gives away for promotion, and crayons. I then proceed to tell the sellers that I know they would want all of us to be able to concentrate with our undivided attention to this matter and that it would be necessary to be uninterrupted for approximately 45 minutes to one hour. If possible, I try to phone the seller ahead with this information about the children and tell them I will be bringing some coloring tools. This enables the seller the opportunity of perhaps getting additional help for the children ahead of time or at least preparing the children so that they are not interrupted. When the seller has made us comfortable and seated us around a table (even a coffee table would work), there can be three possible types of scenarios, and I will go over each of them:

1. You have an offer on your OWN LISTING

2. You have an offer from ANOTHER AGENT

3. You have a CONTINGENT offer

Scenario 1
You Have an Offer on Your Own Listing

You have arrived at the seller's house and they invite you in to sit down. (Never accept an alcoholic beverage if offered.) They do have a dining room table that they have cleared off, and they ask you to go ahead and present your offer. The people present are you and your sellers (husband and wife).

You immediately begin by putting the entire folder in front of you on the table, removing the earnest money check, and putting it in the center of the table.

You begin to explain to the sellers, "First I would like to tell you a little bit about the buyers." (You met them today at your open house, and it is important for you to establish some sort of rapport between the buyers and the sellers, something that will identify them with each other.) You explain to Mr. Seller that Mr. Buyer noticed his large muskie hanging on the wall in the den since *he also* is a fisherman when he isn't working. However, his job transfer has brought him here, and he is really looking forward to coming to the Twin Cities. He has heard so many good things about it. You go on to tell the sellers that you would like to explain what the buyers do, where they come from, what line of work they are in, and what their financial status is. You also explain that you have spent some time *preapproving* them with a loan officer that you called at home. This loan officer feels that these particular buyers look very good.

THIS IS A VERY IMPORTANT POINT TO MAKE.

You go on to say that the buyers *must buy this weekend*, they said. Out of all the homes that they have seen, *"Yours is the one that they decided to write an offer on!"*

After thoroughly going through the Buyers Information Sheet, you say that you are going to proceed with the purchase agreement, and you would appreciate it if they would follow along because this should be familiar to them in the sense that you have given them a sample purchase agreement to read over when you listed the property.

You begin at the beginning and take special note to mention the earnest money which is sitting in the middle of the table. (Unless it is absolutely urgent, *I do not take notes in place of a check.*) I read over the purchase agreement carefully and write down the key points of interest that I feel the seller is taking special point to note.

1. *Earnest* money
2. *Contingent* or *non*contingent
3. *Price* of property
4. *Date* of closing
5. *Inclusions* in the contract
6. Division of the *taxes*
7. Type of *financing*

8. Any *points* included

9. *Tax* proration and special exclusions

10. Date of *possession*

11. *Additional* contingencies

12. Inspections

I go on to list the above points, and after reading over the entire offer **I ask the seller**,

"HOW DO YOU FEEL ABOUT THIS OFFER?"

(I *do not* offer my opinion until I hear what the seller has said. Sometimes even low offers surprisingly will be accepted. Learn when to keep still and when to offer an opinion.)

If the seller has a problem with the price and the terms, such as points, I will list them opposite what the offered terms are. If there is a great deal of discrepancy, I say, "Mr. and Mrs. Seller, I feel that the buyer made an attempt at purchasing this property for some *specific* reasons."

I list the reasons that the buyer has given me. Remember that if you have written a *low offer*, be prepared to back up the offer with good reasons substantiated by the buyer, such as *comparables in the area, internal condition, repairs and/or additions*. All of these things are going to be crucial at the offer presentation if the offer has come in low and there is a wide gap.

Go over the points in the purchase agreement that are the biggest objections.

Finish the purchase agreement by saying,

"You may do one of three things, Mr. and Mrs. Seller":

1. *ACCEPT* this purchase agreement,

2. *REJECT* this purchase agreement, or

3. *COUNTER* this purchase agreement.

However, it is considered to be in good taste to resolve this one way or another *before I leave* because the buyer has been good enough to put his offer *in writing*."

Scenario 2
You Are the Listing Agent and an Offer Is Made by Another Agent

You call the sellers, identify yourself, and tell them that *"from an appointment that was recently made,"* a buyer came through with another agent and has written an offer with his or her *own agent*.

You first ask the sellers if it is convenient for them to come to your own office. This is the best *neutral setting*. Should this be agreeable, you then proceed to reserve a conference room for the other agent, your sellers, and yourself.

WHEN THE OTHER AGENT ARRIVES, I USUALLY:

1. ask the other agent to *tell* us a little bit *about his or her buyers.*

2. ask the other agent if he or she has *prequalified the buyer* and if so, record on the file the name and phone number of the lender.

3. ask the other agent to please put the *earnest money in the center* of the table.

4. proceed to ask the other agent if he or she wants *me to present the purchase agreement.*

5. If he or she says it does not matter, I say that *I would be happy to present it,* and I take it from there.

6. If he or she wishes to present the purchase agreement, *I take out my legal-size notepad* and begin to list the items that are most important, including:

   a. Earnest *money*

   b. *Price* of property

   c. *Date* of closing

   d. *Inclusions* in the contract

   e. *Contingent* or noncontingent

   f. Division of the *taxes* and specials

   g. Type of *financing*

   h. *Points* included

   i. Date of *possession*

   j. *Exclusions*

   k. Any additional *contingencies*

   l. *Supplement* pages

7. When I have gone over the offer from the other agent and clarified the points of agreement or conflict, I ask the other agent the following questions.

   a. How important is it for your buyer to *close on this date*? (if there is a discrepancy in closing dates)

   b. Does your buyer have the means to *put down more earnest money*?

   c. How did you and your buyer arrive at the *price of the contract*?

   d. Are certain items that you have written in *as inclusions very important*? I would like to add that these items may or may not have been on the listing agreement.

   e. If this is a *contingent offer* (subject to the sale of another property), I ask to see a picture of the subject property it is contingent on, a *copy of the listing contract*, if it's *listed* at this time, and a list of any homes for sale in the immediate area of the contingent property. How marketable does that contingent home appear to be? Is it either a *48 or 72 hour contingency*, so I can continue to market the listed property until this particular buyer can make his or her offer noncontingent?

   f. I prefer to sell a home to a buyer where the *taxes are usually prorated* from the date of closing. This means that a buyer pays from the time that he closes, and the seller pays up to closing.

g. *What kind of financing* is involved? Has the buyer been qualified for the down payment, monthly payment, points included, and so on?

h. If there are points included, I try to look at the offer from all aspects. If the offer has come in full price, the buyer is conventional, and the seller is asked to pay a couple of points, it's *time to negotiate*! I try to remind the seller that the offer is extremely good, the buyer is well qualified. If you do not want to pay all the points, is there a chance that you would be willing to *split the points*? I also remind the seller that this buyer looks exceptionally well-qualified and the contract is *noncontingent*.

i. THIS POSSESSION IS A MOOT POINT. Possession depends on two things: where is the seller going or has gone? Does the buyer have a lease, or closing date on his or her own house already? Try to remind the seller of the importance of an offer that is "in hand," *noncontingent*, and the importance of the qualifying factor in the case. Try to show the seller, through the other agent, that the buyer truly wants to be accommodating too!

j. I try to take care of exclusions ahead of time, but if at the last minute during an offer presentation the seller says, "I forgot to tell you I am going to exclude the fireplace screen because it was a gift and a very old antique, but we will replace it with another," I ask, "How important to the buyer is this exclusion?" *Remember that this must be in writing.*

k. *ADDITIONAL CONTINGENCIES:* There are going to be many cases in which the purchase agreement is subject to, or contingent upon the *attorney's opinion, the wife or husband, or seeing the home inspection.* Should the offer be contingent on an inspection first?

In these cases, make sure the rest of the offer is favorable. Put a date in for the contingency removal. For example, "This offer is contingent upon the successful approval of buyer's attorney on or before (date)."

l. There often may be supplements to the contract. In these cases, read them over carefully and make sure that any type of inspection report or survey report has a date upon completion for it to be made. There should be a time allotment for finalization. Should the offer be subject to a survey?

Scenario 3
You Have a Contingent Offer

CONTINGENT OFFERS are sometimes the best offers if you can take care of all the loose ends and manage to successfully represent the buyer at the other end of the situation too.

A **contingent offer** *is often contingent upon the buyer having a house to sell first.*

Often this home is not even listed yet!

A *contingent offer* may also be contingent upon approval by another individual, such as a husband, wife, partner, parent, appraiser, inspector, or someone who holds a vested interest.

Sometimes the offer is contingent upon the buyer getting approval for financing and/or securing the funds for the down payment by a particular date.

Often an offer is "contingent upon the buyer being relinquished from lease obligation."

CONTINGENCIES NEED ONE CRUCIAL THING:

A *DATE* at which time they are *CANCELED* or *REMOVED*.

Should you have a *contingent offer* in which the buyer has a home to sell, you have just met him or her at an open house, and perhaps have not had the opportunity to develop much of a rapport yet, try to:

—— *view the buyer's* home as quickly as possible,

—— *do a CMA* on the buyer's home for your own satisfaction,

—— *ask the buyer* what he or she expects to be getting from the sale of his or her home, or

—— *have the buyer* list his or her home simultaneously with you as you prepare the purchase agreement.

Sample Offer Presentation

THIS IS A SAMPLE OF THE WAY AN OFFER WAS PRESENTED FROM START TO FINISH:

THE PROPERTY DISCUSSED HEREIN WAS A LARGE WALK-OUT RANCH STYLE.

Origination: owner had come through an open house of mine.

—— I did a CMA for her and she insisted we *list the property high*.

—— The home has currently been listed for over *three months*.

—— There have been *39 showings* and *five open houses*.

—— We have had *three price reductions*.

—— *Eight days* after the third price reduction, we received the following. This is the way that the *offer presentation* went from start to finish, at which time it was finally *accepted*.

Saturday

3:00 P.M. I have just checked my phone mail which I do *every few hours*). An agent from another company has called to tell me that she has an offer on my property.

3:15 I called the seller to ask *when we could present the offer*, and the seller, a single woman, asks if we could come over to her home at 5:00. I called the other agent to confirm.

4:50 *I arrived at the seller's home to present the offer*. I asked to sit at the kitchen table and waited for the other agent to arrive. I brought the seller all of the appointment slips for the property and told her that the consensus of the agents showing the home thus far was that the home needed a lot of work, and if another agent were to write an offer on the home, the work needed would probably be reflected in the offer written.

The property was currently listed for $238,900.

5:00	The other agent arrived. We all sat down at the table with the seller. Coffee, soda, and water were offered. I asked the other agent to tell us a little about the buyer. As she told us about the buyer, she put an earnest money check in the center of the table. The check was made out to the **listing company**, and the amount was for $3,000. I reviewed the offer for a moment, and the agent asked if I would present the offer.
5:15	I explained the offer to the seller and the offering price was $215,000. I began *a net sheet*.
5:25	The seller asked to *talk with me alone*. The other agent momentarily waited in the living room.
5:40	The seller said that the offer was *ridiculous*. She couldn't possibly make it with this amount, and she wanted to counter at full price. I explained that we had a much better chance of keeping this very good buyer if we *meet the buyer in the middle*. I explained that the buyer looked excellent because:
	1. his offer was NONCONTINGENT and
	2. he had already been *prequalified* with good credit.
6:15	*The seller listened to me* and countered the offer at $228,000
6:30	*I called the other agent* with the counter.
7:00	*The agent called back* with counter from her buyer at $220,000.
7:15	I called seller *who countered back again* at $224,000. *"I'm not giving the house away,"* she said.
7:30	*I made another call to the buyer's agent.* The agent thinks that the buyer stood firm on $220,000, however, she would let me know shortly.
7:45	*The buyer's agent called back.* The buyer came up to $221,000. "That's it," she said.
8:00	*I called the seller* and said, "The buyer really likes your home. However, he has seen many properties now and feels that he is paying a good price for a home that needs a tremendous amount of interior work. Another issue that we will have to deal with is the *appraisal. Your home is the biggest one on the block.* The appraiser will take this into consideration, and may come in low with the appraisal. Why not take a few minutes to reassess the situation and call me back. I know that the money is tight. *You could have a large estate sale* because you wanted to sell so many things. That would help a lot too. I'll wait for your call."
8:45	The seller called back and said, *"I'll take $222,000 and not one penny less."*
9:00	*I called the other agent* and informed her that the counter now *stood firm* at $222,000.
9:30	The buyer's agent called me back and told me, *"Congratulations, you have a deal.* I'm going to the buyer's home to get the changes signed, and I will drop the papers off at *your home mailbox shortly."*

9:45	I called the seller. The seller was nervous now. She didn't know why she accepted such a low offer, but she said she guessed it was all right. *She insisted that I go over to her house with the papers to sign before the day was finished.* I told her I would be there between 10:45 and 11:00.
10:50	I arrived at the seller's home.

1. *She signed the counter, and we had a deal at $222,000.*

2. *I left her with a copy of all papers she signed.*

3. *I took the highlight sheets I made up on the home with me.*

4. *I left the lockbox on the door for the appraiser.*

5. *I put a sold sign in the yard.*

11:30	I called the office message center to leave a message for the secretary that the property had been sold. (Some agents continue to show until the buyer's mortgage is approved.)
12:00	I turned out the lights and went to bed.

ANOTHER FINE DAY IN REAL ESTATE ADVENTURELAND!

Sample Problem Closings

1. *SELLER DIDN'T AGREE TO LEAVE THE LAMP IN THE LIVING ROOM.*

   It wasn't attached but it was on the wall, and the buyer thought it was staying. Buyer is visibly upset upon seeing this at the *final inspection* the day before closing. (Always make sure that you allow your buyer a final inspection before he or she closes on the home.)

   AGENT TELLS BUYER THAT HE WILL CONTACT THE SELLING AGENT, AND THEY WILL WORK OUT A SITUATION WITH WHICH EVERYONE WILL BE SATISFIED.

   Agent calls listing agent and decides upon price of lamp, and whether seller would consider bringing it back. Would agent be interested in splitting the difference. If not, it becomes a case of whether or not you care about having the repeat business from that client based on how happy he was with you.

2. *SELLER DECIDED TO STAY AN EXTRA DAY, AND EVERYONE HAS AL-READY MADE ARRANGEMENTS WITH MOVING COMPANIES.*

   When it comes right down to it, there's not really a lot one can do. It's best to talk it over with the agents, and if there is still no compromise, volunteer your own time to help or to contribute a day's worth of food to help things go more smoothly. Always keep clients aware that you would do most anything to keep the transaction running smoothly.

3. *BUYERS WANT TO BRING THINGS OVER AND START PUTTING THEM IN THE SELLER'S GARAGE.*

   Not a good idea. Seller is responsible until closing for anything stolen or damaged, even if buyer gets his or her own insurance. It tends to complicate the situation. Best to wait until closing.

4. *THERE IS A LIEN AGAINST THE PROPERTY WHICH THE CLOSER FAILED TO DISCOVER. CLOSING MUST BE POSTPONED AND EVERYONE MUST BE NOTIFIED.*

   Again, this is actually out of your hands. Remember though, it is most important to *keep abreast of the mortgage lender to see how the loan is progressing.* Stay close to the telephone and reconfirm to buyers and sellers the fact that you are willing to hand carry or deliver any documents necessary to consummate the transaction. You may have to reschedule times and dates. Stay calm and assured that all will go well. Never buy into anger or frustration. *A function of your job is to eliminate hassles that frustrate the buyer or seller.*

5. *THE FURNACE BROKE THE DAY BEFORE THE CLOSING.*

   Most contracts read that the seller is responsible for all mechanics of the home to be in proper working order at time of closing. It will have to be fixed or replaced. Stay on top of everything, relating the status back and forth between buyer and seller.

6. *AT THE FINAL WALK THROUGH, THE BUYER SEES THAT THE DOORBELL IS NOT WORKING. THERE WAS NO MENTION OF THIS PROBLEM BEFORE.*

   The seller will have to fix doorbell.

7. *THE SELLER WANTS TO CLOSE THE DAY BEFORE THE ACTUAL CLOSING DATE, AND THE BUYER WANTS TO CLOSE TWO DAYS LATER. NO ONE WANTS TO BUDGE.*

It's always best to leave the decision on which day is actually available in *the hands of the closer*. Sometimes it puts weight on a delicate balance between the buyer, the seller, and who should really be in charge if it has to be changed.

8. *THE MORTGAGE WAS PAID OFF, BUT NOT RECORDED. THE CLOSING IS HELD UP UNTIL PROOF OF PAY OFF IS SECURED.*

Not much you can do here except *make sure from the onset* (if you are the lister) that the mortgage satisfaction is intact and perhaps try to check with the other agent if it is not your listing. Keep the peace, and again, volunteer your time to get any and all documents transported as quickly as possible.

9. *BUYERS AND/OR SELLERS WERE UNHAPPY WITH SETTLEMENT COSTS AND FEEL THAT THEY WERE MISREPRESENTED.*

This is so *important* because it involves their *trust in you. You must be sure that the figures you gave them were accurate.* Also check with the loan officer to make sure that the buyer figures were what he expected at closing. Check with the closer beforehand and have him or her give you final payoff figures for the seller. (These should have been given to seller a day or two before closing.)

10. *WHY CAN'T SELLER GET HIS OR HER CHECK AT THE CLOSING?*

Some attorneys feel that no one should receive funds until all papers are recorded. Make sure you and your clients are aware of this.

11. *AT FINAL INSPECTION THE SWIMMING POOL DID NOT SEEM TO BE IN PROPER WORKING ORDER AND IT IS NOT IN SEASON TO CHECK IT.*

If there is a discrepancy and the seller is aware of the fact that there might be a problem, funds can be held in escrow until the pool can be checked or fixed and then remaining funds returned to seller.

12. *LENDER HAS STIPULATED THAT SELLER MUST REPAIR A RETAINING WALL BEFORE CLOSING. THE WALL IS SUBMERGED IN SNOW.*

Again, a contractor can be contacted and funds held in escrow for the approximate amount satisfactory to buyer and seller, and remaining funds can be returned to seller when the job is finished.

13. *BUYER CAN'T DECIDE WHETHER OR NOT TO TAKE TITLE INSURANCE OUT BEFORE CLOSING BY OBTAINING AN OWNERS POLICY.*

Explain to the buyer that the mortgage company has taken its own policy out on the property. However, if there were ever any undisclosed heirs, forged signatures or just plain errors in recording, an Owners Policy would *protect him or her*.

14. *SELLER LEFT THE DRAPERIES AS SPECIFIED IN THE PURCHASE AGREEMENT, BUT TOOK THE DRAPERY RODS.*

Seller must return them or make concessions for them at the closing. If all else fails, agents should try to compromise the best they can.

15. *THE SALE FELL THROUGH. WHO WILL PAY FOR THE ABSTRACT, SURVEY, OR TERMITE INSPECTION?*

The person to whom it is *charged*.

16. *THERE IS A SEWER LINE ON THE PROPERTY. NOTHING IS MENTIONED IN THE CONTRACT AND NEITHER THE BUYER NOR SELLER WILL BUDGE.*

It usually comes out of the commission. This is a case in which the seller feels he is already losing money, and the buyer says he never was told about it. The agent should always stay on top of everything.

17. *IT'S TWO DAYS BEFORE THE CLOSING. THE APPRAISAL CAME IN LATE AND LOW ON THE PROPERTY.*

The first thing you do is contact the lender and tell them you want an independent appraisal done. You are allowed in most places to do this. Go to your office and pull your own comparables. Fax them to the lender to make sure that they are given to the appraiser.

18. *THE ATTORNEY FOR THE BUYER MAKES UNREASONABLE REQUESTS JUST THREE DAYS BEFORE THE CLOSING.*

It is imperative from the start that you maintain a good rapport with everyone involved with the closing, *especially the attorneys*. Try to stay abreast of the situation and work with the other agent and attorney, keeping the buyers and sellers removed from it. If there continues to be a stalemate, talk with your own company attorney or a good real estate attorney with whom you have developed a relationship. (All agents should have contact with a good real estate attorney for difficult legal advice.)

19. *THE SELLER'S AGENT WAS NEW AND IS NOT DOING FOLLOW-UP BEFORE THE CLOSING. THINGS HAVE BEEN LEFT UNDONE.*

Sometimes you will work with a new agent who is not comfortable with all the work that must be done in order to have the closing run smoothly. *Work closely with the other agent from the onset. Make yourself available* if they seek your help.

20. *THE SELLERS ARE GETTING DIVORCED AND DON'T WANT TO SEE EACH OTHER AT THE CLOSING!*

Often this can be handled with a little tact and finesse. Simply explain the situation to the closer ahead of time and ask if it would be convenient for the sellers to sign off separately ahead of time. This saves much time and unnecessary embarrassment. They may also choose separate rooms.

Checklist for Purchase Agreement

1. Original purchase agreement completely signed

    a. Attached   _____

    b. Out for signatures   _____

2. Copy of purchase agreement   _____

3. Supplements to purchase agreement   _____

4. Earnest money check   _____

5. Note to be redeemed   _____

6. Copy of earnest money check   _____

7. Interest bearing account for earnest money   _____

8. Listing agreement and computer sheet   _____

9. Housing disclosure report   _____

10. Sellers disclosure report   _____

11. Well disclosure report   _____

12. Sellers net sheet   _____

13. Buyers worksheet   _____

14. Condo/townhouse bylaws   _____

15. Contingency removal sheet   _____

16. Lender information   _____

17. Is/is not subject to contingency   _____

18. Picture of subject property   _____

19. Remarks _____

    _____

    _____

20. Date sent to title co   _____

Worksheet for Purchase Agreement
Final Closing

File Number _____

Seller's Name _____

Single _____ Married _____ Divorced _____ Widowed _____

Forwarding Address _____

Current Address _____ Phone _____

City/State _____ Zip _____

Buyer's Name _____

Address _____ Phone _____

City/State _____ Zip _____

Earnest Money: Check Attached _____ Amount_____

Interest Bearing Acct _____ Noninterest Bearing _____

Date Deposited _____

Buyer's Attorney_____ Phone _____

Seller's Attorney _____ Phone _____

Condo _____ Association Name _____

Townhouse _____ Address_____

Present First Mortgage at _____

Phone Number _____ Balance _____

Assumption Approval Necessary _____ Date Rec'd _____

Contract for Deed Holder _____

Home Improvements _____

New Financing

Lender _____ Branch_____

Loan Officer_____ Phone _____

Type of Loan _____ Points _____

Purchase Agreement Date_____

Selling Price _____

Closing Date _____

Commission_____

Other Agent _____

Anatomy of a Closing Transaction

1. Final acceptance of offer by buyer and seller

2. Signed purchase agreements delivered to both buyer and seller

3. Real estate office notified that property is sold

4. Sold sign put on the property

5. Completion of all papers necessary to be sent to closing departments and title company

6. Mortgage payoff notice sent to lender

7. Home retracted from computer and marked sold

8. Loan application made by buyers; fees collected for appraisal and credit report

9. Earnest money deposited by listing company

10. Lender for buyer requests verification and credit report on buyer and also orders appraisal and title policy

11. Past drawings necessary

12. Mortgage company receives credit report and appraisal; documents reviewed for evidence of clear title; final application signed by buyer; loan file sent to the underwriter for his or her review

13. All payoffs on loans against the property ordered; fee owner contacted if seller has contract for deed; seller contacted to settle any title problems

14. Loan file of buyer either approved, suspended for needed information, or rejected outright

15. Closing department for seller receives all figures for payoffs against property; prepares documents; gets all tax information; assessments verified

16. Loan approved; selling agent notified; buyers notified

17. Closing department sets closing date; all parties notified by mail

18. Loan package ordered from lender

19. Closing documents forwarded to title company

20. Final search done; final figures entered on closing statement

21. Lockbox and any highlight information on home retrieved

22. Closing day! Mortgage documents and sellers documents signed; funds collected and dispersed

23. Package prepared for lender, recording, accounting, and title insurance

24. Lender's servicing department issues loan payment book.

25. File documents with county; issue final title insurance policy.

Settlement Day

WHAT BUYERS NEED TO BRING TO CLOSING

1. picture ID of self and drivers license
2. year's paid homeowners insurance premium
3. certified funds made out to "self" for exact amount
4. decision to buy or not buy a separate owners policy for title insurance
5. clarification that utilities are in buyer's name as of closing date

WHAT SELLERS NEED TO BRING TO CLOSING

1. picture ID of self and drivers license
2. proof of any unpaid utility bills (A water bill becomes a lien on the property if not paid off.)
3. proof of payoff on any tax lien, tax assessment, late taxes due, and any late penalty due
4. all keys to all doors to property
5. garage door openers
6. warranties on appliances left at the home
7. abstract on property or owner's duplicate if torrens property
8. payoff notes or mortgages not recorded (shows as a lien against the property)
9. any rent adjustment with seller if lease-back situation
10. servicing contracts (such as heating or air conditioning) that the buyer may be assuming or taking over
11. townhouse or swimming pool membership that has yet to be assigned to buyer
12. termite inspection certification (also sent to attorneys and/or closing department)
13. itemized list of any personal property left with house (should be in accordance to contract)
14. any accumulated taxes or insurance funds should go to seller unless otherwise designated
15. survey copy if ordered

Writing an Offer

6:00 A.M.—arrived at 123 View Lane.

Both clients seemed a bit nervous and said, "We don't think we will be doing anything tonight. We just wanted to talk to you and *not rush into things*. If we miss this one, it's OK. We just started looking."

I said,

> *"I understand. I thought we would look at three or four homes that have sold in the neighborhood here and a couple more that are currently for sale.*

I knew that I would have to be easygoing, not hurry too fast, yet *not* take the normal steps in walking through a home and coming back with a CMA. Tonight I would have to:

1. *list the home before I leave,*

2. *get a purchase agreement signed before I leave, and*

3. *present everything before everyone got "cold feet."*

I showed them the houses. They agreed that these homes were certainly *similar to their own home.*

I asked them what they paid two years ago, and they said, "About $218,000." I told them the market had not appreciated much since that time. They probably would be looking at around the $220s figure. They told me that when they bought the home two years ago, it was listed at $225,000. I said that probably sounded about right for now. *They agreed.* I then did a *net sheet* for them based on a figure of $220,000.

After I made them a net sheet, we sat and talked about the home I met them at. "What would you want to offer on *that home*?" I said.

> *"Well, we were talking about it," said Ann, "and we would want to offer, oh, I don't know. What do you think honey?" she said to her husband. "Oh, I don't really think we talked much about that, did we? We might be rushing these things."*

"Let's do this" I said.

> *"Let's say you had an offer coming in on your own home right now. What would you consider an 'insulting beyond words' offer?"*

He said, "Something in the two hundred teen range."

"Oh," I said. "Then ten thousand less is insulting?"

"For our home, it is," they both said.

"Then we should keep that in mind when bidding on the other home. We can't come in too low. That would be insulting. Yet, you still want to know that you got a good deal, right?"

"Well," said Mrs. Buyer, "let's try an offer at $325,000. "That's not a bad starting point, and if we get it, that's great! We will have to sign the listing in advance though because if they take a contingent offer, they will want to know that we have our house on the market. Isn't that right?" she asked me.

7:30—left their house.

9:00—met at sellers' home at 452 Morexal for offer presentation.

Another offer had also just come in on seller's home, so seller had now received two offers.

1. offer was $319,000 non-contingent
2. offer was $325,000 contingent

*They talked for one hour and **finally countered my offer** at $335,000.*

10:10—*I called my buyers from seller's house.* My buyers came up to $333,000 and crossed out stove.

10:30—*sellers finally accepted,* but not before seller's agent suggested that they think about both offers overnight, and let everyone know in the morning.

I said, "One offer should be countered."

10:45—sellers came back and countered my offer. They said, *"Your offer is cleaner-looking with stronger buyers that are prequalified."*

11:00 P.M.—offer ended.

11:45—*secured all initials. Property was now "sold contingent" upon my buyer's home selling.* My buyer's home sold two weeks later, and *we removed the contingency.*

Important Information for Purchase Agreements

1. *Always put a deadline on your purchase agreements* with time and date for final acceptance so that the offer is either accepted, rejected or countered by a certain deadline, and neither party is left hanging.

2. The words *"subject to" and "contingent upon" are considered to have the same meaning,* for example, "this is subject to an inspection" would be the same as "contingent upon an inspection." The 48 hour contingency addendum stands apart, however, as a separate function.

3. *If a buyer gets an inspection report earlier than the stated days,* the buyer's *stated time to register objections begins then,* not at the end of the days stated in the addendum.

4. *A property may continue to be shown between final acceptance and removal of "subject tos," but the buyer and seller must agree to that in writing.*

5. If the buyer registers objections in writing, as called for within the stated timeline, a solution to the objections may very well extend beyond the deadline.

6. When showing a home, try not to ask the seller anything to do with actual real estate. *All inquiries should go through a listing agent.*

7. If the closing date should change, sign an addendum or an amendment showing the new date. *Do not leave anything verbal.*

8. *When the property is sold, get a listing extension beyond the closing date.* This avoids situations in which the property does not close, but then the buyer and seller get together after the closing date.

9. In some states, to file for homestead for the next year, the buyer must own and occupy the new home before June 1. *Be cautious to set the closing date* at the end of May. If the closing must be delayed until June, determine *who will pay the homestead for the next year.*

10. *In order for a property to be considered "sold," the delivery of an acceptable purchase agreement must be made to either agent.* Until the delivery is made, *another offer may be accepted.* A verbal acceptance or promise will not prevail. *Never wait overnight to deliver a copy of the accepted agreement.*

11. *If an offer has been presented, countered, and another one is written, the seller must be told about the second one.* If the seller doesn't want to look at the second one until the first one is handled, this is all right. It is the seller's decision.

12. *You must always notify a seller in writing with a list of names and addresses for your buyers within a certain time frame.* Various states have different time frames. *This list is in force only as long as the property is not listed with another broker.*

13. *When putting in date and time of possession,* make sure that both buyer and seller agree before final acceptance is in effect. For example, if a buyer asks for possession on the same day as closing, it's best to put P.M. closing or A.M. closing so as not to overlap with movers.

14. *Make sure that there will be no surprises at the final walk-through,* such as a stove that does not work, lights that won't go on or faucets that will not turn, *that could circumvent the closing and cause delays.*

Closing Gifts

MONOGRAMMED DOOR KNOCKER

MONOGRAMMED STATIONERY WITH NEW ADDRESS

LARGE WICKER FRUIT BASKET

LARGE PERENNIAL PLANT/TREE

MONOGRAMMED PICTURE HOLDER

SUBSCRIPTION TO "HOUSE BEAUTIFUL" (GIVE CARD AND INSCRIPTION AT CLOSING)

JUICE MACHINE

OLD-FASHIONED MALTED MILK MIXER (AN ALL-TIME FAVORITE)

MONOGRAMMED PEN AND PENCIL SET

PERSONALIZED LETTER OPENER

PERSONALIZED DESK SET

SUBSCRIPTION TO NATIONAL GEOGRAPHIC (FOR THE BUYER'S CHILDREN)

YEAR SUPPLY OF BOTTLED WATER (LOOKS IMPRESSIVE, YET INEXPENSIVE)

AM/FM RADIO

MONOGRAMMED GLASSES

ANSWERING MACHINE

REMOTE TELEPHONE (THESE CAN BE PURCHASED AT WHOLESALE FOR UNDER $100)

PICTURE OF NEW HOME IN CHARCOAL

DINNER RESERVATIONS AT A RENOWNED RESTAURANT

RESERVATIONS FOR AN UPCOMING PLAY

GIFT CERTIFICATE ON ONE YEAR ANNIVERSARY IN HOUSE

THEATER TICKETS

ONE MONTH MEMBERSHIP AT A LOCAL HEALTH CLUB

ONE MONTH MEMBERSHIP TO CABLE T.V.

ONE YEAR MEMBERSHIP TO A DESSERT CLUB

ONE YEAR SUPPLY OF CAR WASHES

DINNER ON MOVING DAY

Closings

Address	Close	Price	Commission	Comments Closer/Agents

Closing Progress Report

Date _____

Buyer _____ Seller _____

Property Address _____

Purchase Agreement Date _____

Closing Date _____

Mortgage Company _____ Loan Officer _____

Date of Loan Application _____

Comments _____

_____

_____

Points (Locked Date) _____ Floating _____

Appraisal Order _____

Appraisal Completed _____ Amount_____

Documents Received _____

_____

_____

Documents Necessary _____

_____

_____

Closing Company _____

Address _____ Phone _____

Closing Date _____ Time _____

Comments for Closing

Directions _____

_____

_____

What to Bring _____

What to Wear _____

What to Expect _____

Additional Comments _____

_____

_____

Feedback Fax on Showings

Agent Picture

Company Name

Company No.

Date

Time

333–3333

Kindly Inform Us as to

Your Opinion and Your

Customer's Opinion of

The Home at:

_____

_____

_____

Opinion: _____

_____

_____

Price: Ok: _____ High: _____ Low: _____

Showing Agent

Name and Phone: _____

_____

_____

Date: _____

Time Shown: _____

Epilogue

I hope that you have enjoyed this book as much as I have enjoyed writing it. I have looked through my own daily planner book. At the beginning, inside the front cover are three of my favorite pieces that have *kept me going for years*. I am going to end this book by including these three pieces.

They really do say it all.

RULES FOR BEING HUMAN

1. *YOU WILL RECEIVE A BODY.* You may like it or hate it, but it will be yours for the entire period that you are around here.

2. *YOU WILL LEARN LESSONS.* You are enrolled in a full time school called life. Each day in this school you have the opportunity to learn lessons. You may like the lessons or think they are irrelevant and stupid.

3. *THERE ARE NO MISTAKES, ONLY LESSONS.* Growth is a process of trial and error, experimentation. The failed experiences are as much a part of the process as the experiment that ultimately works.

4. A lesson is repeated until it is learned. A lesson will be presented to you in various forms until you have learned it. When you have learned it, *YOU CAN GO ON TO THE NEXT LESSON.*

5. *LEARNING LESSONS DOES NOT END.* There is no part of life that does not contain lessons. If you are alive, there are lessons to be learned.

6. "There" is not better than "here." Once your "there" has become a "here," you will simply obtain another "there" that will look better than "here."

7. *OTHER PEOPLE ARE MERELY A MIRROR OF YOU.* You cannot love or hate something about another person unless it reflects to you something you love or hate about yourself.

8. *WHAT YOU MAKE OF YOUR LIFE IS UP TO YOU.* You have all the tools and resources you will need. What you do with them is up to you. The choice is yours.

9. *YOUR ANSWERS LIE INSIDE OF YOU.* The answers to life's questions lie inside you. All you need to do is *look*, *listen*, and *trust*.

10. **YOU WILL FORGET ALL OF THIS . . .**

Author is unknown
(found on a refrigerator door)

LAWS FOR LIVING

by Shirley Briggs

1. *NEVER TURN CONTROL OF YOUR LIFE OVER TO ANOTHER PERSON!*

2. *CULTIVATE BALANCE IN YOUR LIFE.* Nourish your mind, body, and spirit.

3. *FORGIVE YOURSELF* for everything you did and didn't do. Then forgive all others.

4. *LOVE EVERYONE* unconditionally. Start with yourself.

5. *BE GENTLE WITH YOURSELF.* Set realistic goals, but realize they sometimes will be achieved in the midst of seeming failure.

6. *SCRIPT YOUR OWN LIFE.* Seek guidance from others but remain true to yourself.

7. *SEEK WORK WHICH SATISFIES* and allows for growth.

8. *LEARN SOMETHING* new every day.

9. *TREAT YOURSELF TO A NEW EXPERIENCE* once a month.

10. *DEVELOP THE ABILITY TO BOUNCE BACK* quickly from life's challenges.

11. As much as possible *LIVE IN THE NOW* not the past. Live life with a light touch.

12. Seek the company of those you love and dare to *ALLOW YOURSELF TO BE LOVED.*

13. *REEVALUATE WHERE YOU ARE.* Release things and relationships that no longer fit.

14. *TAKE TIME TO PLAY.* Happiness is impossible without a spirit of fun.

15. *LIVE LIFE BY THE GOLDEN RULE.* You can only keep what you give away.

16. *GO WITHIN YOURSELF* to your core of peace and listen to the voice of silence.

17. *SHARE YOURSELF WITH OTHERS.* Have no expectations from another person.

18. Cultivate and maintain a sense of personal identity. *LEAN ON NO ONE.* Become a leader of self and create your own path.

19. *GIVE A SMILE* to every living creature you contact. Give them a *positive* word or remain silent.

20. *NEVER TRY TO CHANGE ANYONE* except yourself.

21. Develop a *SENSE OF TOLERANCE* for every human being.

22. *CONTROL YOUR LIFE* with love.

23. When approaching a fork in the road of life, *CHOOSE THE PATH* that has a heart.

And finally, *"TO SUCCEED IS TO ACHIEVE ONE'S GOAL."* Ralph Waldo Emerson (1803–1882) said it best when he wrote:

> *"To laugh often and love much; to win respect of intelligent persons and the affection of children; to earn the approbation of honest citizens and endure the betrayal of false friends; to appreciate the beauty; to find the best in others; to give of oneself; to leave the world a bit better, whether by a healthy child, a garden patch or a redeemed social condition; to have played and laughed with enthusiasm and sung with exultation; to know even one life has breathed easier because you have lived. This is to have succeeded."*

My very best wishes for a happy and successful real estate career!

Sincerely,

Barbara Nash-Price

Index